Politically Speaking

Politically Speaking

CROSS-CULTURAL STUDIES OF RHETORIC

Edited by Robert Paine

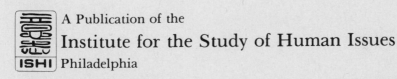

A Publication of the
Institute for the Study of Human Issues
ISHI Philadelphia

Manufactured in the United States of America

Published in the United States by ISHI,
Institute for the Study of Human Issues, Inc.

Published in Canada by the
Institute of Social and Economic Research,
Memorial University of Newfoundland,
as No. 10 in the series *Social and Economic Papers*

Library of Congress Cataloging in Publication Data

Main entry under title:

Politically speaking.

  Bibliography: p.
  Includes index.
  1. Political oratory—Addresses, essays, lectures. I. Paine,
Robert.
PN4193.P6P64   1981   808'.066324021   80–25411
ISBN 0-89727-017-7

For information, write:

Director of Publications
ISHI
3401 Science Center
Philadelphia, Pennsylvania 19104
U.S.A.

Contents

Acknowledgements

We wish to thank the Canada Council and the Vice-President's Fund at Memorial University of Newfoundland for grants-in-aid that enabled two colloquia to be held late in 1976, one in England on the Harlow campus of Memorial University, and the other on the home campus in St. John's, Newfoundland.

Gary Norton helped arrange the colloquia; Joan Lloyd and her staff at *The Maltings* took care of us during the Harlow colloquium; Shirley Fraize, Jeanette Gleeson and Shirley Atkins, all of the Institute of Social and Economic Research at Memorial University, provided secretarial and stenographic support; David Macdonald compiled the References and the Index—our thanks to them all.

We are particularly grateful to Sonia Kuryliw Paine for her painstaking text editing.

The Canadian edition of this book has been published with the help of a grant from the Social Science Federation of Canada, using funds provided by the Social Sciences and Humanities Research Council of Canada.

R. P.
St. John's, Newfoundland

This is the actor's art, drawing tight the invisible thread between player and public. But . . . it is also an art of government, and it uses an acquired skill in language.

George Watson, *The English Ideology*
(1973: 132)

1

Introduction

ROBERT PAINE

> . . . the true rhetoric of any age and of any
> people is to be found deep within . . . precepts
> that condition one's stance toward experience,
> knowledge, tradition, language, and other peo-
> ple.
>
> *Encyclopaedia Britannica,*
> XVth edition (Sloan 1974: 802)

I

Rhetoric is devoted to persuasion, and politics as rhetoric is the *leitmotif* of this book. This means releasing the study of politics from a study of its institutions and concentrating instead upon the way in which politicians attempt to sway, and even mould the experience and knowledge of their public.

In approaching rhetoric the contributors have held to a course that is not that of linguistics, formal logic or formal rhetoric. This might impart a naïveté to our writing as seen from the different perspectives of these other disciplines, but the job could not have been done in any other way. All but two of us are social anthropologists: David Lloyd-Jones is a political scientist, Ian Rodger a free-lance writer.

Our focus is upon the organization of 'meaning' in the verbal culture of politics: how it is selected, constructed and communicated— or 'lost.' Thus whether the rhetoric is purple prose or plain talk, establishment or radical, the chapters are about different cultural forms of rhetorical persuasion, about the setting of rhetorical 'traps,' and about how rhetorical strategy and the actual performance of a speech take account of the occasion or context.

Certainly our wish is to sharpen the perspective of political anthropology, but we hope that what we have written—and how we have written it—will have an appeal beyond anthropology, and even beyond the ranks of academe. The discipline of rhetoric—not to mention anthropology—is a minefield of arcane terms and every effort has been made to keep our manner of saying things within ordinary bounds.

II

With 'context,' 'strategy,' 'performance' and 'persuasion' as key notions, the words of rhetoric, in our view of them, are *moulden*. But in another view of rhetoric, notably that of Maurice Bloch, its words, like those Pantagruel offered Panurge, are *frozen* (Rabelais 1946: 620).[1] Bloch's view is given in his Introduction to the other anthropological collection of case studies in political rhetoric (Bloch 1975), and it seems appropriate to draw attention here to the epistemological issue between these two views of rhetoric. In doing so, we may also clarify further the position adopted in this book.

For Bloch rhetoric is "formalised language," meaning "an impoverished language . . . where many of the options at all levels are abandoned so that choice of form, of style, of words and of syntax, is less than in ordinary language" (1975: 13). Formalization of language also controls—such is the conclusion—discourse, to the point of eliminating it. Rhetoric is wedded to a Cartesian imperative of the self-evident—in this case, the self-evident "power of compulsion" that is embedded in the social structure (pp. 11, 19). Status arrangements predetermine everything. This seems to mean that oratorical power cannot be attributed to the speaker; instead Bloch sees it as emanating from (and reflecting back onto) the culture itself.[2] Thus the political orator finds himself operating within a system of communication "which has largely given up the power of creativity" (p. 18). A particular puzzlement with Bloch's position is why he identifies formal language as the language of politics, for "if oratory were as formulaic as Bloch seems to suggest, oratory and practical politics would be incompatible" (Burling 1977: 699). Indeed, Bloch (*op. cit.*: 24) concludes that the oratory "implies acceptance of who is top[;] it [oratory] does not produce it."

Certainly there are notions of formalization in various chapters of this volume, but the disagreement with Bloch is fundamental. It reaches even to the epistemological standing of the social world: something 'given' or something negotiated? The principal difficulty arises over the way Bloch associates formalization with an absence of negotiation between speaker and audience. Bloch sees coercion (*op. cit.*: 12) where we see persuasion; whereas he sees formalization as a 'given,' which constrains the speaker, we see it as an outcome of rhetorical artistry and political acumen by which an audience is constrained; that is to say, the politician strives to have his audience see the world through his interpretation of it in his speeches. Formalization of language is an instrument to this end in the general sense of introducing restrictions of form; but there need be no implications of language impoverishment such as Bloch attaches to formalization.

Contrary to Bloch, we see political rhetoric not as based upon an *a priori* acceptance of "who is top," but as directed to the attainment of that acceptance. This *a priori* element in Bloch's view of rhetoric as praxis has several serious consequences. One is the assumption that the code used by a speaker is autonomous (hence the elimination of discourse as well as of rhetorical creativity); in our view this is something towards which the politician strives—usually without ever attaining it. Another consequence is that rhetoric is relegated to an epiphenomenal place in politics: just as "the medium is the message" for McLuhan (1965) so, for Bloch, the social structure is the message. That this is the conclusion one arrives at from reading Bloch is particularly regrettable because he set out to pioneer, in anthropology, the "significance of what kind of speech is involved in political interaction" (*op. cit.*: 4). He raised an impediment instead.

III

Our disagreement with Bloch may be usefully set in the larger context of the prolonged historical debate, in the West, over the meaning and worth of rhetoric. It has been dominated by the opposition between the Aristotelian and Cartesian traditions: rhetoric for Aristotelians is a mode of discourse capable of "proving opposites" (Burke 1969a: 52); whereas in the Cartesian view, because "disagreement is a sign of error" (Perelman 1969: 2), rhetoric is afforded little validity or utility, if any at all.[3] Thus the central issue is "the epistemological status of opinion as opposed to truth" (Perelman 1963: 158), and for the opponents of the Cartesian position, "it is the *idea of self-evidence* as characteristic of reason, which we must assail" (Perelman 1969: 3; original emphasis).

Although this battle is won on most fronts today,[4] Cartesian notions of proof and reason in the past led generally to the dismissal of rhetoric as an influence in the conduct of human affairs (Burke 1969a: xiii; Perelman 1969: 5; Sloan 1974: 802). It was not until the 1930s that the pendulum began to swing back, and a comparison of the entries under *Rhetoric* in the XIth (1910–11) and the XVth (1974) editions of *Encyclopaedia Britannica* suggests how general changes in the intellectual climate reproduced themselves in a changing conception of rhetoric.

The XIth edition entry opens thus: "The object is strictly persuasion rather than intellectual approval or conviction; hence the term, with its adjective 'rhetorical,' is commonly used for a speech or writing in which matter is subservient to form or display." In the XVth edition, which consists principally of sections by Thomas O. Sloan and Chaim Perelman, a 'reply' is found: "form is subordinated to content, to the action on the mind, to the effort to persuade and to convince" (Perelman 1974: 805). Both editions cite Samuel Butler's derisory comment that "all a rhetorician's rules / But teach him how to name his tools," the XIth to note, without refutation, "the assumption is . . . that . . . these tools must be devoid of practical use," the XVth to dismiss it (Sloan 1974: 799). The XIth edition concludes: "The conditions of modern life, and especially the invention of printing, have to some extent diminished the importance which belonged in antiquity to the art of speaking, though modern democratic politics and forensic conditions still make it one which may be cultivated with advantage." In the XVth, the emphasis is strident: "the new media . . . and the new orality of modern life" are recognized (*ibid*.: 802).

With the place of persuasion re-established, a return has been made to the classical appreciation of rhetoric, with some important elaborations. For example, there is now a concern for audiences— whereas before emphasis was almost exclusively upon the speaker (or writer)—and for the 'situation' of an utterance. In short, "a text must [be made to] reveal its context"; truth and meaning themselves are informed by context (Sloan 1974: 799). Not surprisingly, the idea of 'persuasion' itself is expanded; Burke's treatment of it, for example, veers strongly towards the psychological and persuasion is linked to the process he calls "identification," which "ranges from the politician who, addressing an audience of farmers, says, 'I was a farm boy myself,' through the mysteries of social status, to the mystic's devout identification with the source of all being" (Burke 1969a: xiv).

Although such developments within the discipline of rhetoric owe something to the social sciences, they are, at the same time, developments to which social science should respond.[5] It sometimes seems as though anthropology, in this respect, is still very largely at a journey's beginning: one looks for more explicit attention in our writings to the manifold role of rhetoric in social behaviour such as is found in Rosaldo (1973) and in the case studies in Bloch. Yet the current attraction in anthropology of Kenneth Burke is of significance here (for a commentary, see Overington 1977) as, too, are the enterprises of the "ethnography of speaking" (for overviews, see Bauman 1975; Bauman and Sherzer 1974). Nor should it be forgotten that for some time anthropologists have been studying rhetorical aspects of cultural behaviour without ever calling them such. In the concluding chapter an effort is made to forge links between insights from the anthropological work and other insights from the discipline of rhetoric itself.

IV

To conclude, our discussion will be conducted at two levels throughout;[6] the first we might call *speaking politics*. At this level the implications for our enquiry—that it is about politics and not, say, astronomy—are made clear. Politics is a domain of competing ideologies and reputations. As there is likely to be considerable subjective motivation and interpretation attached to these matters by the persons involved, it is *not useful* to regard the accounts that people give of what they are doing in politics, or their reasons for doing it, as answerable to true/false criteria. The second level may be regarded as that of the *politics of speaking*; it directs attention to the way a speaker—whether his subject be politics or astronomy—works for the attention of his audience. Here the important issues are those of aesthetics (a sure route to culturally specific codes of ethics) and semantic structure; in short, we are dealing with the possible designs a speech (or other forms of persuasion) can take. The success of any political speech depends largely upon the speaker's grasp of the two levels and, ultimately, upon his ability to bring them suitably together.

In a book of this kind there is a real danger of spoiling a good case through errors of commission, and I hope that we have not so extended the key concept of rhetoric as to lose our readers. Not all activity is made out to be rhetorical: non-symbolic activity is not, 'speaking about' is not, and propaganda is not (see Chapter 2). On the other hand, the reader who comes to sense the redundancy in the phrase "political rhetoric" will have deciphered the principal message in this book about politics. The intent is not to denigrate politics; on the contrary, it is to view it as a vehicle for the circulation of symbolic statements about the social order.

Notes

1. My thanks to George Park for the reference to Rabelais, and especially for his advice on the general arrangement of this Introduction.
2. The only explanation that Bloch offers for this statement lies in his

references to "traditional authority"and the tautological status of "explanation" in such circumstances (1974 and 1975, *passim*). This would present us with the possibility that politics are handled in a radically different way in societies with traditional authority than in the world about us, were it not for evidence to the contrary from other essays in the Bloch collection (1975) and even from Bloch's earlier writings (see Werbner 1977). Underlying the vagueness and the contradictions here is the inadequacy of "traditional authority/society" as a taxonomic distinction.

3. For example:

Even as Aristotle is teaching one man how most effectively to make people say "yes," he is teaching an opponent how to make them say just as forceful a "no" [Burke 1969a: 52].

"Whenever two men come to opposite decisions about the same matter," says Descartes, "one of them at least must certainly be in the wrong, and apparently there is not even one of them who knows; for if the reasoning of one was sound and clear he would be able so to lay it before the other as finally to succeed in convincing *his* understanding also" [Perelman 1969: 2].

4. In philosophy, the existentialists and phenomenologists "have strongly challenged . . . such dualities as knowledge and opinion, persuasion and conviction, reason and emotion, rhetoric and poetry, and even rhetoric and philosophy" (Sloan 1974: 799); and in science the challenge of structuralism to positivism now means that "scientists, like others, are always operating on the basis of a belief, as only another paradigm can replace a paradigm" (Krohn 1977: 79–80; cf. Nisbet 1976).

5. There is no entry for rhetoric in the *Encyclopaedia of the Social Sciences*.

6. A point first made, in seminar, by David Alexander.

Rhetoric and Politics

2

When Saying Is Doing

ROBERT PAINE

> The basic element of politics is, quite simply,
> talk.
>
> Peter M. Hall, *Sociological Inquiry* (1972: 51)

I

It is sometimes held that what politicians do, rather than what they say, is the proper subject of politics. This book is not devoted to the contrary view but it does resist, as simplistic, not just the view that it is 'doing' that counts but that 'doing' can always be reliably distinguished from 'saying.' For one thing, we may learn of what has been done (or suppose that something is being done) only from what we hear. Most important of all, there is a sense in which 'saying *is* doing' and this is the kernel of rhetoric. Here I am deliberately contrasting rhetoric with most of our speech acts, which are merely 'talking about,' and suggesting its similarity to music and drama: the 'doing' and the effect are inseparable. The task before us is to demonstrate the connection of rhetoric with politics.[1]

In general, to approach politics through its rhetorical aspects allows one to re-address some familiar views, such as the nature of legitimacy in politics. We take the view that political legitimacy is mainly the problem of getting people to listen to, or rather, to accept what is said. Indeed, approaching politics in this way draws attention to the place of discourse in politics, but with this probable result: rather than demonstrating discourse, the rhetoric provides a public impression of discourse when in fact there may be none. This underwrites the strong element of performance one is likely to find in the process 'saying is doing.'

The apparent paradox in this situation should not be lost. Politics itself is generally thought of as propositional (because of its strong bargaining aspect). At a general theoretical level, the explanation is simple: there is complementarity between symbolic and pragmatic action in any undertaking, and performatory speech is to propositional speech as symbolic action is to pragmatic action. Rhetoric, then, belongs to the symbolic side of politics, and symbolic systems of action, it is known, reduce peoples' perception of available choices. However, by attending to the constraints in the 'speaking' relationship between politicians and their public, it should be possible to give a grounded explanation that shows how the dominance of the performatory mode actually comes about.

A politician wishes to put a claim on his audience through his speeches by making what he says appear relevant and useful, just and necessary. It follows that the focus of any sociologically oriented study of political speech must be on how the politician draws that necessary element of commitment from his audience. This means considering precisely what he is trying to achieve each time he makes an address: co-operation (from a civil servant?), consent (from Parliament?), approval (of as much of the electorate as possible?). Such differences are likely to be reflected in his mode of rhetoric. This immediately raises the question of what the politician reveals about himself and his plans as he approaches particular audiences. But the more important question is probably what he manages to reveal to his listeners about themselves. Audiences are likely to draw comfort from hearing themselves in a political speech; when this does not happen they may reject both the speaker and his speech—pejoratively as "it's just rhetoric!" At all events, among the first questions a political speaker has to consider are: "what's permitted?" and "how will it be understood?"

His success will likely depend on the relation he contrives in his speeches between content and form. We can think of this as approximating the relation between the 'what' and the 'how' of things said, so long as it is remembered that powerful content is often a matter of appropriate form. In short, legitimation of a political message comes particularly through its form. The riddle of political persuasion is what quality in *that* speech by *that* politician tipped the scales and lost him the attention of his audiences—or, not only won its attention but led it to identify with what he was saying. To solve the riddle the code of the form of the speech has to be broken. This means recognizing not only that rhetoric is persuasion but also that persuasion rests upon the ability to organize the experience of those who are to be persuaded.

Perhaps the most important argument for approaching politics through its rhetoric touches upon what may be a gross prejudice within some social science circles in connection with the study of politics. The prejudice shows itself when questions are asked about the social and economic bases of political power to the neglect of what every practising politician, or salesman, or teacher never doubted: that 'saying is doing' (and hence is an act of power). Hard-data social scientists may even consider that all that matters in an election, for example, is the result—as shown by which of the candidates win.

A view of politics as rhetoric is therefore needed to qualify such reductionism and, at the same time, to highlight an important part of the construction of politics as a cultural reality. Certainly it can be demonstrated, sometimes even without much difficulty, that a result at the polls is obtained relatively independently of the rhetorical inputs into a campaign; but the error is to suppose, on that account, that rhetoric is politically irrelevant. A good deal more happens, or is accomplished, in the course of an election than the results. Candidates have to 'fill time'—several weeks or months of it—with public politics. How they choose to do this provides primary data concerning politics as a cultural process (in the explanation of which the root metaphor of a dramaturgical model—namely, performance—is appropriate); and this would still be true even if we supposed that the choice expressed at the polls was unaffected by these public performances. In short: rather than who wins, the question of concern to us is *what* is winning. To view politics, even its electoral campaigns, as a cultural process is to bring to mind how, aside from the formal winners, there are "moral victors, . . . excelling in electoral performance without ever taking office" (Gold's chapter in this volume).

II

It is in their need to persuade that politicians are likely to be drawn to rhetoric; let us therefore consider the forces behind persuasion.

First of all, persuasion ideally begins with a suspension of disbelief among the members of the audience, then it moves to the inducement of their collaborative expectancy, and finally it achieves their complicity with the speaker. The writings of Kenneth Burke tell us how this can happen. For instance, he invites us to imagine a passage built around a set of oppositions: ". . . 'we do *this*, but *they* on the other hand do *that*; *we* stay *here*, but *they* go *there*; *we* look *up*, but *they* look *down*,' etc."; and he suggests, "once you grasp the trend of the form. . . . you will find yourself swinging along . . . even though you may not agree" (1969a: 58; original emphasis). Then there is the triggering affect of words as labels that become justifications for action; for example,

". . . to call some occurrence of a death 'murder' is to justify (explain, motivate) the search for an individual who intended to kill." Thus, ". . . language is itself the motive for the search" (Overington 1977: 134; *pace* Burke). What must not be overlooked, however, is that any such labelling needs explaining itself, for it is there that the particular construction of meaning takes place. We can assume that a speaker does not chance on the words that 'trigger'; rather he chooses them deliberately to unite the knowledge and experience of his audience. Much the same point has been made from the study of folk tales: the originality in a folk tale—including the performance of telling it—owes a great deal to its quality of appropriateness (Hymes 1974: 21).

"You are drawn to the form," says Burke. This is why an audience begins to swing along, "and this attitude of assent may then be transferred to the matter which happens to be associated with the form" (*loc. cit.*). So the orator lures the audience into his game; the performance is shared. This is possible only because the audience—not just the orator—is itself bound by cognitive constraints; the trick for the orator is to know how to exploit this fact. It is precisely because form *is* important to all audiences that a politician can get through to his audience with a message of content. Were this not so, then the command that speakers have over audiences would be far more widely spread than it is—becoming merely a function of each speaker's access to information (that is, content). Such a situation would also be more open to the propositional mode.

The politician must see, then, that the form of his speech mediates its content rather than either quelling it or allowing it to run free. Strong content is dependent upon effective form. On the other hand, if an audience believes it hears form rather than content, it is unlikely to give the speaker the commitment he seeks.[2] The word *style* seems serviceable when we consider these relations between form and content; a speaker, we might say, 'attacks' (metacommunicatively) an audience with his style. But audiences are not defenceless. One speaker's style can be compared with another's, and audiences will do this, as much as they are able, on their terms. The control that each politician can exercise in this process is therefore crucial to him particularly because, though he is likely to appeal to his listeners in their 'code,' he does so with the intention of himself becoming the medium through which they interpret the world.

The politician has to persuade his audience; but to succeed he does not necessarily have to persuade it towards his own opinion. Demosthenes seems to go so far as to say that the responsibility for what a politician says rests upon his audience: "Your orators never make you either bad men or good, but you make them whichever you choose; for it is not you that aim at what they wish for, but they who aim at whatever they think you desire" (cited in Perelman 1969: 24). However, a politician still has to persuade members of his audience that he represents their opinions (whatever he may subsequently do with them); indeed, he may have to explain to them what opinions they really have, and in doing this, he may verify and justify their beliefs for them. Finally, it is still he, the orator, who must evoke from his audience that sense of commitment, which is an integral part of what I mean by persuasion. As has been said of Demosthenes himself: "When Cicero spoke, the people said, 'How well he speaks!'; when Demosthenes spoke, the people said, 'Let us march!' " (Adlai Stevenson, cited in Duncan 1962: 175).[3]

This task of political speech may be made clearer by comparing the experience of being persuaded with that of being convinced, particularly with respect to the disposition to act. Whereas it is reasonable to suppose that a 'persuaded' person is (under ordinary circumstances) disposed to act, he who is simply convinced may still not allow himself to be persuaded: what he has accepted as 'true' he nevertheless does not deem as appropriate or compelling for his own behaviour. However, a person who is not convinced may, in deference to the circumstances, allow himself to be persuaded. Rousseau, in *Emile*, recognized it as useless to convince a child without also persuading him. In the same way, political speech is directed to persuasion rather than conviction. The speaker tries to place his claim on a particular audience in a particular context without worrying whether his argument will be recognized by others, or in all circumstances (cf. Perelman, *op. cit.*).

Thus, to Burke's (*op. cit.*: 50) view of rhetoric as "inducement to action" can be added the *inducement of the appropriate context*, from which will flow the behaviour or action that the politician desires from his audience. We can look upon context itself as a resource of the political speaker—not as a given resource but one moulded, even constructed by him. The key to this resource is the form of *argument*, a hallmark of rhetoric since Aristotle, in which one or more of the propositions are suppressed, that is, left implicit or assumed. It is argument by *enthymeme* ('holding something in mind' or 'leaving unstated'). An enthymemic argument presents a truncated or abbreviated syllogism; for example, the syllogism, "all men are passionate/all saints are men/therefore all saints are passionate," can be reduced enthymemically (by the suppression of the first or second proposition) to either, "all saints are men/therefore all saints are passionate," or "all good men are passionate/therefore all saints are passionate." The enthymemic form does not (as the example also shows) necessarily entail a falsehood; rather what is omitted is implied.

Now, it is precisely this feature of leaving certain things implied that gives the enthymeme its importance as an instrument of persuasion, rather than of conviction. It is left to the members of the audience—who thereby become involved in the making of the argument—to supply the implied proposition or to supplement it with one nearer their own beliefs and prejudices. Such persuasive implying is still more obvious in slogans, which do not appear to have received much attention from logicians. But as an enthymeme presents a truncated syllogism so, I suggest, a slogan may be regarded as a reduction of an enthymeme. In expressing one proposition ("better red than dead" or "black is beautiful"), slogans necessarily leave unstated *all* the associated propositions that would belong to a syllogistic argument. This dramatic 'isolation' of an explicit proposition gives slogans their potency as cognitive triggers. One notes, too, that whereas enthymemes can have the appearance of discourse, slogans put an end to the thought of discourse. Intended to remove doubt, they proclaim particular 'truths'— unqualified and because they are undemonstrated, assumptive. But a slogan is a summarizing statement and so, it might be objected, has not that which is left as assumed in the slogan already been argued through? Certainly this can be so; however, I think the essential point in the present context is the probability of a close complementarity between enthymeme and slogan in the process of persuasion: either a slogan is extracted from an enthymeme or an enthymeme is constructed from a slogan. This leaves little place for the examination of first principles. To the contrary, what is sought by the speaker (and usually his audience) is a broad mobilization of shared sentiments; selected for their high emotional charge, they are likely to be left unexamined.

This slide into greater degrees of 'impliedness'—which can have a forceful impact on audiences—culminates in the use of single words or phrases that, in themselves, contain no proposition but are such that they are likely to induce a proposition by inference. These include words such as "democracy," "the workers," "the Party," "terrorism," "law and order," "immigration," "fair play," "the just society," and so on. As slogans, they are all heavily value-laden, yet they need to be distinguished from those slogans that carry an explicit proposition. The reason is that a speaker can use them *as though* they were nothing else than what Aristotle called "topics": simple signals of what a speech is to be about and provided by a speaker prior to engaging in persuasion. In actuality, however, they are usually co-opted by the speaker into his persuasive purpose. Thus Powellist rhetoric acquires legitimacy at the same time as it places a strong emotive appeal through the use of such topic-like words as immigration and fair play. No position need be adopted explicitly by the speaker while such words—let us call them *banner-words*—are being introduced (here is an important function of speech content). He waits until his banner-words have ignited the prejudices of his audience; then he summarizes for them *their* position—and he may well use a slogan to do so.[4]

Already with the appearance of banner-words, slogans or enthymemes in a speech (or in a speaking campaign), the performance that we call persuasion has begun: the factual and evaluative are entangled; form and content entwined. Styles are discernible—including some choices of tactics in employing an enthymemic argument (which I now use broadly to include banner-words and slogans, as well as enthymemes proper). The most important choice of tactic is which part of the argument to suppress—premiss(es) or conclusion?[5]

The answer may be as simple as this: when the intention of a speaker is to win acceptance of a premiss, he may have cause, in his presentation, to suppress any conclusion (alternative A). But when his intention is to commit an audience to a conclusion, he may have reason to suppress its premiss(es) (alternative B). It is an hypothesis that I want to examine, but before looking at an example of each of its alternatives, let me also put in the form of an hypothesis a line of thought prevalent throughout this chapter; namely, that we can expect a political speaker to 'phrase' himself in a way that minimally offends his 'target' audience. Put slightly differently, this means that in order for a politician to achieve his goal—the consensus of as many people as possible—he will arrange his appeals so that they escape examination. We shall see that one way of doing this is for the speaker to leave either his premiss(es) or conclusion unstated.

Comparing now the slogans "black is beautiful" and "better red than dead" (as examples of alternatives A and B, respectively), we must concede at the outset that both—and not just the second slogan—present a conclusion; but the hypothesis is not, I think, impaired by that. For it is only in the case of "better red . . ." that the conclusion appears to include an evaluation of its alternative (non-red). Moreover, it dramatizes this conclusion in terms of another alternative: life or death. Precisely because it refrains from an evaluation of its alternative, the conclusion in "black is . . ." is left open politically: 'white' as well as black may be beautiful; and the message stops short of saying (for instance), "better dead than nigger."

Our hypothesis also suggests that in the conclusion of slogans such as "better red . . . ," its associated premisses, about 'being red' in this case, will be suppressed. Surely this is what happened in England at the time of this slogan, and the reason is fairly obvious: 'being red' would have been found offensive, if examined, by segments of the target audience that was being urged to act against the policy of nuclear deterrence. A slogan of the type, "black is . . . ," is hypothesized as the converse case. Here it is not political action (yet) that is being urged, but the acceptance of a new premiss—a new way of thinking about oneself as a black person—and the potential consensus could be threatened by the drawing of political conclusions from the premiss (such as black power). In this case, what is opened to examination and urged upon the public *is* 'being black.'

I suggest that the difference between alternatives A and B is also likely to be a sequential one, the choice of 'B' indicating a more advanced stage in the process of persuasion than if 'A' were chosen. If this is so, the hypothesis may be used as an aid in deciphering the stage a speaker supposes he has reached in his persuasion of an audience, and thence in the construction of case-histories of persuasion. We have postulated that alternative A should be presented before alternative B, but we should also enquire about possible beginning- and end-points in the persuasion process other than these two alternatives. In other words, what kind of appeal (if any) precedes the use of 'A,' or succeeds the use of 'B'?

A final matter touching our hypothesis is that in *all* enthymemic appeals, the consequences of what is being urged are likely to remain hidden. This would be true even in the case of alternative B, for since it suppresses premisses while expressing a 'conclusion,' the conclusion would be an uninformed one: with little knowledge about 'being red,' the consequences of the conclusion, "better red," are hidden.

Reasons come easily to mind as to why the enthymemic type of argument is so effective. Audiences, on the whole, do not like to be asked to examine arguments *in extenso* any more than they care to listen to a demonstration of 'first principles,' and they are usually given what they prefer: persuasive capsules. So there is nothing unusual about the enthymemic argument; in fact, it is a feature of our everyday conversation. It is also usual for a person placing his appeal in this way to draw his audience closer through a process of identification; this is particularly important in public speeches. President Sukarno, for instance, when using the notion of *pantjasilat* (the five principles of an independent Indonesia) as a banner-word in his speeches would identify himself as the "golden bridge" or as *Ratu Adil* (the just ruler of Javanese mythology) (Lind 1976). Enoch Powell, on the other hand, seemed more concerned to draw his English audiences closer to his thesis than to himself, and he variously identified his listeners as the embodiment of a victimized England (cf. Lloyd-Jones's chapter in this volume).

A politician who would exclude the devices of enthymemic argument from his rhetoric not only shows himself uncaring of sympathetic evocations among his supporters and potential supporters, but also makes it easier for opponents who do not eschew these devices to judge what he says on *their* terms. In using these devices, he may cause opponents to complain that he is 'begging the question' (*who* are workers? *what* is a terrorist?). That matters little; but it would matter if the politician were found by his *supporters* to be imputing a position to them that was not theirs. The error is fundamental, reflecting an incapacity to organize the experiences of those whom one would persuade. It is likely to undo any claim that the speaker may have had on his audience.

To avoid this error means, in the first place, that the politician must court the predispositions of his constituents. Yet to give people the speeches they want to hear is (much current popular opinion on this subject notwithstanding) to take account of only one element in the politics of speaking politics; a politician will also include what *he* wants them to hear. The mergence of these two elements—so that what he wants them to hear is what they want to hear—is a political necessity whose achievement is a rhetorical art. It requires that the politician incorporate the members of his audience in such a way that his and their interests, or causes, appear to become one; it is to this end that a recurrent rhetorical theme is likely to be the defining of 'us' and what kind of people 'we' are. The politician is likely to realize that some of our opinions in this matter are needed to support the fulcrum by which he would move other of our opinions (Burke 1969a: 56).

In this and perhaps other ways, an element of exchange is woven into the essentially performative structure of a political speech. Yet such an exchange is itself highly rhetorical, without necessary validity beyond the context of the speech: the politician who offers reassurances at the hustings is likely to be doing what is *expected* of him in that context without the public expecting to be able to constrain him otherwise. In the maintenance of such a rhetorical sense of exchange, the politician can draw help from the residual factor of vagueness in enthymemic propositions. Often reduced to slogans, these propositions are customarily presented, and often accepted, as the basis for joint action, even as 'shared' promises for the future. It was in this way that, for example, the political rhetoric of the early Trudeau administration in Canada was directed to a shared future; its slogan was "the just society." Even if the country was not, or not for long, politically united by it, at least the slogan was symbolically irrefutable, and a good deal of political capital accrued to the government while the opposition searched to change the definition that this slogan put on political debate.

In other words, politicians make assiduous use of ambiguity. Cohen (1969) associates ambiguity in political life with deliberate "mystification"; however, the dependence of politicians on ambiguity has much to do with their need to negotiate with their public, especially where it is plurally composed. In one speech or in the same campaign, a politician may have to mediate situations that are themselves ambiguous and may have to appeal to different-minded sectors of his public. Although no politician wishes to be judged as ambiguous, it is an important resource for most of them. Thus, "as a candidate, Jimmy Carter's ambiguity brought him support from across the political spectrum; each group could see in him what they wished" (*Montreal Star*, 19 November 1977).

Ambiguity in the speaking of politics, then, is an artifice for handling the contradictions endemic to politics; it is connected with the *legitimation* of meanings. But politicians who cynically exploit this moral paradox—or who fail to see it—may do so at some peril. For in the end it is themselves they have to legitimate, and politicians *in power* are expected to go beyond appeal to action, and here ambiguity, if not concealed, can reduce credibility. The same reporter on Carter suggests how, now that he is President, "all . . . are seeing what he does," and his continued ambiguity is reinterpreted as vacillation and uncertainty.

In concluding our discussion about enthymemic persuasion, note should be taken of its limitations for public debate. The root cause of this is the arbitrariness of persuasion which has validity only for a particular audience; groups arguing with each other on this basis are likely to end up without even the sense of a common problem. Instead, each side is likely to hold high its slogan as an emblem of non-negotiability: while some cry "rather red than dead," others howl "a red under every bed." In a phrase of Ricoeur's, this is discourse "by stimulus" rather than by anything else (1971: 533). In Canada today, the provincial government of Quebec has the avowed objective of political sovereignty; this is occasioning a great deal of public talk, a principal consequence of which is, however, a mounting rhetorical deadlock (as indicated by the antipathetic slogans of "separation" and "unity"). This tendency to deadlock issues underwrites the essentially performative and non-propositional character of rhetoric. The journey towards a point of deadlock serves an important political function, but on arrival at that point, the role of rhetoric in the political process essentially ends.

III

I turn now from the art of persuasion to more epistemological questions about rhetoric that are important for the approach in this book to politics. Let us begin by reviewing the position stated at the beginning of this essay.

Quintessentially, rhetoric is action (*vide* Adlai Stevenson's view of Demosthenes' rhetoric). Thus far we have considered this notion of action in the context of *saying is doing*; however there are ways in which one 'says' through doing rather than by saying;[6] examples are protest marches and Mao's swimming of the Yangtze. Sometimes it is a case of using word *or* deed, but of greater impact is their use in combination (there are likely to be speeches at the end of a march, and *The Thoughts of Chairman Mao* will be there on either side of the river). Indeed, the relation between word and deed is ideally directed towards an effect beyond mere combination: we bring them together so that one will confirm the other—as Christian iconography so richly illustrates.

Perhaps, then, we can come a bit closer to the nature of rhetoric by considering it also as *saying while doing*. To establish this position we compare it to that adopted in linguistic philosophy on performative utterances. We are told that these utterances are such that to say something is, indeed, to do something (and not just to talk about); examples are "I do . . ." as uttered in a marriage ceremony, "I name . . ." as uttered in the launching of a ship, "I bet . . ." as uttered in a wager, and "I give and bequeath . . ." as stated in a will (Austin 1962: 5). Yet the efficacy of each is dependent upon an accompanying deed—giving and receiving the ring, breaking the bottle of champagne, the handshake, and placing the signature. This is no hair-splitting point: the enormous rhetorical effect of De Gaulle's calculated indiscretion, "Vive le Québec libre!," owed much to the fact that he said it while standing on a balcony in Montreal, addressing a mass audience congregated in the square below. Such drawing together of word and deed, in context, gives rhetoric its potency; the doing and the effect are inseparable.

Interweaving of speech and action has been noted as fundamental also to the structure of the *magical rite* (Tambiah 1973: 222).[7] What are we to make of this? First, it is as performances that rhetoric and magic share this characteristic, and I suggest it is when word and deed confirm each other that the parties (actor and audience) to a performance are most likely to be drawn into a relationship whereby they themselves confirm each other. Certainly there are other similarities between magic and rhetoric, as performances, that encourage one to pursue this thought: as magic can destroy magic but not the belief in magic, so rhetoric can destroy rhetoric but in doing so once again delivers its audience over to a belief in rhetoric; magic and rhetoric are ordinarily unimpaired by scientific or rational argument that could demonstrate falsity in their performances and thereby separate the parties to such performances. A key factor here is the way the force of common assumptions (prevalent among an audience) is mobilized in the course of magic or rhetoric. This is well understood in magic, and with respect to rhetoric I have tried to show how much of its art also depends on providing audiences with the chance to supplement what they hear with their own beliefs, experiences and social knowledge. Success in this process means that a politician (like a magician) can sound socially informed without actually having to be so, and for his audiences, it means they are able to enjoy a suspension of disbelief about what they hear.

We can call upon this perspective to determine the relation between rhetoric and *propaganda*, not linguistically, but rather with respect to the audience's relationship with the speaker. What is meant when an audience condemns a speech as "propaganda"? One supposes that this word is popularly used only in a pejorative sense, and it is a stronger pejorative than "rhetoric" ever is. Most important of all, it carries a different sense than "rhetoric" which, as a pejorative, typically refers to a lack of earnestness or genuineness on the part of a speaker, or to a speaker who confines himself to commonplaces at the same time as he over-garnishes what he has to say. This is rhetoric as purple prose rather than as action. The charge of propaganda, on the other hand, seems to refer to an audience's perception of a speaker's assault on their common assumptions. This can happen in at least two ways: a speaker is judged to be 'begging the question'—propaganda as bad performance; or he is perceived as attempting to undermine the audience's loyalties and their commitments to action; this is propaganda as a kind of counter-performance. Haw Haw, Pound and Tokyo Rose were considered by many, during the Second World War, as propagandists on both these accounts—but not by those who were persuaded. Rhetoric persuades.

This raises the distinction between persuasion and *coercion*—not an easy one, but one which seems to be widely held as important for the delineation of rhetoric. Although the outcome intended of rhetoric is usually that of inducing conformity to a point of view, we like to characterize the means as persuasive rather than coercive. By what reasoning? If it is that persuasion is voluntary and coercion involuntary, we are in all likelihood being culturally simplistic. For any universal rule as to where and how coercion takes over from persuasion has to take into account the cultural specificity of logic and apperception, and different levels of experience within a culture. We are, however, on safer ground when we relate the distinction to the perception of situations of choice. There is a *prima facie* case of coercion when few choices of either speakers or ideologies are perceived as available; on the other hand, when there are overlapping audiences and speakers competing for their attention, persuasion (and with it, the art of rhetoric) is at a premium. Coercion and persuasion, then, may be regarded as positions on a gradient of perceived availability of choice.

Rhetoric and propaganda are themselves not distinguishable through reference to this variable of choice, and both occur in situations of varying degrees of choice. Propaganda is rejected rhetoric. Should there ever be a situation without any perceived choice, it would be sociologically pointless to speak of rhetoric. Though there is this important coda: rhetoric is itself devoted to the reduction of an audience's perception of choices.

Let us look again at the underlying notion of rhetoric as *action*. I particularly have in mind the effect by which a speech justifies an audience's beliefs, or—what is of greater pertinence politically—the justification people find in a speech for the persuasion it exerts over them.[8] However, there is rhetorical action (in this case usually non-verbal) of an assembly of people as well as of their speaker; in the fulfilment of rhetoric, the action of the one follows as a consequence of the other. The flow is not always, or only, from the speaker to his audience. Protest marchers 'take' their speakers to the platform. The possibility should also be kept in mind that non-verbal actions (like the carrying of banners, saluting or the laying of wreaths) may be more persuasive than verbal ones inasmuch as the former are more self-evident, or entirely so. Ultimately though, the two forms of rhetorical action are interdependent: who would listen to Labour-Day speeches without the parades—and who would deliver them? By the same token, who would find a justification for marching without the speeches?

As the Labour-Day example suggests, the actions of both speaker and assembled crowd may lie in the compulsion of an *occasion* that serves the need—which we all feel from time to time—to reaffirm our beliefs. In this instance, the occasion itself is *a fortiori* to the parades and the speakers, and we persuade ourselves. But in others—De Gaulle speaking in Quebec is an example—it is the rhetorical action itself that generates an occasion, and in doing so persuades us to accept at least some of the major consequences of our beliefs. And in yet others, of which "England Expects . . . " (prior to the naval engagement at Trafalgar) would be an example, history redeems the rhetorical action as the herald of what became an occasion.

Common to each of these senses of occasion is the dramatization of shared values. Aside from its possibly being a spur to pragmatic action, the role of rhetoric is that of agent in the ritualization of politics. Here we recognize ritual as, at once, symbolic action and a justification for what we have done or have to do. If occasions draw upon rhetoric, it seems that it is only in association with an occasion that a particular rhetorical performance can have longevity. Since 1871, for example, Labour politicians in England have made the annual journey north to speak at the Durham Miners' Gala (described in this volume by Rodger). There they address the largest assembly of people in Britain, whose views are in sympathy with their own, and for that they willingly pay the price of choosing words to match the occasion.

Of course, changes in media in our day have produced carefully stage-managed moves away from political oratory as a formal occasion. With the invention of radio, audiences could stay at their firesides and listen—the politician had to learn how to 'chat'; and now that television brings the physical presence of the politician in close-up, we may think we possess our politicians more than ever. We are probably wrong about this—in all ways *except the rhetorical.* The reason is that it is with respect to the rhetorical that the politician seeks to oblige us; he knows that the media now dispose us towards a relationship of familiarity with him; he realizes that we are likely to expect him to voice some of our secret thoughts as though they were also his (for example, Roosevelt's "The only thing we have to fear is fear itself"); he also knows that his best chance of continuing to possess us is in obliging us in these ways.

Even if we allow that the political speaker is guided by the W. I. Thomas dictum that "If men define situations as real, they are real in their consequences," one question still remains. *Who* does the defining? Demosthenes can be read as saying it is the orator's audience, and we have paid attention to this point of view. As a conclusion, however, it is insufficient, even erroneous. For the orator interposes his definitions between his audience and their sense of the situation and of what is real. In other words, there is a strong factor of differential power in the process we have described as persuasion; this is one reason why any inference about the presence of rhetoric as evidence of a society of "free" men (an idea that Burke has suggested) must be heavily qualified. That the successful political orator may leave us satisfied through the manipulation of our own predispositions still means that we can end up as committed to him as though he held a pistol at our heads.

Notes

1. Among a number of people who read an earlier draft of this chapter and offered suggestions for its improvement are John Comaroff, Lin Jackson, David Macdonald, and George Park.

2. This balance that must be struck between form and content is often lost through underrating content—*viz.* "The manner is not only a thing of moment, but of greater moment than the matter" (written by the young Gladstone shortly after entering the Commons; cited in Watson 1973: 125–26). The matter must always be made to matter; artifice may be necessary but when it is perceived it does not ordinarily aid persuasion. There are, then, limits to political "wordhood" (Bloomfield) or to the extent to which the language of a politician may safely focus attention upon itself. Whereas "Rose is a rose is a rose is a rose" (Gertrude Stein) belongs to the rhetoric of literary language, a politician, in his rhetoric, is well advised to turn a rose into a nosegay.

3. Bailey, in the next chapter, refers to this citation as an illustration of the distinction between the deliberative (Cicero: appeal to the mind) and hortatory (Demosthenes: appeal to the will) modes of rhetoric. I use it to illustrate a different point: the *fulfilling* of rhetoric. This I see a Demosthenes doing, whereas a Cicero falls short; and granted the notion of the fulfilment of rhetoric, we can expect it to appeal to both mind and will.

4. Indeed, a speaker may leave his "topic" so vague in the minds of his listeners that when asked what the speech was about, they are unable to say, though they may well recall a slogan or two.

5. The technical definition of enthymeme is a syllogism in which either a premiss or the conclusion is suppressed.

6. Cf. "administrative rhetoric" (Burke 1966: 301–2) and "rhetoric of actions" (Lloyd-Jones 1976: 11–12).

7. Specifically, *speech* is "in the form of utterances and spells" (cf. the slogans and enthymemes of rhetoric) and *action* is in "the manipulation of objects" (cf. Note 6).

8. The notion of *justification* in association with *action* I have adapted from Ellul's (1965) writing on propaganda; but whereas Ellul considers action as it emanates from an audience that has been persuaded—"the aim . . . is . . . to provoke action" (p. 25)—our view is that rhetoric itself is to be considered as action. Technically, this is the difference between perlocutionary (Ellul) and illocutionary utterances (see Austin 1962; Finnegan 1969; Tambiah 1973).

3

Dimensions of Rhetoric
in Conditions of Uncertainty

F. G. BAILEY

This essay will distinguish three dimensions of rhetoric and the contexts in which they are likely to be used. The three dimensions are *hortatory/deliberative*, referring to the orator's objective; *grandiloquent/tempered*, concerning his style; and *cardiac/pseudo-cerebral*, words that recognize the fact that persuasion can be addressed to the heart or (apparently) to the head. The main context considered is that of uncertainty.

Reason, Deliberative Hearings and Exhortations

Rhetoric is etymologically and historically linked with the spoken word, but the term refers to any persuasive tactic or resource that uses symbols. Thus cracking a skull—to invent a crude example of Burke's "administrative rhetoric" (1966: 301)—is not a rhetorical mode of persuading the victim although it may become so for the bystanders; indeed, it may have been done just to impress them.

In the presence of a rhetorician, *caveat auditor*. Those who are wary of rhetoric share a common opinion that the rhetorician is not in search of truth but is out to gain an advantage. He is a sophist, they say, who stoops to deceit and half-truth and employs sleight of tongue. His art guides the audience away from propositions that are empirically verifiable in the direction of what will 'sell,' what will excite, what will move that particular audience to action. What he says may by chance be in accordance with some empirical truth, but truth is not the first consideration. Rhetoric, it seems, would have no place if all decisions were reached by reason, if all men could see reason, and if seeing reason moved them to action.

Other opinions are kinder. Rhetoric, designed to capture the attention and the approval of a listener, is an aid to teaching. Also it can be, in itself, an object of aesthetic appreciation, a performance and a source of delight. The sophists, the founders of the systematic study of the art of rhetoric in the Greek world, mounted this defense: although rhetoric is a neutral instrument, a tool that can be used for good or bad ends, it behoves the just man to make himself skilled in the art so that he can better make truth prevail and better protect himself against being gammoned by the unjust man. The same arts can serve both the detective and the burglar, and it is a poor detective who does not know the burglar's standard tricks. The argument is incontrovertible, even if it commends the use of rhetoric only in a back-handed way.

The next argument finds more positive merits in rhetoric. Certainly rhetoric is the use of persuasive devices (figures of speech, the structure of an address, symbols, and so forth), but it is more than a mere set of tools. If one steps back from the single exhortation and looks instead at a succession of such exhortations—a hearing—then rhetoric is revealed as a form of argumentation, a way of testing ideas and evidence, and therefore, like the syllogistic mode of reasoning, a way of reaching a decision. The hearing in a law court proceeds in just this way (Berman 1968). Politico-administrative decisions, when taken by a council or a committee or a leader-in-council, are also reached through argumentation, the persuasive presentation of opposite points of view. Even when the decision is taken by a leader alone, it is said (and this is in line with one's intuitions) he is likely to rehearse rival arguments in his mind, along with their rhetoric, as a way of deciding what to do. In short, it is maintained that rhetoric is a form of deliberation, public or private, designed to reach a decision in matters which require action. Let us call this the *deliberative* use of rhetoric.

The contrary view, with which we began, can be stated more forcefully. Rhetoric is not a form of deliberation and has nothing to do with discussion. Indeed, insofar as the rhetorician allows debate (and therefore questioning, and therefore doubt) he is likely to fail in his purpose, which is to bend people to action. Rhetoric is a means of conveying to an audience a decision already reached, and conveying it in such a way that listeners will not only like the decision but also act upon it. The object of the rhetorician's address is not the intellect but rather the will. Duncan (1962: 175) cites Adlai Stevenson: "When Cicero spoke, the people said, 'How well he speaks!'; when Demosthenes spoke, the people said, 'Let us march!' " Cicero appealed to the intellect or to the palate, Demosthenes to the will. Let us call this *hortatory rhetoric* and so distinguish it from the deliberative mode.

Both kinds of rhetoric are opposed to decision-making by *reasoning*, which proceeds by logic and offers propositions about facts for empirical validation. Is it possible to identify the dimensions, the variations of which will distinguish between reason, deliberative hearings and exhortations?

Let us begin with a man, at a committee meeting, who wishes to turn the occasion into an exhortation to be delivered by himself, to close off the possibility of reasoning and deliberation, and, most of all, to exclude other people's exhortations. There are of course non-rhetorical expedients, the use of which depends upon force: controlling the agenda so that only the one speaker is allowed; adroit appeal to Robert's Rules, which, when used by a master, castrate with remarkable speed and efficiency; and various other forms of intimidation both inside and outside the committee room. Such practical actions are not, in themselves, symbolic and therefore are not rhetoric, although once practised successfully, they may gain symbolic value. Our present search is for strictly rhetorical artifices that inhibit the free exchange of ideas and allow only one side of the question to command attention.

These devices can be categorized by target or by form. Those that concern target fall into three classes: the cardiac, the pseudo-cerebral and the cerebral (reason). When the content is cardiac, the proponent (in this case the person who wishes to make this an occasion for exhortation and to inhibit free discussion) appeals to the heart rather than the head; he seeks to arouse passion and strives to excite emotion. His assumption, a reasonable one, is that people in a state of excitement are inhibited from applying scientific doubt. There are four emotions on which he can play, and they are linked in two pairs: love and hatred, fear and derision. All require the proponent to argue by asserting, as distinct from demonstrating, an association (or even an identification) between his proposal and some item, the validity of which his hearers (he hopes) would never think of doubting.

Some of the following are fundamental values in particular cultures: patriotism, free enterprise, anti-colonialism, the sacredness of the family, Christian charity, courage, honesty, equity, democracy, and whatever else. The doubter or questioner only reveals his own immorality and untrustworthiness. When there are powerful symbols available to the rhetorician, through metaphor or metonymy, the more convenient it is for him: flags, crosses, historical events (such as Valley Forge, Stalingrad, El Alamein, the Black Hole of Calcutta, July 4th or July 14th), historical figures (such as Stalin, Benedict Arnold, Churchill, Machiavelli, Garibaldi or Gandhi), motherhood, brotherhood (nowadays also sisterhood), blood, purity, faeces, and so on.

These symbols give the hearer a sense of being in touch with something firm, unshifting, reliable, almost—a paradox—concrete.

The same sense of concreteness can be achieved by the device of personifying. The rhetorician gives the listeners a person (sometimes a creature) with which they can identify. An example is Enoch Powell's notorious little old English war widow who, in a once respectable back street of Wolverhampton, bravely endures the insults of her immigrant "Negro" neighbours, keeps the door knob polished, the step whitened, and shovels up the highly symbolic message that comes through her letter box from time to time for use as manure on that bright, pure white English rose, which despite the squalid surroundings, flowered in her backyard (Smithies and Fiddick 1969: 41, rose added; Lloyd-Jones's chapter in this volume).

Another set of rhetorical contrivances explicitly closes off options by appealing to fear, to a sense of helplessness. These can be presented relatively unadorned, as in the invocation of authority: why debate alternative courses (to that favoured by the proponent) when the authorities will certainly not allow them to be put into practice? Constitutions and other forms of regulation also fall into this category, and custom and precedent can be used in the same way.

A related argument is that which invokes peril. To ignore the proponent's advice is to invite calamity. Any division of opinion will encourage a common enemy and allow him to prevail. Such arguments generally call for a more grandiloquent presentation than the straight invocation of authority. Powell used the colored immigrants in just this way. A notorious example is that of the Jew in Hitler's oratory: at one and the same time a peril, an explanation for all that had gone wrong, and a potent symbol of impurity and evil (Duncan 1962: 247).

Love and respect, fear and hatred are responses to powerful people who dominate those who feel the emotions. The rhetorician can turn in the other direction and, through derision, belittle the opposition. Ridicule cuts off an opponent from sources of authority and legitimacy, and puts him beyond the pale of the community of listeners. It also diverts their attention away from his proposal. Its dangers for the rhetorician, as Hitler noted, are that it may induce complacency and weaken the will to act (Duncan 1962: 241). For example, compare the indulgent image of Italians with the adrenalin-moving epithets for Germans, presented by allied propaganda in the Second World War.

All these are devices that are simple to identify. They are the "agit" part of Lenin's "agitprop," appealing to passions and emotions while bypassing the intellect (Smith 1968).

So much for cardiac devices. The pseudo-cerebral contrivances are those that give the appearance of using the forms of logic and the procedures of scientific reasoning, but in fact select or distort or shorten these procedures so that all sides of the question are not considered. One set of such artifices closely resembles cardiac appeals to fundamental values and legitimizing authority, but draws its symbols not so much from the everyday world of religious and social experiences as from authoritative philosophies. It appeals nearer the intellect because it purports to provide explicit premisses on which to reason. The speaker generally need not go into detail: "Marx writes . . ." or "If we are to follow Adam Smith . . ." are the rhetorical equivalents of flourishing a bank book or reviewing the troops, indications that the credit or the force is available if anyone is unmannerly or foolish enough to express doubt. The philosophies most useful for this purpose are those which provide an explanation for everything that happens (Popper 1961). These same philosophies are most likely to command religious (that is, never-doubting) adherents. Notice that there is also present one variant of the appeal to authority: since these philosophical systems provide inescapable laws of historical development, it is a matter of common prudence to go along with them.

There are more subtle varieties of pseudo-cerebration. All involve diverting critical attention, either in a kind of hyperbole, by asserting that the question at issue is only a part of a much larger concern, or using what might be called *structural metonymy*, by focusing on a relatively minor matter and so diverting attention from the main question. The hyperbolic track leads in two directions: either, as described above, to an appeal to the authority of a transcending philosophy; or to (that well-known strategem of those about to lose an argument) widening the issue so far as to produce mystification and collective paralysis.

Another contrivance treats as primary what, in fact, is derivative. If the proponent can get people deeply involved in an apparently constructive debate about a relatively minor matter, the major questions may never be asked. If your colleagues begin to take sides on the question of whether the new course on belly-dancing for men should be taught separately or along with the co-eds, you may never be asked the obvious question of whether or not such a course belongs at all in a university. I think this is one of the meanings that Burke attaches to "identification" when he gives the example of the shepherd: people are so fixated on pastoral loving care that they forget the lamb's terminus—the butcher's block (1966: 301).

Metonymy in a narrower form has a similar effect. Hearing a certain building purified as the "White House," the listener is discouraged from recalling the dirty linen that names and events would otherwise bring to mind. Both methods, hyperbole and metonymy, enable the speaker to avoid stating his argument explicitly. Thus, to quote Bentham (from

Burke 1955: 98), the address "without the form [has] the force of an assumption." When detected, such an act is called *petitio principii*: begging the question.

All these devices, in both the cardiac and the pseudo-cerebral categories, stray from the matter-of-fact, step-by-step presentation of propositions logically connected and/or offered for empirical testing. They incline the listener to empathize, arouse an attitude and incite action; all inhibit questions from empirically minded individuals. There is a further expedient common in university committees, in which a high value is set upon scientific rationality. It resembles those diets that make you slim by having you eat nothing but french-fried potatoes: hunger dies from a surfeit. If the committee members want facts and figures, provide them, pressed down and running over until no one can make out which end of the tool is the handle and which the cutting edge. There is a fine account of this method in a book by Ely Devons (1961). To call this scientific rhetoric is apt. It appeals to authority (the inevitable is 'demonstrated' at the same time as it invokes a procedure that commands legitimacy and that has become a symbol of modernity in scholarship: obscuring by mystification (emulating the squid which conceals itself in a cloud of ink) and focusing attention on what is derivative (the method) rather than on what is primary (the question at issue).

There are other forms of rhetoric that draw partly from the authority of science[1] and partly from human nature. The great virtue in the scientific attitude—exercising doubt—appears in a more common guise as cynicism: refusing to have the passions aroused and writing off exhortation either as a tasteless façade erected to conceal the deformities of self-interest, or as "too sappy to put over on an adult mind" (Merton 1949: 281). The situation can be remedied by the use of what Merton calls the "propaganda of fact": a plain statement of an empirically verifiable fact and therefore 'scientific.' An example is: "He invented a new drug, and he tested it first on himself." But the form of the statement—a statement of fact in the indicative mood—is the extent of the science. Put the statement in context, and the listener is being exhorted to think: "What a brave and dedicated man!" (It can come out as: "What an idiot!") But more is involved here than the simple and familiar use of an indicative form for an imperative mood, like the message addressed to a booking clerk: "I want a ticket to London." The listener is being manipulated as a novelist manipulates his readers, by the tactic of indirection: not telling him (and so boring him or rousing his resentment) but rather giving him the satisfaction of working things out for himself. Thus the rhetorician can avoid the "sappy address" and still put one over on the "adult mind." Indeed, the more adult the mind thinks itself, the more complicated and technical can be the information conveyed to lead it towards a conclusion. It can be a very effective way of appealing to that form of authority that is a demonstration of the inevitable. To identify it, we can mingle two rhetorical terms and call it *suggestio veri*.

So far we have examined the cardiac and the pseudo-cerebral as devices that help the rhetorician discourage free discussion. I turn now briefly to form, a category which includes figures of speech, such as metaphor, simile, hyperbole and meiosis, metonymy and others. In fact, there is a formidably long list (see Fowler 1937). Some of these, such as *suggestio falsi* and *suppressio veri*, refer to content. But what are we to make of such purely verbal mannerisms as alliteration, or of such speaker's mannerisms as apostrophe or other artifices which are "doctrinally neutral" (Burke 1966: 296)? I do not know whether one or more of these is of particular use in sealing off a discussion, but it does seem that the frequent employment of some of them in an address is an indication that the speaker is trying to 'hype' his audience (a convenient verb indicating the inducement of a state of ecstasy). Others, like persiflage or bathos, are used to de-hype (or sober up) the audience, possibly as a way of making a transition from the cardiac to the pseudo-cerebral or even to the cerebral modes of presentation.

This suggests that the figures of speech and their associated structural devices, by their frequency and intensity, indicate the dominant mode of the address: whether in its appeal it is cardiac, pseudo-cerebral or cerebral and, in its form, grandiloquent, tempered or plain (to use Cicero's categories). The grandiloquent, like Hitler's oratory, eliminates discussion; the tempered allows discussion; the plain encourages it. An hortatory address will therefore be grandiloquent, a deliberative address should be tempered, and the communication of scientific results should be plain.

These are the choices before a speaker. Is there any internal logic between these three modes, such that one can predict the mode used by the opponent from that chosen by the proponent? At first sight, it seems that there might be. A virtuoso display of grandiloquent oratory will surely put the members of the audience in such a state of ecstasy, will so numb their brains, that they can respond only to more of the same kind: a Gresham's law (or the reverse) of rhetoric. Indeed, this rule holds for many political exchanges besides the verbal: firearms are to be countered with other firearms, not fists. But I do not think that it is entirely so in the case of rhetorical modes: I have sat too often in committees and watched with admiration while a colleague, in a matter-of-fact way, punctures the last speaker's balloon and gently wafts the gas out of the window, leaving the atmosphere pure enough for plain reason. It is true that some kind of *rite de passage*, some transitional speaking may be required, but if we are to understand why one or another mode of address carries the day, we must direct our attention not so much (or at least not only) to the grammatical requirements of rhetorical communication— to questions of syntax—but more to the contexts of uncertainty that rhetoricians and their audiences experience.

Contexts of Uncertainty

Certain contextual features encourage the use of emotive appeals to potent symbols and to fundamental values; other features promote matter-of-fact discussions in which all are concerned more to find the truth or to solve a problem than to make their own opinion prevail.

If the context has no external 'authority' exercising a constraint on both proponent and opponent, then speakers are freer to use an hortatory mode. In this proposition the concept *authority* includes not only persons (such as judges, or an audience that will vote one way or the other) but also the sharing of common values and membership in the same community.

Sometimes the opponent is not in fact present to make a reply. He is defined by the proponent as an enemy and a person outside the moral community, the cause of misfortune and the embodiment of evil. Campus radicals and their administrators tend to treat one another in this fashion. The administrators of a particular campus in a "multiversity" (Kerr 1972) externalize the central administration in the same way. Likewise, through his oratory and in a grimly literal fashion, Hitler excoriated the Jews.

Why should such rhetoric be hortatory? First—for those who like pedantry—it is so in a literal sense: if the opponent, being absent or excluded, cannot make a reply, the address must be an exhortation, for the other forms of rhetoric call for discussion. Secondly, the address is intended not to change the mind of an opponent, but to convince or to reinforce the convictions of an audience, whose members have already (the rhetorician assumes) excluded the opponent from their moral community. Therefore, he need not temper the address in the hope of making the opponent more pliant by massaging him.

On the other hand, if the opponent is a member of the community and cannot be easily excluded, and if the proponent is likely to meet him again in other debates, then he will be more inclined to try (or at least to go through the motions of trying) to convince him. In order to do so, he will employ a more rational approach. In other words, the proponent will be less reluctant to search for common ground from which to launch his argument. The reason for this restraint is that hortatory appeals tend to be addressed to ultimate values or ultimate authorities and so do not leave room for compromise. An opponent revealed as the embodiment of sin is to be destroyed, not met halfway. Therefore, if the context makes compromise expedient (or a show of willingness to compromise), the speaker, to be effective, must stop short of grandiloquence and employ the more tempered discourse of pseudo-cerebration or reason.

It is not always possible to do so because ultimate values and ultimate authorities, in any particular society, do not constitute a single consistent set. This is true in many universities where there is an irreconcilable dilemma between the demand for teaching and the demand for research. Once a discourse reaches an irreconcilable level (or, in the view of sensible and pragmatic persons, sinks to these depths), there remains no mode of interaction other than assertion and counter-assertion, its effectiveness depending on grandiloquence and hortatory skills.

Yet the continued orderly existence of any society is contingent, in part, upon the capacity of its members to pretend that they share an ultimate agreement, which becomes the ultimate source of stability and certainty. In other words, as is well known, some things are sacred. We live under the ultimate guidance of "the Bible" or "the constitution" or "the law" or "Marxist-Leninist principles" or whatever else. We create roles to impersonate and promulgate ultimate values in the persons of judges, or administrators who must bear the final responsibility. The person in such a role (and the code which he represents) is likely to push debaters towards moderation, towards argumentation based on pseudo-cerebration and towards tempered discourse because in that way the myth of shared common values is less likely to be damaged. You can go so far as to remark that your honourable friend sometimes has trouble in walking and chewing gum at the same time, but you cannot call him "that skunk from Grand Rapids" because skunks are part of no man's moral community. The phrase also brings into question, by its extreme incivility, the continued existence of that community. But the mode of pseudo-cerebration has at least the simulacrum of a belief that it is possible to start from common agreed-upon principles (even though occasionally one cannot find them).

An audience in certain circumstances is a kind of authority and its expectations about what it should hear will determine which mode of rhetoric will be effective. Other things being equal, if the mode is grossly out of accord with the audience's expectations, the speech will be judged "in poor taste" or even "meaningless." (There are conditions in which the speaker can get away with, or even profit from, doing the unexpected. Briefly, the art lies in making statements that astound the audience and so catch its attention, but at the same time being sure that the audience, upon reflection, will come to understand what was said and why it was appropriate to have said it.)

What governs an audience's expectations? First, audiences vary according to their culture and sophistication. Some have had much experience in listening to detailed argument and consider themselves insulted by anything less. They want reasoning, or at least pseudo-cerebration. Others do not have the capacity, or choose not to exercise it. There is a comical account by Dr. Bunzel (Bunzel 1975), the president of San Jose State University, in which he describes his attempts to convince a committee of the Assembly of the California Legislature that the university's procedures, which maintain a degree of confidentiality in personnel files, are not only expedient but also just and equitable. In a very literal sense the committee showed itself on that occasion unwilling to listen to reason.

Secondly, the expectations of the audience will depend upon its composition, in particular upon the degree of heterogeneity. It is generally assumed (and I think, correctly) that the larger the audience the more likely it is to contain varieties of people, and that in such a situation appeals should be made to the most common factor (which, from the point of view of reasoning, is also likely to be the lowest). In other words, when the audience is large it pays to make the appeal through motherhood, sex, faeces, patriotism, and the various other grossly hortatory symbols.

Thirdly, the balance between exhortation and reasoning will depend upon the nature of the problems. Where to land the apparatus on Mars, how to prevent theft in the library, or how to make the bookstore show a profit are problems that should (at least in principle) induce a more reasoned debate (since all parties have presumably agreed to what they want) compared with such complicated issues as the proper use of graduate students as teaching assistants, or the appropriate balance of time and energy allotted to teaching, research and committee service. This expectation is thwarted often enough, but by and large Burke (1955: 51) is probably correct when he writes ". . . in proportion as the rhetorician deals with a special subject matter, his proofs move away from the rhetorical and towards the scientific."

Fourthly, one must consider the political significance of both the audience and the occasion. In university committees there is a marked gradation in the level of exhortation between the usually small committees that conduct their affairs behind a screen of confidentiality and the larger committees that work in the full light of publicity. A larger committee—a university senate to which every faculty member belongs is the example I have in mind—tends to exhibit the features of a debating society, even when it has the power and the responsibility to make decisions that will have practical consequences. The senate is a place where differences and contradictions in fundamental values get an airing. Exhortation and grandiloquence about high policy flourish, whereas detailed argument and close reason about implementation meet with inattention or even ribaldry. It is a place for ventilating, reinforcing and embellishing ideologies: the practical plans to be drawn up in the light of those ideologies (compromise between rival ideologies is therefore required) are made and implemented elsewhere.

The 'reality' argumentation occurs in smaller committees or in 'cabinets' of administrators. In such gatherings debate about fundamental ideologies is considered a waste of time and differences are quickly suppressed in the interest of finding solutions to practical problems and putting the solutions into action. The members of a 'back-room' committee of this kind do not have to worry whether their statements will keep their personal image bright before the audience, because there is no audience. To a much greater extent than in larger gatherings, their arguments can be addressed to finding the best solution rather than to humbling a rival and so inflating one's own reputation. In fact, a too obvious desire for victory in debate would diminish the image of a practical, reasonable and, above all, realistic servant of the institution, and without this image, he would not be invited to serve. Therefore the grandiloquence and the heart-stirring appeals to passion are curbed, for they get in the way of cool calculations, inhibit compromise and expose long-standing animosities that paralyze small groups. The larger gatherings, unrestrained by the need to find a solution to immediate problems, can afford sustained disagreement. In smaller groups grandiloquence provokes mild ridicule, and even the briefest of exhortations causes embarrassment.

So we come back to asking what conditions require decisions to be reached by deliberative rhetoric as opposed to reasoning. When there is no agreement about the axioms from which reasoning can proceed towards a decision, there is no alternative to the use of rhetoric. By definition, there is no scientific way of settling such issues. Questions about ultimate values, what is intrinsically right and good and just, are of this kind. They are not matters of fact but matters of opinion. The more ultimate values are brought into question, the higher rises the feeling that earth's foundations are about to crumble, and the result is a rise in emotion and level of exhortation. Conditions of uncertainty, in which the parameters are unknown and the worst is anticipated, tend to numb the capacity for calm reflection and critical thought and the willingness to listen to detailed reasoning. The people need reassurance, they need to have their passions aroused, and they are open to exhortation and grandiloquence.

Even small back-room committees sometimes find themselves in this impasse, and there are various rhetorical routes for bypassing it. One often hears statements from chairmen such as, "I hear what you are saying and it is a difficult and important question. But I think we, having taken notice of the question, should arrange for a discussion elsewhere, because the issues are too big for this group to reach a decision." Alternatively, "I do not think we have all the information we need to settle that. Why don't you and I and Jack and maybe a few others get together next week and work it out, and then we can report back." The adroit chairman will take care not to report back, or if he does, to do so in such a way that further argumentation is inappropriate.

There are other situations where the fundamental goals and the axioms from which to begin reasoning are not matters of debate, because everyone is agreed upon them, but they are so complicated that they cannot be used to lead to a rational decision. In principle it may be possible (since everyone is agreed about the goal), but in practice no one can achieve sufficient intellectual control over the many variables to make a genuinely rational argument. To give one example, all those involved in decisions about strategy agreed that the goal in the Second World War was to defeat Germany. But the debate about saturation-bombing of civilian targets as against the use of resources in other fields was settled not by rational argument, but by the clash of rival rhetorics and the destruction of personal reputations (Snow 1962).

The issues that come before legal officers and the law courts are often as complex. Who is telling the truth? Where does equity lie? What will be the future consequences of this decision for the law and for society? The difficulties are compounded because the ultimate questions concern right, good and justice—all matters of opinion, not fact. Administrators face the same decision when compelled to choose between conflicting advice from different experts. Each area of expertise can proceed to its decision by reasoning within its own accepted paradigms, but there is no meta-science resolving the conflicts between the different bodies of knowledge, only the art of the administrator. In short, in such cases there is no way of making a decision except through the use of rhetoric and making the choice according to the most persuasive opinions.

If this is so, in what respect can we say that one decision, among those arrived at in this way, is better than any other?

On questions of ultimate values, one can conceive of no absolute standard of "better": the adjective means nothing without the addition of "in the opinion of X."

On the impossibly complicated politico-administrative and legal questions, a decision by rhetoric (victory going to the most powerful and effective advocate) simply adds other imponderables to the equation: Will Winston be in form? Will George get his nose too much into the sherry and again foul everything up by putting on his *macho* act and making our side look ridiculous? Our man is just a beginner—that's all we can afford—and they have got money enough to hire a Queen's Counsellor. With Ralph on our side, there is no way we can lose. In short, the complexities of the original issues are compounded by the varying abilities of the advocates and the chances of their day in court.

So why make decisions in this way? Or at least, why pretend that this is a reasonable way of reaching a decision? The answer is that we are essentially talking about practical reasoning, not about how many angels can dance on the head of a pin or whether God made the world and then withdrew from it leaving us to do what we will, but how to raise funds to cut the dry rot out of the cathedral roof timbers. No decision means no action, and no action means that one day the cathedral roof, lead and all, will come down on the Bishop's head.

Then why not spin a coin? Why not consult an astrologer? There are statesmen who do that, but most of us would feel that such a recourse leaves matters too much to God; and anyway, it is said in Christian religion (and often lived out by the practitioners of such passive religions as Hinduism), God helps those who help themselves. So we work to make a decision and we have faith that by feeling the weight of different points of view, somehow the right one will be selected. The alternative is inaction, the final despairing admission that there is, after all, no order in things.

Thus deliberative rhetoric becomes a part of that sustaining human myth that, even if only a little, we do control our own destinies. Anyway, short of these religious heights, it could be added that since right always turns out to be defined as might, then by finding out who is mighty, at least we have a better chance to implement a decision, even if it later turns out not to provide the anticipated benefits.

To conclude. In one way or another, grandiloquence is a function of uncertainty: there is no supreme certainty-giving authority to moderate the extravagances of the rhetorician; the audience is a bewildering mixture, so play safe by aiming at the universal passions; there is no agreement, only a confusing discordance about fundamental values; no rational decision can be made in the face of such complexity. Conversely, the more people feel that their problems can be solved, therefore posing no ultimate threat to their continued existence, the less (leaving aside the aesthetic appeal of 'performance') they are receptive to hortatory rhetoric. Between these two extremes comes deliberative rhetoric.

Note

1. "Rhetoric" may be used in another way, which, although convenient, somewhat stretches the meaning of the word. The practitioners of each scientific discipline have a characteristic style of communicating their ideas. The several natural sciences have, what are in effect, protocols for use in publishing results: thus there exists a mode of communication that may be called "scientific rhetoric" (Hexter 1968). Since the propositions of science are supposed to be addressed to the intellect and not to the will, one might argue that "rhetoric" is less appropriate than "style." But there are two reasons for being inflexible about this usage. Firstly, certain scientific propositions do turn out to be matters of opinion, of faith and of will (see Kuhn 1970; and Snow 1962). Secondly, in certain cultures and in certain situations the mere use of a scientific style is itself a rhetorical device, inclining the listeners towards faith and away from the quest for proof.

The Head and the Heart

4

Rhetoric and Ritual Politics: The Durham Miners' Gala

IAN RODGER

> . . . anyone who is not inspired and carried
> beyond his own limited aspirations by the
> Durham Miners' Gala is incapable of under-
> standing with heart as well as head, what
> membership and leadership of the Labour Move-
> ment is all about.
>
> Sir Harold Wilson (Quoted in *The Guardian*,
> 29 December 1977)

Introduction

Most studies of the nature of rhetoric concentrate on its use, or misuse, by individuals. It is an attractive and absorbing exercise to analyse the linguistic and dramatic techniques individuals employ, and to compare the varying styles which they use at open-air meetings, in parliaments, and in radio and television transmissions. It is easy to assume, when conducting such studies, that rhetoric is a device controlled solely by the individuals seeking to manipulate a political or social group—or a nation.

When we compare, however, the use of rhetoric by individuals in different cultures, it becomes obvious that their audiences are not wholly passive but predetermine the quality and style of the rhetoric used to address them. It can be said that rhetoric often affirms, or refers to, what is regarded by the listeners as a known truth. It follows that individuals employing rhetoric must know something of their audiences' concep-
tions of these truths. If they are to be successful, they must possess far more than a linguistic or oratorical competence. They must know the emotional temperature of their audiences. They must be acquainted with their audiences' social and political folklore, including past

utterances that were once effective but that have become inappropriate or even the subject of banal jokes. A British politician, for example, who tries to evoke the Dunkirk Spirit on the relatively less dire occasion of economic crisis or industrial unrest is liable to immediate ridicule. Long before the Second World War ended, the majestic phrases of Churchill's 1940 speeches had become the subject of barrack-room and music-hall (vaudeville) burlesque, and it would be a foolish politician who evoked these phrases on any occasion that was demonstrably less fraught than those which faced Britain in 1940. An American politician likewise has to know that the calculated rhetoric of the moon landing has already become a debased currency and that a similar fate has overtaken some of the statements in President Kennedy's inaugural speech.

But this is not to say that people who resort to burlesques of these rhetorical utterances are without respect for past heroes like Kennedy or Churchill, or no longer honour the occasions that inspired their speeches. A good politician who seeks to claim the mantle of past heroes and to assert that he is party to the received truths of his audience must know precisely where the jokes stop and veneration begins. The politician must also take care to adapt his delivery to the occasion and venue of his address. Just as the actor in a movie may employ minute gestures to indicate emotions and meaning which would be invisible and meaningless in a theatre, the politician must adopt a behaviour suited to the occasion and the expectation of his audience.

It follows that we cannot safely arrive at a description of rhetoric that can apply equally in all cultures, or even on all occasions within a particular culture. The charged drama of Hitler's shouted orations to the Nuremburg rallies in the 1930s in Germany would be excessive, intolerable and politically counter-productive at a German political meeting today. The style of Martin Luther King, which derives from sermons to Black congregations in the southern states, is inimical to most English-speaking listeners outside the United States. They may be moved by recordings of his speeches, but it is more the art and technique of his delivery and the knowledge of his tragic death that is affecting. Such listeners are not party to the known truths which King shared with his audience; nor are they acquainted with the intimate pattern of dialogue between speaker and quondam preacher, and with the intricacies of response to deliberately repeated phrases—all of which achieves the catharsis of a chorale in a cantata.

If we accept that rhetorical styles relate specifically to individuals and their cultures, it is important to consider rhetoric not only from the point of view of the individual's use of it but also as a concept understood, received and accepted by the audience. If we accept that the individual must know his audience well to use rhetoric effectively, we must presume that there is a shared knowledge between speaker and listeners. One of the obstacles to such an approach is that rhetoric is often regarded pejoratively. Rhetoric has incorporated the adjective *false* in its definition. This mistaken meaning has arisen, in part, because it is in the nature of continuing dialogues between politicians and their audiences that effective and 'good' rhetoric can, like lightning, strike only once in the same place. Last year's tocsin can become next year's tired joke. Phrases that once launched revolutions and wars enter the museum of a society's memory. Politicians who carelessly employ such phrases in a new social and historical context are readily identified as people using false rhetoric. It is our misfortune that many politicians throughout the world are lazy word-spinners, whose language diminishes the art of rhetoric. It would be a mistake to presume that rhetoric is present only when it is badly used and it would be a further mistake to assume that it is employed only in highly charged emotional situations.

The mention of the styles of Martin Luther King and Hitler, for example, should not lead us to conclude that rhetoric appears only when politicians shout (cf. Park's chapter in this volume). In cultures disposed to the hyperbole of understatement, rhetoric is no less present. The use of the understatement in such cultures can be a rhetorical device in itself. The art of rhetoric is practised as much by those who appear to say very little in one cultural context as by those who appear to say a great deal in another. There are many occasions and situations when politicians share such a common bond of understanding with their audiences that the act of rhetoric is not overt or specific on their part but pervades the occasions in which they and their audience take part.

One such occasion in Britain is the Durham Miners' Gala, which takes place annually on the third Saturday of July in Durham City. The Gala, which is also known colloquially as the Big Meeting, is the largest annual open-air gathering of trade unionists and their families in Great Britain. In its heydey, when the Durham coal field extended to all parts of the county, it used to attract an estimated 250,000 people. Even today, when the area of the coal field has shrunk and only the eastern part of the county bordering the North Sea is still mining coal, the Gala attracts about 100,000 people. With the exception of the years of the First and Second World Wars, it has been held in Durham City since 12 August 1871. It is an occasion that no Labour prime minister in Britain can afford to miss.

The Durham Mines and Miners

Any attempt to examine the social and political significance of the Gala, and the relationship and understanding between those who attend it and those who come to speak at it must take some account of the history of Durham and its mines. Durham contains the oldest worked coal fields in Britain (Fynes 1873; Garside 1971). Coal was being mined for profit by the monks in the fourteenth century. During the sixteenth century, coal was taken from Durham pits to the staithes at Newcastle upon Tyne, from where it was exported by sea to London. Until the development of rail transport, the British economy was wholly dependent upon ship-ping coal by sea from Durham and Northumberland. The metaphor still in use to indicate wasteful activity, "taking coals to Newcastle," is a monument to this trade. It is also relevant that George Stephenson, a County Durham man, first made his mark as an inventor by developing an improved form of pit-head winding gear and that before he built the Rocket steam engine, he first had to design iron railroads for trans-porting coal, which in his day was drawn by horses from the pits to the Newcastle staithes.

Another and more melancholy indication of the great age of the Durham coal field is that the names of Durham villages dominate the early history of mining disasters. These accidents, which sometimes killed off most of the male population in a village, were due more to the lack of knowledge of the dangers of fire damp than to criminal negligence or carelessness on the part of greedy mine owners. In the Middle Ages coal was harvested from drift mines and coal seams near the surface. When these resources were exhausted, mining operations then necessitated sinking shafts so that coal could be extracted at lower levels. Devices such as Stephenson's winding gear made this possible, but the dangers involved in deep mining were not yet realized.

The fact that coal mining is a very ancient activity in Durham County has a bearing on the social history of the area. It is important to realize that coal mining in Durham developed within or close to es-tablished settlements. Generally, mining activities elsewhere in the world start with geological surveys determining the existence of an ore or mineral beneath relatively open country. A shaft is then sunk and the pit-head attracts shanty towns that, in due course, become established settlements inhabited by migrants from other parts of the world. In Durham, "coal-getting" began in or near villages that had been settled as far back as Roman times, or at least as far back as the Anglian settle-ment *circa* A.D. 600. The winning of coal in these villages during the Middle Ages can be compared to the act of wooding in forest settlements elsewhere in Britain during the same period. Though the land under which the coal lay was owned by the lords of the manor, whose descendants were later to invest capital to exploit both the coal and the miners who worked it, there was a common interest in extracting it. It is beside the point whether individual landlords were oppressive or benign towards their tenants. What is more significant is that as mining developed and grew more profitable, the landlords tended to withdraw from close contact with their tenants and concentrated their attention on managing their agricultural estates. (It is worth noting that most visitors to the county are usually amazed to find a remarkably beautiful pastoral landscape surrounding the mining villages.) Generally, they remained isolated socially from the villages, with the result that the villagers tended to look to themselves for mutual support.

Though there has always been a small agricultural work force in Durham villages, coal mining was until recently the only means of gaining a living. The social differences, which sometimes exist elsewhere in mining towns between the miners and those who run shops or provide ancillary services, do not exist to the same extent in Durham villages. The owners of small shops, for example, were, and still are, tenants of their property. During the Lock-Out of 1921, when the mine owners sought to impose a cut in miners' wages, they resorted (in some villages) to the device of enforcing the closure of small shops and tenanted public houses. This atrocious act had the effect of creating common cause among all who lived in the villages. The cutting off of the beer supply led to the creation by the miners of co-operative breweries, which brew the ale known as "Miners' Federation." It is still gloriously on sale in working-men's clubs in the county and is, incidentally, also on tap in the House of Commons.

It is most important to realize the effects that the Lock-Out and the events of the General Strike of 1926 had on mining villages. In places like Chopwell in the northwest part of the county, the "Strike," as it is known, created for a short period virtually autonomous states with individual collectives. In Chopwell, Harry Boldon,[1] the chairman of the Miners' Lodge, even organized the supply of fish in lorry convoys from wharves at Tynemouth and declared Chopwell a republic. This kind of action, which was faithfully depicted by Jim Allen in his series of four plays called "Days of Hope" on BBC-TV in 1976, encourages many people who do not know the Durham miners to think of them only as political militants. But the action they took in 1926, which had a political expedient, was made possible and effective because cohesive and parochial communities fashioned by the harsh regimes of the coal mine already existed.

The practice of working coal in these villages dominates the life of everyone in the community. Children, for example, must learn early in their lives not to make too much noise in the streets while night-shift workers are asleep. The arbitrary absence of men on different shifts means that women, retired miners and older miners working at the pit top are drawn into the social organization of the community. No individual, unless he or she is perverse, can ever feel that he does not belong to this community. One might think that because the dominant political affiliation is to the Labour party, this party would play a considerable part in social life. But the focus of society is to be found in working-men's clubs, which serve a social rather than a political aim. It is often presumed by outsiders that these clubs must be hotbeds of political militancy, but they largely serve more parochial ends. Douglass, who worked in the Durham coal field for some years, remarks in his pamphlet (1973) that Durham miners tend to prefer black jokes about mine safety or in-jokes about local characters to jokes with a more general political reference. He comments that although the only kinds of pit ballads usually heard outside the pits are disaster ballads, "most young miners love to hear songs about their own village and workplace."

This attachment to village life, which is thought to be typical only of rural villages largely or wholly dependent upon agriculture, is common throughout the county. Certainly the bonds exerted by the squirearchy and the Church of England in rural villages have no place here. The Christian message that we are all on this earth to help each other is expressed through the Methodist and other non-conformist churches, but it scarcely needs underlining in a community that is aware, through its daily work, of the practical application of this message. Other habits typical of the rural village are an intense interest in gardening, support for local football and cricket teams, and even occasional poaching. More special to the area are the breeding and flying of racing pigeons, the rearing of whippets, and the growing of leeks, which engages such a passion that it cannot be classified as mere horticulture. The leeks, grown from specially selected and fiercely guarded seed, are fed on secret recipes until they grow to a prodigious size.

In the 1950s, however, miners began to acquire private cars, and the pattern of wholly localized leisure has been breaking down. Before the fifties extra-local activities were limited to forays by bus or hired coach to the larger towns, to race meetings and league football matches in Sunderland and Newcastle; now it is possible to make frequent and unscheduled visits by car. A Tyneside-based comedy series for television called "The Likely Lads" recorded this social change, depicting one of the lads as the classic working-class Geordie preferring the old ways, and the other as a man of pretensions towards a bourgeois style of life. Needless to say it was always the pretensions of the latter that led to his downfall.

A sentimental attachment to the more solid virtues of the past and a distaste for the gimmickry of consumer capitalism are not confined to the North East of England. But the widespread grief and alarm that accompanied the National Coal Board's programme of pit closures in the western part of County Durham, when these pits were found to be uneconomic, were very real. It may be supposed that these closures should have occasioned a wave of relief that the long period of enslavement to coal had come to an end. Yet in many villages these closures were strongly opposed, not merely because the means of livelihood was being taken away from them but also because the closures meant the end of the whole way of life associated with mining.

I recall, for example, an ex-miner from a pit near Spennymoor who was only 25 years old and not therefore someone who had spent a long working life below ground. He wept as he told me of the day his pit closed. He had lost much more than a dangerous job that day. The rhythm of his village's life had been destroyed. The intricate social relationships of trade-union lodges, the local government administration, the local Labour party, the churches, and the social clubs were broken apart. For, even if other work could be found, it meant adjusting to alien work patterns in factories in nearby towns. The tacit trust and understanding of the pit, reinforced by kinship and long association with neighbours, had no place in the alternative world of the factory. Many miners in West Durham found that they could adapt to this world, and despite the tedium of commuting, many of them have now found work in the east part of the county, where the coal seams extend under the North Sea.

It is these village-minded people, with their parochial loyalties, who make up the majority of those who attend the Big Meeting. It should be clear by now that they are not the industrial workers or trade-unionists of popular imagination. They are not urban-based members of the proletariat, whose only bond beyond immediate family ties is their membership in a club or a union or a political party. This is not to say that they are politically illiterate or apathetic. Durham County is one of the strongholds of the British Labour party, and its county council claims to be the oldest continuous socialist administration in the world. The people who continually vote this administration into power and who annually go to the Big Meeting in Durham City do not need or expect to be galvanized into militant action. Unlike the urban-based factory worker, they are not isolated individuals coming together to be told that they have common aims. Just as they already know who they are, where they come from and who they identify with, they also know the political argument in their sleep. They have an abiding manifesto of their own, one which they know so well that it scarcely needs specifying and enunciating.

For them there is nothing novel in demanding better wages for a dangerous job or better working conditions. Disdaining clarion calls to instant action, they take a longer historical view, believing in the inevitability of their gentle victory. Douglass (1973) puts this well when he dedicates his pamphlet, "To the Durham miners who have filled my heart with an unshakeable belief in the liberation of humanity." The programme for the 93rd Gala in 1976, issued by the Durham branch of the National Union of Miners (NUM), quotes Thomas Hepburn, a Durham miners' leader, who said in 1831: "To know how to wait is the secret of success."

The impatient revolutionary might well say that these miners have already waited too long, but such a view is really irrelevant. We are not dealing here with the way others might like the Durham miners to act, but with the way they are. It is important to remember this when examining the rituals of the Gala and the nature and content of the speeches delivered at it. The people who converge in their thousands on the ancient city of Durham on the third Saturday of every July are people who believe that success lies in knowing how to wait.

THE EMPTIED CITY

The backcloth to this annual event is undeniably spectacular. Durham itself is a piece of rhetoric in stone. The city clusters round a loop in the River Wear, which is known to geographers as an incised meander. The loop contains a piece of ground, known as the peninsular, whose summit peaks above the level of the surrounding houses. On top of this peninsular stands the Norman Cathedral, which is guarded on the north side by the castle. This magnificent architectural assembly shouts that here is not only an ancient centre of learning enclosing the shrines of St. Cuthbert and the Venerable Bede, but a fortress. It inspired Sir Walter Scott to say of it: "Half Church of God, half fortress 'gainst the Scot." In the days when the monks and their serfs began winning coal from drift mines, this city was the power base of the North East of England, and the Bishopric of Durham was as much a martial appointment as a theological one. For many centuries Durham's incumbent bore the singular honour of the title of Prince Bishop. In the hierarchy of the Church of England, Durham comes next to the Archbishoprics of York

and Canterbury, and its bishop is privileged, along with those of York
and Canterbury, to take part in the crowning of a British monarch.

Such a privilege is now only a relic from the days when political
power was fused between Church and State, but it has naturally left
other legacies that distinguish the society of Durham City from the
societies of the county's villages. The peninsular remained an
ecclesiastical stronghold for many centuries and is now the centre of
Durham University. In the days when the miners staged their first galas,
the officers and clergy of the Church of England lived on the peninsular
in a style familiar to any reader of the novels of Trollope, but with
conventions of service and respect that were unknown in the pit villages.
The fact that the city was, and still is to some extent, the administrative
centre for the county also contributed to the making of an isolated
middle class there. The enlargement of the university during the past
thirty years has reinforced this bourgeois tradition, which is antipathetic
to the miners and their cause.

When the miners enter the city on foot, having disembarked from
their hired coaches at the perimeter, the city is almost empty. In July the
university is on vacation and its students and most of its staff are absent.
Knowing of the congestion the event causes, foreign tour operators give
Durham a miss on Gala Day. But there is also a deliberate absence on this
day of many of Durham's middle-class residents. Such people announce
their social and political disaffiliation by making it clear in advance that
they will be out of town for the Gala. They will even see to it that they
pronounce it in the accepted pronunciation of "Gahla" and not in the
local style of "Geyla." The social aspirant will make sure that his newly
desired friends all know that he too is leaving the city for the weekend. It
is not socially smart to be caught on the streets on the day of the Big
Meeting. This dissociation from the event on the part of those whom the
miners tend to call "the posh folk" is not merely passive and verbal; it
has physical expression of a rather dramatic kind.

Though Saturday is a normal shopping day, many of the shops are
boarded up. This boarding up is not makeshift. Most Durham shop
fronts have specially designed fixtures to accommodate the boards that
are used only once a year on Gala Day. Late on the previous Friday
night, the streets of Durham have the appearance of a town awaiting a
siege. In the hotel bars and public houses, many of which now elect to
stay closed throughout Gala Day, all furniture and moveable items are
removed by landlords who intend to stay open. If the landlords of the
pubs did not remove their furniture, they would never be able to
accommodate their customers. The great crush of bystanders watching
the procession of miners through the narrow streets has on occasion

broken expensive plate-glass windows. All the glasses normally in use are stowed away and replaced by specially ordered stocks of plastic. Some of these precautions are sensible as fights and vandalism are not unknown. Before plastic became available, it was the custom in some pubs to serve drink "by the neck," that is, only in bottles. In 1955 I recall advancing to a bar on a 'carpet' of discarded bottles, which, though slippery, caused no remark among the drinkers or the pub staff. Behavioural decorum that applies at other times does not apply on Gala Day.

The deliberate absence of many of Durham's residents and the rather formal caution of those who remain to deal with the invasion, evoke an interesting response on the part of the miners and their families. The knowledge that all who may be against them have left the city or are sitting out the day behind boarded windows assures them that everyone who *is* in sight is with them in spirit. When I last went to the Big Meeting in 1976 people nodded at me in the street and smiled and sometimes touched my hand as I passed them—not in acknowledgement of our knowing one other (for we did not), but rather of my presence with them at that time, obviously in sympathy. The feeling of being among so many apparent friends is electric and once caused Sam Watson, a former leader of the Durham miners, to remark that on Gala Day at Durham there is champagne in the air. It is no fancy to regard these smiling people in such a mediaeval setting as members of some army which has, for a day, taken over a city.

THE MARCH OF THE BANNERS

Twenty-five years ago, this image of an army take-over was very real. In the days when coal was worked in all parts of the county, the contingents from the various pits made a point of assembling on all the roads at the city boundary before marching to join the main procession in the centre. This ritual has been disturbed because of the construction of a motorway by-pass on the north side of the city and because there are now fewer pits, most of which are situated only in the eastern part of the county. But the custom of the procession has been preserved. Its destination is the old race course that lies on the east side of the city beside the river. The procession is not stage-managed and it needs no marshals to command this or that contingent. Each contingent is self-contained and self-regulating. An order of procession agreed upon in advance can be easily adjusted to changed circumstance, and a contingent that finds its way blocked will wait patiently for its turn to join the procession.

Each pit (village) contingent has its banner and its brass band. These bands are a matter of great pride, and some of them compete in

The Durham Miners' Gala
(Courtesy of Ian Rodger)

national contests and are therefore nationally known. Those villages in which this musical tradition has died out hire bands to lead their contingents. The bands, in uniform and assembled in formal order, precede the silken banners of the union lodges which proclaim the name of the pit (and therefore village) they represent. Many of these banners are forty and fifty years old. They vary in size but average between six to seven feet in width and five feet in height. They are hung from a horizontal pole supported on each side by two upright poles. The pole carriers, an office of some honour, support the base of the poles in a leather socket; other attendants hold the stays, which are secured to the upright poles, taut and steady in case of wind. Pride of place immediately behind the banners goes to union officials, followed by miners who may or may not be accompanied by their wives and/or children. In earlier times, these contingents were wholly male, and formally dressed in suits and ties. Recently, however, dress has become more casual.

The air of friendly informality, which allows members of a contingent to call out to friends watching them pass by, does not mean that those who are in the procession and those who watch it are unaware of the meaning and purpose of the event. The magnificent banners are usually housed in the union lodges, and are otherwise seen only on grim days of industrial strike or on days of grief when a man has died in the mine. On Gala Day in Durham, grief-laden events of the past year are recalled for all to see and remember. If a pit has suffered a death through accident during the year, a black drape is attached across the top of the banner. The relatives of the deceased are usually invited, if they wish, to walk immediately behind the banner. It goes without saying that most of those who see this banner with its black drape will be familiar with the story of the tragedy it recalls. Older people also reflect on tragedies occurring in the more distant past when these banners pass by. I recall the moment in 1976 when the Easington banner returned from the meeting and was preceded by a group of teenagers dancing in a ring in front of the band. An old lady, recalling the Easington Colliery disaster, turned to me with her eyes full of tears and said: "The silly bairns. They weren't even born." Easington did not carry a black drape that year but the earlier deaths were still remembered.

Though the mere sight of these banners can evoke much emotion, I must make it clear that despite the long history of accidents, disease and industrial strike, the emphasis of the pictorial message and of the slogans on the banners is almost uniformly pacific. The central feature of these banners is usually a picture of a rest home or home for aged miners, or of some past and usually long-dead political figure. The Seaham banner, for example, displays an oval portrait of a seated Christ attended by children in nineteenth-century clothing, and is captioned: "Suffer little children to come unto me." The New Herrington banner shows a miner approaching a gate labelled Economic Emancipation, which is being opened by an angel figure, labelled Trade Unionism, handing him the key. The Boldon banner carries two pictures that compare early miners' homes with those built during the past twenty years, thus proclaiming practical progress in this sphere of welfare. The Easington banner carries portraits of Keir Hardie and Robert Smillie, and Blackhall's banner celebrates more recently dead political leaders (Attlee and Bevan). Banners from the pits that are now closed carried similar messages of quiet restraint. One of the very few that carried a blunter message was that of Chopwell. Said to have been designed by Harry Boldon, whose acts of 1926 have already been mentioned, it had a figure of Christ on the front with the caption, "Come unto me, all ye that are heavy laden, and I will give ye rest." On the back were depicted Marx, Engels and Lenin, with the caption, "Man is born free and is everywhere in chains." Even this banner, with its more direct message, conformed, like all the others, to a style of decoration derived in part from the pre-Raphaelites and in part from the scroll work of Canal-Boat art. The colours were sombre and rich and the lettering suggested a religious rather than a political intention. There is no place at all for modern agit-prop art depicting scenes of heroic strife and working-class struggle.

It is worth adding that the occasion of the Gala is not one at which people carry placards or shout slogans. Even the evangelists of the various minority parties of the Left who, on other occasions, rarely miss the chance to shout their views and sell their magazines, tend to maintain a low profile at the Gala.

Those who have accepted a Marxist interpretation of English working-class history, whether they be Marxists or not, will no doubt find this lack of overt political statement puzzling and the predominantly Christian flavour of the banners rather bewildering. This general deference to the ideals of the Christian ethic, however, would not surprise Mr. Tony Benn, M.P. and current Minister for Energy. In a speech in 1976 commemorating some Levellers who were shot at Burford, Oxfordshire in 1649, Benn traced the origins of the English Labour movement to the tradition of Christian dissent which goes beyond the Levellers to the Lollard movement of the fourteenth century (Benn 1976). The Christ figure depicted on the banners belongs to this tradition of Christian dissent, which is an alternative to the official Christ of the Prince Bishops of Durham. This figure is the champion of the meek who shall inherit the earth and who, along with Thomas Hepburn, know how to wait.

It is doubtful whether many or any of the onlookers at the Gala reflect, in such a conscious manner, upon the figure on the banners. And it is certain that they do not engage in much political discussion among themselves. Prior to the event, the local newspapers confine themselves to giving details of changes, the names of speakers, the numbers of pubs that plan to be open, car-parking arrangements and so on. The event itself is scarcely discussed. And when the crowds gather on the narrow pavements of the ancient streets to watch the procession, there is little argument between individuals of one faction of left-wing politics and another. Watching the bands and the banners go by is more akin to the experience old soldiers have when they see their old regiment march past with its battle honours flying. People naturally take most pleasure in seeing their own village contingent, but the other contingents offer a reflection of their own community, and people will often check with a fellow bystander to find out whether this or that band has passed. This excuse for conversation often leads to the question, "Where are you from then?" The names of the villages on the banners are thus exchanged on the pavement. This is very important. Gala Day brings together people from different settlements who share a common experience of life, labour and history. Exchanges between villagers confirm the merits and qualities of the culture which they all share. During the week following the Gala, those villagers who did not go are made to feel sorry that they missed the event. Nobody is criticized for missing the speeches; there is just a regret that they missed this communion of marching miners.[2]

In contrast to trade-union demonstrations elsewhere, which can stimulate counter-demonstrations and invite rigid control by the police, the Gala is an occasion for pumping the flesh, for nodding and winking and the slapping of backs. The police, who can appear with surprising speed to break up a drunken brawl, are not much in evidence in the streets. Most of them are, after all, local lads, and people from other parts of Britain attending the Gala generally comment on their civility and good humour. There is really no way in which the ebullient visitors to Durham City can be contained. The guest speakers and the prime minister, if Labour is in power, are housed in the Royal County Hotel with the union officials, where they have some protection from the milling crowds. But there is no protocol or corps of bodyguards to protect even a prime minister from being suddenly chatted up on a first-name basis by some gatecrasher. As a reporter for the *Newcastle Journal*, I once interviewed Clement Attlee, who was rather an austere and withdrawn person. Our conversation was suddenly invaded by a very large miner brandishing a slopping pint of beer, who slapped the Labour leader on the back and leered into his face: "Haway. Clem. You're a canny lad." The Gala is not the place for solemnity and awesome respect for political leaders. The leader of the Labour party, even when he is prime minister, is to the people of County Durham on this day only "one of us," and he and the guest speakers, usually well-known members of the party, are referred to by their first names.

As soon as the first contingents have made their way through the crowded streets and across Elvet Bridge towards the race course, the guest speakers and the prime minister take up their positions on the balcony of the Royal County Hotel for the salute. Those of the official party who cannot manage to push their way to the balcony, lean out of the hotel windows. As the bands march past, playing almost anything from *Abide with Me* to a Beatles tune, the banners dip forward in salute and the leaders wave and nod from the balcony. This act of respect is really rather cursory, for the marchers are busily scanning the other windows to catch sight of friends and acquaintances in the union organization.[3] Not meaning to show disrespect to the leaders, marchers and union officials call out to each other. It would be a foolish politician who complained that he did not come all the way to Durham to be so disregarded. The middle-class socialist intellectual from the South of England has to be careful not to appear too distant and aloof. He knows, of course, as anyone in the party must, that he is being greatly honoured by being invited to speak at Durham. Northeastern England is one of the great power bases of the Labour party, and though President Jimmy Carter may have served some American political purpose when he visited Washington, County Durham in 1977,[4] there is no doubt that Prime Minister James Callaghan served his own ends in delivering the American president to the people of the Northeast. However, the Durham Gala is really a domestic occasion devoted entirely, as far as politics are concerned, to cementing relationships between the miners, their leaders and the Labour party. The speeches must be devoted to this end and to the affirmation of known truths.

THE SPEECHES

The guest speakers are chosen and voted upon by the Durham Branch of the NUM. At times of internal dissension within the Labour party, it is possible for political observers to assess the general mood of the Durham miners by noting the speakers they have chosen. When Labour is in power, the more tendentious speakers are generally not chosen. It is assumed that barring some extraordinary crisis, "Wor Clem," "Wor Harold" or "Wor Jim" (our Clem Attlee, our Harold Wilson or our Jim Callaghan) will be in Durham on the third Saturday of July, and though he usually speaks, he does not suffer the indignity of being balloted.

Delivering a speech at the Big Meeting must be a daunting experience. The speaker should find comfort in the knowledge that he is addressing the largest assembly of people in Britain whose views are in sympathy with his own. Only the politically ardent make their way to the race course for the speeches, whereas many of their friends and neighbours, whose political affiliations are the same but who treat the Gala as a day out, will remain drinking in the pubs or will take their children to the fairground roundabouts and dodgems at the far eastern side of the race course. The speakers can therefore be sure that they have only the ears of those who really care. Though this must be some comfort, the conditions in which they speak are surely testing.

The rostrum is usually sited at the western end of the race course so that the speaker has the towering mass of the cathedral behind him. The audience, standing on the flat and dwindling away towards the river banks, gives the speaker no certainty as to the limits of audibility. He is equipped with microphone and amplifiers but it is hard to obtain rapport and feedback from this open-air gathering. Though he may have been chosen to speak because he is thought to embody the heart and soul of socialist thinking on some current issue, he is expected to enunciate the more classic truths. The Big Meeting is not an occasion for Labour leaders to announce new departures in policy. Rather, it is an occasion for the reaffirmation of ancient virtues, for the assertion of the merits of solidarity and for remembering the very ancient and continuing aims of the Labour Movement. Reference to "the movement," and not to any one particular left-wing party, is an essential piece of the rhetoric of the occasion. The term serves to encompass new developments such as the inclusion of members of the Communist Party, who may happen to be within earshot, as well as the whole spectrum of the living Left, referring back in time to the Chartists, the Levellers and even the Lollards.

The rhetorical mood of this occasion is thus encapsulated (historically and emotively) when, from the platform, against the wind and the sky and that cathedral, a speaker starts a sentence with, "We, in the Labour movement. . . ." And there is usually a pause after the "We." For the "We" is in itself a piece of rhetoric preparing the way for the banner statement "in the Labour movement." The use that can be made of the key reference to "the movement" is well illustrated in a report in *The Sunday Times* on 17 July 1977 of speeches heard at the Gala on the previous day. As the report does not suggest that the speeches were confined to the reiteration of known truths but instead stresses the element of confrontation between Mr. James Callaghan, the prime minister, and the other speakers, it is necessary to say something about the immediate political context of the occasion and about the manner in which the event was reported.

Throughout 1977, British miners were seeking substantial pay increases at a time when the government they supported was seeking, for reasons of economic strategy, the limitation of pay increases. It is of some political significance that the Durham branch of the NUM chose Mr. Arthur Scargill, the leader of the Yorkshire miners, to speak at the 1977 Gala. Mr. Scargill has a national reputation as a militant trade-union leader, and the Durham miners were no doubt fully conscious of the implications of inviting him. Though they are not regarded as militant by the Yorkshire miners whom Mr. Scargill represents, they made use of the occasion to provide Mr. Scargill with a platform to debate the issue of their pay claim in the immediate company of the prime minister.

It must be said too that *The Sunday Times*, in common with most national newspapers, is hostile to any Labour Government, and that it would not miss an opportunity to depict a Labour prime minister in public dispute with his most devoted supporters. The report concentrates on the conflict of views expressed by Mr. Callaghan and Mr.

Scargill and says nothing about the social context of the occasion that serves the aims of consolidation rather than confrontation. Those who might doubt this assertion should carefully examine the sentence in the report that suggests that Mr. Callaghan was jeered by 100,000 miners and their families. This is a deliberate attempt to exaggerate the number of people present at the race course so as to suggest that Mr. Callaghan was jeered by the total mining population present in Durham City on that day. As I have already pointed out, the number of people attending the speeches form only a part of the total.

The headline to the report in *The Sunday Times* was "JEERING GREETS CALLAGHAN'S PAY PLEAS TO MINERS," and the report read as follows:

> The Prime Minister and Yorkshire miners' leaders, Arthur Scargill, stood on opposite sides of the pay divide at Durham miners' gala yesterday—Callaghan claiming that the tide was turning in the battle against inflation and Scargill standing firm on the miners' £135 a week demand and describing the Chancellor's latest mini-budget as a "sop."
>
> Heckling and jeers from the 100,000 miners and their families greeted the Prime Minister when he said: "For the sake of the whole country—and miners are part of the country, they are not separate, they are part of the whole national family—the government's first priority is to get down the rate of inflation which was destroying us three years ago. That is the objective we have set ourselves and the tide is beginning to turn. We are winning this battle."
>
> Callaghan's strong personal plea to the miners included the announcement of Government approval of a scheme to allow underground miners to retire at 62 years of age. An Energy spokesman said later that the scheme, which starts next month, will mean that men volunteering for early retirement will get a lump sum of £300 and two thirds of their pay until 65. Surface men with 25 years underground work will also be eligible.
>
> When the Prime Minister told hecklers that: "He laughs best who laughs last" a voice in the crowd shouted, "You can afford to." Callaghan was jeered when he said: "I know some people are not satisfied but the great bulk of the people are satisfied." He went on. *"The lions can command the lions' share under a system of free collective bargaining but the Labour movement and the Socialist movement is about more than the lions. It is about the weak and the sick and about those whose bargaining power is not strong.* That is why I am proud to say that we are going into the next phase of incomes in a free bargaining period in an orderly way and *marching side by side with the trade union movement.* There will be no differences in this matter. There will be every attempt to ensure that the return is free but orderly. The twelve months' period will be maintained."
>
> Before Callaghan rose to speak, Arthur Scargill, who marched to the rally behind the banner of Boldon Colliery, told the rally that if miners

accepted any further form of wage restraint, it would mean more vicious cuts in standards. Scargill said miners needed a minimum 56 per cent increase in gross terms simply to retain the position they held nearly three years ago. And he added: "I am arguing for £135 a week for miners this November not as an objective, not in the form of seeking, but as a positive claim. We have now been told by Mr. Healey that wage increases must be limited to ten per cent next year and we have been given a sop by way of a tax reduction, which is half way to what it was in 1974, when it was 33p in the pound.

"I want to urge the whole trade union movement and, in particular, my own union, to ignore the advice and pleas of the Government for a further wage restraint policy." Laurence Daly, the general secretary of the N.U.M., said the transition to free collective bargaining would be "an extremely painful and difficult job" but in the long run it would be possible to find the right road between individual freedom and collective responsibility. He said the TUC will make its comments on the Chancellor's proposals when its economic sub-committee meets next week. He said the committee will find itself critical of Healey's statement about incomes in the next phase. "We must be careful when we return, as we will, to what some people call free collective bargaining that those at the top do not reap the benefits of sacrifices we have made."

This report suggests that there was an open and insoluble conflict between the Labour prime minister and the miners, who are normally regarded as some of the most ardent supporters of a Labour Government. There is no doubt that the adherence of the Labour Government to a policy of wage restraint was already arousing the anger of the miners in 1977. This policy was to lead later to the disaffection of many Labour supporters and to the consequent victory of the Conservatives in the general election in 1979. But at the time at which Mr. Callaghan was confronted by Mr. Scargill at Durham, the wage restraint policy had not become nationally unpopular.

Mr. Callaghan was therefore presented, at Durham, with a special opportunity to dissuade the miners from pursuing a wage claim which would lead to the collapse of his policy if it were granted. If his Government gave in to the miners, it would not be able to restrain other trade-unions from campaigning and demanding similar wage increases. Thanks to the invitation which had been extended to Mr. Scargill by the Durham miners, Mr. Callaghan was faced with an open public debate on this key issue. There is no doubt that the views of Mr. Scargill and of the Yorkshire miners who had elected him to office were extremely popular. In 1974, the miners' opposition to a somewhat similar policy of wage restraint applied by Mr. Heath's Conservative Government had led to a general election which resulted in a Labour victory. The part they had played in this victory made them regain a political self-confidence which had been virtually absent since the General Strike in 1926. Mr. Scargill was therefore voicing a common belief in the industry that mining deserved very high wages, that the union should employ its industrial clout to obtain them and that, in any case, a Labour Government owed the miners a better deal. It was also felt that by returning to a system of free collective bargaining, whereby strong unions like the miners' could use their muscle, the miners would be better off.

It is significant that Mr. Laurence Daly, the NUM's general secretary, was less convinced that a return to a free-for-all in wage bargaining was necessarily a good thing. He is reported as saying that he thought the transition to such a system would be "an extremely painful and difficult job." He reminded his listeners that such a system might not be as beneficial as some people imagined because it might benefit some workers while harming others. His remarks provided a persuasive introduction to the arguments which Mr. Callaghan put forward.

It may be supposed from the newspaper report that Mr. Callaghan met an entirely hostile reception. There is no doubt that he was jeered when he admitted that he knew that some people were not satisfied with the government's policies. But he was most surely heard in attentive silence when he made his reference to "the lions' share" in the passage in italics.

It is in this vital part of his speech that he refers to "the movement" and couples this reference to the known truth that the Labour movement is concerned not only with the strong but with the weak, the sick and those whose bargaining power is not strong. He offered a return to free bargaining for wages in the future but again stressed that this could only be achieved by "marching side by side with the trade union movement." To those who are not familiar with the dictionary of emotive terms and rhetoric which serve within the Labour movement in Britain, this passage in his speech may not seem very remarkable. It appears merely to reiterate various home truths. But it is this kind of reiteration which can allow a Labour politician to escape from a difficult situation. It is certainly true that, in time, Mr. Callaghan's policies were seen to have failed his party but the consequences of his speech at Durham were quite considerable. The campaign to return to free collective bargaining suffered a setback. Although the Durham miners cheered Mr. Scargill and welcomed his act of ceremonious rhetoric in marching with the Boldon banner to the race course, they undoubtedly returned home with second thoughts about pushing their government too hard. Mr. Callaghan had reminded them of the need to look after the weak and the sick, and he had used the emotive phrase, "the movement."

The importance of this particular rhetorical occasion was not appreciated by the many people in Britain who are unfamiliar with the Labour party's private rhetoric and who know nothing about the Durham area. Speeches at the Durham Gala are rarely reported at length in most of the national newspapers. Despite the fact that the North East of England represents one of the most solid bases of power for the Labour party, the Gala receives little coverage nationally. Although it is a remarkable spectacle, and yearly attracts the leading Labour politicians, this lack of coverage is not wholly surprising. On most occasions, the dialogue taking place on the rostrum is often a rather private conversation among members of the party and their supporters. The occasion of Mr. Callaghan's open dispute with Mr. Scargill was an exception, and was brought about by the special circumstances of a government economic policy which obstructed the ambitions of some of its most faithful supporters.

The event provided *The Sunday Times* with a nice story, and the fact that Mr. Callaghan was jeered would doubtless lead many people to assume that his visit to Durham was a failure. But this is to ignore the impact of the remainder of his speech which appealed to the traditional principles of the socialist movement. His plea for caution also echoed the observations of Mr. Daly. Despite the fact that Mr. Scargill has great personal appeal and despite the attraction of his more militant stance, the Durham miners did not subsequently support a free-for-all in wage bargaining. Mr. Callaghan therefore achieved his objective, which was to persuade the NUM not to go it alone and threaten strike action to gain higher wages. It is clear that in the following year, his policies were to prove highly unpopular and it might be said by some that he should have heeded Mr. Scargill's arguments in order to sustain the Labour party in office. But this is to raise other issues and to obscure the short-term effects of his deft use of rhetoric at Durham.

Conclusion

It may be thought that Mr. Callaghan's rhetorical exercise was scarcely louder than a whisper. Yet those who presume that rhetoric requires the style of the demagogue and that it must be full of empty phrases must recognize that some occasions require a rhetorical style that many would find almost inaudible.

Any Labour politician who is invited to speak at the race course at Durham had better know that his listeners will have a very sharp ear for false promises and wild imagery. The social experience and working conditions of the Durham miner persuade him to favour understatement rather than exaggeration. The difficult and dangerous nature of his work, in which he depends upon swift and often unspoken co-operation from his fellows in the mine, creates an attitude of mind which distrusts loose talk. As he also inhabits closely-knit village communities of some antiquity, in which meanings are often conveyed by nods and winks rather than by lengthy explanations, he is accustomed to an economy of style in expression. In this respect, he is quite unlike many urban and suburban industrial workers who may or may not know their neighbours or share the same work experience. A speech which would likely appeal to an audience of alienated and deracinated urban industrial workers would not be a success at Durham.

Frequenters of political demonstrations and meetings who visit Durham Gala for the first time often comment on the festive good nature of the gathering and on the lack of any sense of strife and aggression. It must be remembered that, in any case, all potential enemies have chosen to withdraw from the scene. There is no visible opposition. There is no need to shake fists at anyone or chant slogans in order to orchestrate a sense of common purpose. The mere presence of thousands of people is in itself an unspoken slogan. To be in Durham on Gala Day is to be, by definition, a part of the movement.

Someone visiting the Gala for the first time is likely to conclude that it is more of a social than a purely political event. In the bars and cafes and in the streets, there is little political discussion. Remarks about the visiting speakers may be confined to observing simply that "Wor Jim [meaning Callaghan] looked fine." I recall being tremendously moved by a speech made in 1954 by Barbara Castle M.P., but when I commented on the speech later to a man in a pub, he said: "Oh, she's a canny lass"— and no more. It has to be made clear that saying somebody is canny is high praise indeed in the North East of England. No doubt, on some other occasion, among close friends, he would have indulged in a lengthy conversation but he felt no need to do this at the Gala.

Doubtless, the apparent distaste for political debate on this occasion is the reason that the Labour party makes little use of the Gala to recruit members or canvass support. Even the minority socialist parties restrain their customary evangelical zeal. They are not actively prevented from selling their newspapers and magazines; it is simply that active politicking somehow seems out of place. A large number of people who attend the Gala have come to enjoy themselves. Many do not even attend the speeches at the race course. Some choose to drink all day, while others prefer to take their children to the fairground. It might be thought that such people have no political interests but this assumption would be a mistake. All of them are members of a community that has shared a terrible history of mining disasters, strikes, lock-outs, and industrial strife known to all. Such people do not need a history lesson or a political lecture. The speakers whom they have invited must know that they come to affirm rather than to preach. The rhetoric employed must be subtle and merely nod in the direction of the known beliefs of the audience. Mr. Callaghan knew well where exactly to make his reference to the aspirations of the movement so as to link them to his declared policy of maintaining a balanced wage policy.

I believe that the study of political rhetoric cannot be limited to analysis of the speakers' individual styles but that it must take account of the nature of the audience. If the lightning of effective rhetoric is to strike, the clever politician must know the nature of his audience in advance. For rhetoric is not merely in the gift of the speaker. For him to declare what he regards as a known truth is not enough; he must know what kinds of truths are already known to his audience. He must know enough about his audience to avoid saying too much and thus earning the response that his rhetoric is false.

It seems to be thought by some people that audiences are merely passive assemblies awaiting linguistic manipulation by their politicians. But on many occasions it is clear that audiences predetermine the nature and style of the speeches they hear. The style required at Durham on the third Saturday of July is not one which could be used well elsewhere. Different social groups and venues require slightly different styles. The idea that the politician can generate his rhetorical style in the isolation of his office and then apply it to a waiting audience undoubtedly derives from considering the conditions which presently prevail when he is called upon to make nation-wide broadcasts on radio and television. On such occasions, local cultural differences and prejudices have to be set aside and the speaker has to resort to bland formulae.

It is instructive that politicians today seem less eager to make these face-to-face addresses to the nation. They have learned that they cannot, in this manner, succeed in pleasing all of the people all of the time. They clearly prefer to be seen pressing the flesh in a local context and to be filmed speaking to a specific audience whose character can then be described by the television reporter. In this way, they are seen acting in an apparently sincere relationship with a particular group or community. The rhetoric they employ may strike some viewers as inappropriate and even false but its use should be understood when and if the social circumstances are explained. If, for example, Mr. Callaghan's speech at Durham had been seen on television and its reporting had paid some attention to the social history of the Big Meeting, he would have profited his case more surely than by appearing in a TV studio interview. He would have been seen and heard performing on a stage which is, itself, a part of the rhetoric of the British Labour movement.

Notes

1. Personally communicated to me by Brian Sutherland, Boldon's grandson, who was a fellow student with me at Durham University.

2. A relatively new development on Gala Day is the parading of jazz bands, which takes place after the pit-village contingents have passed through the city to the race course. These bands are composed of young girls dressed in bright uniforms in the style of North American majorettes. Some beat drums while others play kazoos and paper-comb instruments in unison. What is significant about these jazz bands is that they largely come from villages where coal is no longer mined. A girl at the head of each band carries a placard with the name of her band's village. Holding this jazz-band parade in Durham on a day when there is a crowd at hand has obvious advantages, but it is difficult to resist the suspicion that for some of the ex-pit villages, this is a means of participating in Gala Day.

3. People familiar with town fairs and similiar events may wonder what role is played by city and county councillors. Such people take no formal part. They may, however, visit the Royal County Hotel informally.

4. President Carter gave a well-meant but hilariously sounding version of the Geordie greeting, "Haway the lads!" when he visited Newcastle. It was a rhetorically successful gesture to use the phrase.

5

"Weaklings Wax Biggest with Words": U.S. and Norwegian Populists

GEORGE PARK

Under such a title[1] I dare only be brief—and yet I have so much to say: I must therefore beg pardon in advance for presenting my evidence in condensed form, to allow better discussion of its implications. I shall be less concerned, in any event, with the surfaces of the texts than with what might be called, aping Chomsky, their deep rhetoric. Underneath my own rhetoric is a more than casual interest in the possibility of populism as an instrument of enlightenment. One of my purposes in this comparison, accordingly, is to show that the possibility is real (the Norwegian case), though in the birthplace of populism it may seem always to have miscarried.

It has been a fairly simple matter to settle on the appropriate texts, since what I am seeking is "deliberative rhetoric," as defined by Bailey in Chapter 3, not the rhetoric of simple political salesmanship. I am therefore content to use George McKenna's collection, *American Populism* (1974), on the U.S.-American side,[2] paying attention to all the twentieth-century items except those representing right-wing populism—a phenomenon apart. A Norwegian symposium, *Norsk Populisme* (PAG 1972), is available on the other side, but because it represents only the perspective of the PAG (Populistiske Arbeidsgrupper i Bergen), I have added texts which speak for the Popular Socialist party, the North-Norwegian movement and Christian populism. An inclusive strategy was wanted, as a narrow comparison of texts could not serve my broad objective.

The ideal method of treatment is not so easily found. The texts are not sufficiently comparable to permit (as perhaps two speeches from the same rostrum might) useful content analysis, in rigorous style. My method has therefore been to address three questions to each body of texts, searching all of them for the evidence, which I then summarize and illustrate.

Three Questions

The three questions I shall pose to the texts repesent a coherent package of dichotomies:

Where the rhetorical appeal is mainly:	emotive	instructive
1. The focus of concern is:	identity	programme
2. The presupposed value criterion is:	grace	enlightenment
3. The personal image projected is:	exemplary	astute

I find that Bailey's distinction between *cardiac* and *pseudo-cerebral* (Chapter 3) is not as winsome as others might make in much the same sense, though I find it unambiguous. All rhetoric appeals at once to heart and head: if a politician reads out statistics he does not thereby eliminate the gut reactions of his audience, and even in his "Cross of Gold" speech, William Jennings Bryan required some mental effort from his listeners. But all rhetoric does not keep a nice balance, and one important measure of the political significance of a polemical utterance is the amount of skew on this dimension. In order to suggest a dimension of the rhetoric itself, rather than a supposed etiology, I have chosen to focus on *emotive* and *instructive* modalities to represent the broad distinction I want; they are sufficiently close to Bailey's to benefit from his discussion of types.[3] Mine are not terms which require elaborate explanation—bold examples of either type would be reliably rated by independent judges. At the same time, most political rhetoric intended to influence ongoing policy debate would probably combine both qualities. My questions to the texts are therefore more specific and aim at areas of choice inhibiting a middle position.

A populist who is trying to attract a following may focus his concern on *identity* with known values, causes, or quasi-group interests; or on a *programme*. While projecting a party platform, one speaker may be content to emphasize solidarity with grand and established interests, whereas another may want to define the safe path between conflicting or confusing alternatives; where the point of the one speech is only to urge men forward upon a set course, the other offers the skills of the pilot for making a difficult passage. The perennial aim of populism is decentralization of economic and political power, but the means are various and seldom self-explanatory, ranging from the single tax or free silver to reshouldering burdens or tightening belts. Even the populist without a special gimmick or panacea must have an itinerary, and must treat an occasion of speaking or writing as one for instructing the public or one for manipulating identities and alignments.

What he will do is likely to reflect his sense for the qualities of the audience (question 2) and his sense of self (question 3). Some speakers patently do not expect much cerebral effort from an audience, but some assume that their audience is aware of pressing problems and looking for hard answers. Should a populist decide the people want instruction, persuasion by argument and a cogent demonstration of the failings of opposition programmes, he will have made a particular assumption about his public values in the political sphere. What matters is intellectual clarity, far-seeing leadership and resistance to false argument—in short, *enlightened* policy. But when a populist instead expects the people to seek grandiloquence, persuasion by faith and the courage to call the opposition "enemy," he has made a different assumption about his public. What matters then is stature not argument, image and imagery not discriminating logic. Politics becomes a field for conversion not instruction, since men and women judge the truth of a statement by its sponsorship not by its content. The people want a pressing issue swept away, not analysed: they seek not enlightenment but *grace*. Political grace, like divine grace, is showered from above, inspiring confidence and generating its own reward.

Max Weber's "charismatic leadership" presupposes the phenomenon of political grace, but it is hard to envision lasting charisma where the grace was not matched by intellectual clarity—and in general, Weber's type suits legend better than reality. We cannot assume that a leader's projected image will regularly correspond to his sense for the public preference in policies. Bryan pursued the politics of grace with very fancy talk. McGovern, another failed U.S. presidential candidate, was committed to the cause of enlightenment but took more care to show where his heart was than to display a sharp head. The relevant types of leadership, or of projected self-image, may be labelled *exemplary* and *astute*—with the proviso, of course, that a morally exemplary image need not be an unintelligent one nor an astute persona morally disenchanting.

But does not every politician try to claim both qualities of leadership? I think the balancing act is especially difficult for a populist, who would establish rapport with a definite (if, possibly, an imaginary) public rather than simply win votes wherever they might be found. Perhaps the (retrospective) charisma of President Kennedy derived mainly from his having established credible claims to both exemplary and astute leadership, though his rating for either one may not have been outstanding; but I think each quality appealed to a different public, and that a genuine populist could not have managed the act.

A populist does have a choice of images though he may not have a choice of publics. One populist who claimed astuteness without exemplary personal qualities was the right-wing alcoholic Senator Joseph McCarthy: if he was more concerned to claim than to disclose information, he was not wanting in grace, for all that. Unfortunately, the grace projected on a leader by his public cannot directly feature in an analysis of *his* rhetoric and so may leave little definite record. But it must be true in every case that some reciprocity inheres between a successful politician and his public, and is refracted in his performance: at least if you consistently fail with one tactic and win with another, pragmatic counsel is apt to prevail. But a sharp mind is cousin to a sharp tongue, and it is not always easy to win friends by 'showing brains.' The problem is magnified for the populist in a society where plain people are suspicious of fancy talk. But fancy or elaborate speech from the mouth of a Polonius does not project°intelligence, whereas plain talk can. If political rhetoric carries no message below its surface, it may carry no message at all.

Populism in the Twentieth Century

Populism is reform-from-below and so may be found akin to socialism. But populism differs fundamentally in lacking theoretical roots: without a universalistic, utopian plan for a world discontinuous with our own, the movement is not radical, however revolutionary it may be in mood. The cult secret of Marxist socialism, giving it a perennial appeal, is hidden in *Das Kapital*, a theory of Confucian splendour which the ordinary Russian or Chinese cannot understand, but which prophesies revolution by cataclysm. In the nineteenth century this was the future—death and rebirth to a beatific world. In the Russia or China of today the cataclysm is now, a liminal period in which the law belongs neither to the past nor to the future. Populism does not propose the suspension of laws, natural or positive; the movement just wants to get the rascals out of power so that people can live as they have always wished. Populism even of the right is not conservative, since it regards some powerful institutions of the established society as pathogenic; but populism is defensive. So far, no populist movement has achieved an institutionalization remotely like that of Marxist socialisms—the conditions for doctrinal clarity have usually not been forthcoming. Populists seek to restore lost values through resistance to the encroachments of central direction in the affairs of ordinary people. Though proponents usually have their share of evangelical fervour, they seem to assume that the people know what they want by way of ends. They do not address alienated—spiritually impoverished, immiserised—publics wanting elementary instruction on what the good life is or ought to be.

It is easy to see that this assumption restricts the ledge in time upon which a populist leader can expect to perch above the revolution. The situation is deemed to call for no heroes—no torch-bearers, no catechists, no midwives to some terrible labour of rebirth; all that is wanted is a man with a key to the gates. The people will take care of the rest. We should not be surprised that Marxists find this sort of thing insufficiently serious. The populist leader takes the stage briefly and has done. If he stays he probably will not stay as a populist. A populist who did make it to the White House would have to consolidate his strength in the usual way, spreading his party over far more ground than it was meant to cover. And is not every little island run either by a general or by a former populist?

This is possibly an unsympathetic question, and I have trusted the reader to take it as a rhetorical one. But I expect the redolence of populism for most will be that of the Americas, where politics has never been placed above the rat race, and long tenure of office must be machine-made. Recently *populism* was borrowed by a Norwegian sociologist (Brox 1972: 97) to refer to a decentralization movement in his own country, in which he had a positive interest. Whatever else it may have, that movement has not the American redolence of flimflam and fly-by-night tent meeting. Since Norwegian populism can be credited with having kept Norway out of the European Economic Community, in opposition to both socialist and conservative establishments, we must take the movement seriously. But I anticipate, perhaps. The difference between the two styles of politics ought to come out of an examination of the texts that I have chosen. The question that we cannot ask directly of the texts, but that must guide us through all this, is whether the differences are deep and significant.

Précis of the Texts: U.S.

The materials I shall use to represent U.S. populism are organized by McKenna (1974: 153–206, 245–308) in two sections as follows:

1. Populism and the New Deal
    Senator William E. Borah, "The Farmer's Enemy": a magazine article published in 1936. The farmer's plight can be blamed on greedy monopolists and careless politicians.
    Senator George W. Norris and the anti-injunction law of 1932: taken from his autobiography, 1945. The law was badly wanted but was opposed by powerful interests.
    Senator Huey P. Long, "Share our Wealth!": his open letter of 1933. So much wealth is owned by so few that levelling could make us all rich.
    Senator Gerald P. Nye's defense of isolationism: his farewell speech to the Senate, 1944. The Senate faces a major task in controlling the scramble for easy profits at the end of the war. It never should have begun.

2. The New Populism (Left-Wing Examples)
    C. Wright Mills on the U.S.A. as a centralized state: Chapter 1 of *The Power Elite* (1956). The men in power today exercise a wide discretion in the way they govern a disunited mass.
    Carl Oglesby, "Trapped in a System": speech for anti-war marchers in Washington, 1965. Liberalism has failed, and its institutions as well.
    Jack Newfield and Jeff Greenfield, "The American Myth Is Dying": Chapter 1 of *A Populist Manifesto*, 1972. A broad alliance is to be formed to fight an unjust distribution of wealth and power in the U.S.A.
    Senator George McGovern, speeches from his 1972 presidential campaign. "My Stand": The people want no ideology but an end to the credibility gap. "Acceptance Speech" at the Democratic National Convention: The country has strayed from the path of democracy and virtue—"Come home, America!"

Précis of the Texts: Norway

From the Norwegian material, I have chosen the more polemical/ political contributions to the Bergen study groups' symposium. From each of the other sources I have selected a summary chapter or section that gives a fair showing of the author's rhetorical style and concerns. Since the language barrier may prevent some readers from referring to these texts, I annotate them here, translating the titles. (I make no effort to imitate the rhetorical colouring of a piece, restricting myself to what might be called the prose message.)
    From the PAG symposium, *Norsk Populisme* (1972), the three polemical pieces reviewed here are:

1. Sveinung Time on "New Political Alignments in Norway" (pp. 9–17): Keynesian capitalism has produced the wrong kind of goods and work situations; a party system perpetuating cleavages which offer no real choice to the voter; and central direction of the many by the élites, left-theoreticians included.

2. Sverre Rörtveit on "The Parliamentary System in Norway" (pp. 126–44): The state has been a tool of the capitalist class, and Labour (movement and party) has failed to gain control of this tool even while instituting many economic controls—the effect of which has been to stabilize and strengthen capitalism. Bureaucratic expertise is never politically neutral, and socialists have lacked counter-expertise as well as backbone. A mass movement armed by a new vision and its own expertise can use parliament to turn the state into an instrument of the revolution, which will peacefully form a populistic, post-capitalist society.

3. Audgunn Oltedal on "Populism in Norwegian Politics" (pp. 155–70): Norway has been depoliticized by a preoccupation with economic development, which was considered the special province of technical experts. Thus techno-capitalism has been having its way without regard for conservation, and democratic ideals have been perverted. Populism arose on a broad party front as a movement based on recognition of the need for community at the local level, and sought to undermine capitalism by structural reforms which would break its inner logic. Populism opposes party cleavages which artificially divide the people, and doctrines which call for taking power rather than generating insight and a broad popular demand for an end to capitalism.

The other exemplars of populist rhetoric I include in this review are:

1. Ottar Brox, *Politikk* (1972). Brox is a sociologist, a Popular Socialist, at this writing a member of Parliament, and a leader of the populist movement in its championship of a new approach to the development of marginal regions (North Norway) and in its fight against "submission to the bureaucrats in Brussels." The full title of his book translates as *Politics: Contributions to a Populistic Argumentation*. I consider three essays:

(a) "On Populism" (pp. 97–98): In its model of a national society, populism's key idea is the local community, whereas that of Labour is the economic/occupational sector, and that of orthodox Marxists is class. Populism is conservative relative to basic cultural values but radical in its opposition to a "development" that would strengthen the hold of monopoly capitalism.

(b) "Revolutionary Tactics in Norway" (pp. 99–105): A proper revolution will give ordinary working people the power to enjoy self-reliance under traditional—even "petty bourgeois"—values. This is to be done by gradually changing the rules of the game in favour of ordinary people, not by foisting on them a utopian vision which is, in fact, an opiate. The revolution is to attack the premisses of today's institutions, not the institutions themselves, and to set constraints but not declare war on the powers that be.

(c) "Must We Crush the Class State?" (pp. 106–14): The varied conditions of ordinary life today suggest many possibilities for radical change on a local scale, not entailing direct assault on the state or major strongholds of capitalism. Change should begin in the peripheral regions, where new energies could be channelled into small co-operatives, defended by wily economic strategies, not mere idealism. Radicals should create "socialist islands in a capitalist sea" and gradually free men from the tyranny of job-market politics, rescue the local community and shift the balance in favour of decentralized production.

2. From the Christian populist Bjorn Unneberg's *Green Socialism* (1971), I have taken the title-chapter for consideration. The author has taught in the Folk high school system, and is oriented to Center/Farmer party youth. He does not use the term "populism" in this book.

"Green Socialism" (pp. 61–76): Socialism is a much abused but still viable ideal, and "green socialism" sides not just with those alienated by the industrial production process but with all whom the social order cuts off from significant self-determination. Man is sensitive to his social milieu: families, work groups, local communities, nations, and international communities each may be found in better and worse forms. The EEC is increasingly centralized in Brussels and oriented to capitalist efficiency; the UN is bureaucratic and legalistic, doing little for common justice. "Green socialism" aims to use economics, political science, sociology, ethics, and ecology to lay bare the faults accumulating in the Norwegian social milieu, and to develop better patterns—a challenge especially to Center party youth.

3. Finn Gustavsen, *Rett På Sak* (1969). This translates as *Straight to the Point* or *Right On*. It deals intimately with some of the restlessness within socialist ranks that generated the (later so-styled) populist movement. The final chapter carries the political autobiography of the

Popular Socialists' parliamentary leader through the summer of 1968, when he was preparing to let someone else succeed.

" 'We Despise Parliament!' " (pp. 237–51): Rightly or wrongly, the Popular Socialists were blamed for this sentiment when the cry rang out in treble voices from the Storting (Parliament) galleries. There *are* good reasons for expressing such contempt: some leaders are unworthy, unfair electoral rules are not corrected, trivialities predominate whereas important matters are hustled through, committees are carefully packed, unpopular issues are suppressed, and undue power still lies in private hands. Parties of the right wing are controlled by big capital, the selection of candidates is dominated by party tactics not ability; and once in, a dull man is hard to get out. All men are imperfect, and short-comings are magnified by power. There should be more frequent rota-tion, and I propose to lead the way; at any rate, a party politician should work outside Parliament as well as inside. Popular Socialism is not pacifistic; it must be prepared to fight for justice when peaceful means have all been tried. The party is for strict industrial democracy and the decentralization of political power; stands against elitism in the party or in any transitional period of society; and urges the undogmatic use of informed socialist thought from all camps, erecting no infallible heroes and spurning solutions which, though appropriate to agrarian societies, are unrealistic for Norway today. The party is glad to be a party of youth, but warns against domination by students rather than ordinary working people. The party can get nowhere without institutional democracy, and can turn it to use against capitalism by moderate means and strong conviction. A crucial step is dissociating Norway from international power blocs.

The Nature of Populism

Where did this political tradition begin? Although populist rhetoric in the U.S. goes back to the revolutionaries Jefferson and Paine, the first Populist party platform was not proclaimed until the Fourth of July, 1892. The periods we have to consider here are the 1930s and the present decade. Both are rather special, but since Washington politics were a world phenomenon by Roosevelt's time, the periods are generally un-derstood. However, since the pattern of populism today does have such explicit origins in the final years of the last century (Goodwyn 1976), and since even McKenna finds populism elusive—"more a mood than a doctrine" (1974: xxv)—it is worth examining the 1892 platform for an irreducible kernel, if it can be found.

This platform called for an *expansion* of government power (Preamble 9) and not, as one might have expected, a contraction. The power of government was simply identified with that of the people. Oppression, injustice and poverty were thought to derive from other sources, and all these evils were to be ended by the extension of government into the economic realm. Specifically, the platform called for nationalizing the railroads, telephone and telegraph, and for establishing postal savings banks. At the same time, the taxing power was to be limited to raising the bare costs of government. Although it is sometimes said (Hicks 1931; Smith 1969: 308) that populist demands were all substantially taken up and won by mainline parties, the only major plank of the actual platform that U.S.-Americans adopted is the graduated income tax; and it has scarcely been effective in preventing the accumulation of massive fortunes, the main *desideratum* of these original populists. The fact seems to be that although they wanted a "restoration" of economic and political power "to the 'plain people,' with which class it originated" (Preamble 6), their analytical sense of the future—how to achieve such a restoration—was as imperfect as their historical sense about when and where power had once rested with the 'plain people.' In retrospect it is easy to see why populism had its origins among small-town and agrarian leaders, for it is *opposition to overriding power, felt to be external.* Here is "revolution" in the U.S.-American sense of rising against 'foreign' domination, directed not against England but the big city, the big corporation and the big—increasingly centralized—government.

If the rhetoric of populism in its later manifestations betrays the same kind of alienation—a reaction to elements of one's own society as foreign—we should perhaps expect the later movements to face the same problems of unity and policy as well. A populist movement can define its 'people' so inclusively that their heterogeneity becomes a problem as soon as the heat of battle is over or a divisive policy issue is encountered. Then the movement may disperse or it may be pulled together by the quality of its rhetoric, which must reflect in good measure the quality of the 'plain people' as well as the leadership.

Ratings of Populist Rhetoric

Wanting to rate each document fairly, I have reduced the emotive/ instructive distinction to three phases, cumulating the separate scores for each text. Although this does not qualify the subjectivity of my ratings, it does give the reader (with text in hand) a fair chance to check me. Since each text must be given three summary ratings, each is considered as a coherent piece of rhetoric seen in three facets; the discussion of these occupies the body of my chapter. The most convenient rating scale is the Q-sort with five positions, the neutral being rated null (0). I have used the ends of the scale (emotive 2 or instructive 2) except where I saw the possibility of counter-arguments to my decision: then I have expressed qualification by using the intermediate positions on the scale (emotive 1 or instructive 1—or when in doubt myself, the null rating, 0).

QUESTION I: THE FOCUS OF CONCERN

Does the text focus the reader's concern on a social cause or movement founded in a self-conscious collective *identity*, or on the credibility of a definite *programme*?

Four U.S. New-Deal Populists. Though Senator Borah's essay is ostensibly an analysis of the position of the farmer in the seventh year of the Great Depression, the title is provocative and the chief concern is to vindicate the farmer, laying the blame for his plight (albeit rather vaguely) at the door of the monopoly capitalist, who was guilty of morally or legally indefensible practices. For the rest, Borah defends the virtue of the ordinary man and the free-enterprise system, though he is not content just to beat on familiar drums and cite black-and-white issues. (Rating: emotive 1.)

Although Senator Norris dwells, in his autobiography, on the persons and circumstances associated with the passage of the Norris-LaGuardia anti-injunction bill, he does so without ever discussing chapter and verse of the bill itself. It is evaluated by its association with good men at the level of sponsorship and by its opposition to the unfair practices of powerful mining interests. Though Norris's nominal focus of concern is pro-labour legislation, he does not comment on the policy implications of this bill, which is presented simply as righting a particular wrong. (Rating: emotive 2.)

In contrast, Senator Long's interesting circular does outline a detailed programme for "sharing the wealth," which was to come from "the reduction of swollen fortunes from the top" (McKenna 1974: 186); but the eight points of the programme occupy only one-fifth of his space. He devotes the rest to swelling the reader's sense of a going movement, which has the blessing of "the Lord, of the Pilgrims, of Jefferson, Webster, and Lincoln" (p. 185). He does not argue any issues raised by the programme. (Rating: emotive 1.)

Senator Nye's farewell speech fell on deaf ears. Though it was the swan song of an isolationist at the peak of his country's war involvement, the text is not gaseous. It is devoted determinedly to programme and policy problems, to reviewing the significant history of Nye's two decades in the Senate and predicting the major policy problems of the post-war years to come. At the same time, halos and tails are dealt out to a number of social categories along the way, and Nye's own position is justified by naming its enemies: the military, the munitions manufacturers, foreign statesmen, and slick political managers. (Rating: instructive 1.)

Four U.S. New-Left Populists. C. Wright Mills is concerned to explicate the phenomena of power, not to invest the powerful with negative personal attributes or mistaken values. He threads a careful path between the institutional/structural approach to power and the common-sense view that powerful men have great (and often dangerous) discretion. (Rating: instructive 2.)

Carl Oglesby devotes his rhetoric to building a movement by disembarrassing his reader of presumed value commitments just to the right of the speaker's own position, while undercommunicating differences with any on his left. His concern is with 'which side,' not 'which path'— that is, with identity not programme. (Rating: emotive 2.)

The Newfield/Greenfield text styles itself as a manifesto and offers "three essential beliefs." But only the first of these is a belief about the predicament of the just man in an unjust society; the others are concerned with contingent questions—potential alignments for a populist movement in today's U.S.A. The text as a whole does not try to provide the intellectual scaffold for a new populism but attempts to hew a path between excesses of liberalism and the New Left's radical fringe. It is an exercise in identity-claiming through name-calling and name-dropping. (Rating: emotive 2.)

Senator McGovern's first text subordinates the actual issues named to the rhetoric of opposition, and heaps all the country's troubles at the door of the "establishment center," whose motives are not made clear. The second, much longer text, buries every general issue it touches in the particularities of current circumstance; the cash basis of politics, the dangers of war, and job insecurity are the main headings, but no general programme of action can be extracted from the text. (Rating: emotive 2.)

Four Norwegian Populists. The PAG rhetoric is evenly didactic, without appeals based on social identity—except that capitalism, or occasionally a "capitalist class," is made the enemy. Positional identity is always argued relative to the programmatic positions and arguments of parties to the left and right, though not with a view to taking up an overall position on that spectrum. The question of the identity (occupationally or morally) of the opposition or the target people/potential recruits does not come up. (Rating: instructive 2.)

Ottar Brox adopts a restrained polemical style. It becomes clear that at a deeper level, he is intensely concerned to connect with an audience: the style of each piece is adapted to circumstance, and Brox expects no rhetoric to penetrate a closed mind. Each text is organized around a crucial distinction between populist and other policy programmes, and aims to clarify thorny issues in what is, cumulatively, a move to establish a new radical rhetoric no longer wedded to "class." (Rating: instructive 2.)

Björn Unneberg eschews any sort of inflammatory style. The "first great revolutionary" was Jesus—that defines revolution. Unneberg turns away from 'red socialism' not because of red bloodiness, which goes unmentioned, but because of its narrow concern with the relations of production. Solidarity is equated with brotherhood and fellowship, and is focused on family, local and regional communities, not on a disciplined party or union. There is thus an underlying message about the value of a Christ-like identity; but the surface of the text is a gently didactic essay defining a programme by deliberating the questions, how much care should "solidarity" command at each level of organization, and where might a balance be found between economic and other concerns. (Rating: instuctive 1.)

Finn Gustavsen's text is addressed directly, but artfully, to the problem of maintaining a radical stance without becoming disoriented—avoiding the twin perils of dogmatism and whimsy. His style is non-didactic: he strikes a note of intellectual uncle-ishness throughout. He claims no mass following but outlines a coherent position for which a small party ought to fight with its wits: "It is not as exciting as guerilla warfare but it is *our* reality" (1969: 251). (Rating: instructive 2.)

QUESTION II: THE PRESUPPOSED VALUE CRITERION

Does the text presuppose a public calculus of values inspired by the idea of *grace* (virtue and the good life associated with a particular lifestyle and inner persuasion) or by that of *enlightenment* (let the people see the world as it really is and they will build the good society)?

Four U.S. New-Deal Populists. Senator Borah presupposes a correspondence between moral and economic merit; he exonerates the farmer as cause of his own desperate plight and inculpates the urban elite—the "farmer's enemy" who has duped him. (Rating: emotive 2.)

Senator Norris's rhetoric is that of moral rights and wrongs, not of salvation through learning. Miners are "misled" not misinformed. Norris's legislation embodied "fundamental decent principles," not any sort of legislative breakthrough, and the good attorney is "eminent," not brilliant. In short, the universal standard is grace, not enlightenment. (Rating: emotive 2.)

Senator Long finds that the poor are virtuous, the rich and the "wiseacres" are not. He opposes the agricultural policies of Roosevelt not on theoretical economic grounds but for being antithetical to common sense and "the laws of God." He urges his followers to convert others (provoking a chain reaction) rather than to debate and discuss. One of his planks is Jeffersonian education, but he presents it as "training for life's work" and for meritocratic standing, not enlightenment or leadership. (Rating: emotive 2.)

Senator Nye is speaking to his colleagues, not to the public as such, and the didactic nature of his text bespeaks a supposition that the Senate must be wary and enlightened, distrusting mere intuition of right. The public remains "the plain people," as such a people of virtue, but needing paternalistic protection against the slickers of the "Plunderbund" who are driven by selfish motives. Thus salvation is through faith in the Common Man not through truth's transforming him. (Rating: emotive 2.)

Four U.S. New-Left Populists. C. Wright Mills is concerned that the facts about a complex and fluid system of power be "made plain." He is an enlightener *par excellence*, always ready to warn that an intellectual task is not simple—then to charge at it. (Rating: instructive 2.)

Carl Oglesby, in his concern to dissociate his position from that of the liberals, who failed him, promises his cerebral listener that he will "take a close look" at them but fails to do so in any sense. "Liberalism" in his rhetoric is no more than a label for all the abuses of federal power he can recall since World War II. The two liberals he does mention (J. F. Kennedy and Adolf Berle) are not cited in connection with ideas but with alignments. The guilty 'liberal' may come away moved, but the astute listener is frustrated. (Rating: emotive 2.)

The Newfield/Greenfield text is concerned to promote a broad alliance of disparate social elements into a "pact between the have-nots." To do this (as is clear to an observer) there would have to be a massive burial of ideological and ethical differences, "a synthesis of many radical and some conservative ideas" (1972: 296). The deep rhetoric here thus appeals to intuition and commitment, not analytical understanding. More problems are buried than are brought to light. (Rating: emotive 2.)

In Senator McGovern's first text he is at pains to blame the Vietnam war on "the establishment wise men, the academicians of the center"; that is, "Ye shall distrust learning." His second text culminates in "the affirmation that we have a dream." No cerebral listener could possibly mistake this dream for an enlightened view of the path ahead. (Rating: emotive 2.)

Four Norwegian Populists. The PAG rhetoric is written (in fact or in effect) by graduate students for graduate students. It is bent on making an intellectual break from the party-political rhetoric hitherto accepted in student debate. Audgunn Oltedal bases an argument for playing down party differences on the grounds that (cardiac) party loyalties inhibit intellectual communication on the local level, where any crucial new "insights" and "bases of conduct" must be formed. (Rating: instructive 2.)

Ottar Brox is in the sociological tradition of C. Wright Mills, and at his most polemical does not substitute the attempt to sway for the attempt to persuade. Brox disavows the assumption that the truth will arm the righteous: a party might be right but lose on the plane of political action because its proponents did not prove "energetic and intelligent enough" (1972: 113). He argues that major institutional changes will follow from changed value premisses—that is, from public enlightenment. (Rating: instructive 2.)

Björn Unneberg is a teacher and pursues his calling in this text. But what he unfolds is a balanced, even timeless world view, not a disclosure of how wrong ideas have shaped today's world awry. Thus "green socialism" becomes the banner of grace, under which the milieu is to be made better by a movement of reconstruction. (Rating: emotive 1.)

Finn Gustavsen's warning against student domination of his party is not directed against thought but shallow doctrinairism: this is not a world like Senator McGovern's, in which the intelligentsia is corrupted by its learning, but one in which that class is isolated from the sources of political wisdom, as Mao found China's students to be. The purpose of dissociating Norway from power blocs is to preserve its policy independence, not just to save its skin. (Rating: instructive 2.)

QUESTION III: THE PERSONAL IMAGE PROJECTED

Does the text intend to establish its author as an *exemplary* leader (qualities of the heart projected) or as an *astute* one (a person with a 'good head')?

Four U.S. New-Deal Populists. Senator Borah does not project himself strongly either as the farmer's friend or as a teacher. He is moderately informative but dodges step-by-step argument in favour of homage to the farmer, demands for protection of his market, and a rumbling insistence that "something is wrong." (Rating: balanced 0.)

Senator Norris projects himself as a faithful public servant who listened to "every syllable of testimony," who exercised canny committee strategies, but who did little personally of the actual drafting of his bill, giving it over to legal experts. He is careful to dissociate himself from the miners' "false leader," John L. Lewis, who is condemned as unpatriotic. (Rating: emotive 1.)

Senator Long presents himself as a poor but earnest man, who has won hard battles and plans yet tougher campaigns on behalf of "every child in this land." He says his movement has and needs no "managers" because it is a holy cause. The humble style of the circular is its chief rhetorical device. It is a personal appeal from the Senator for help, but it carries, not far below the surface, an unmistakable message: pie in the sky. (Rating: emotive 2.)

At one point Senator Nye appeals to his colleagues to strip the world they perceive of its rhetorical colouration and ask what it all "actually comes down to." This is to advise that ultimately one should not trust argument but the inner light of common sense. In spite of his personally beleaguered position, he fails to set up arguments and knock them down, preferring to display elaborate restraint towards his critics in the "smear and hate brigades." In short, the deep rhetoric of this speech projects a man of dogged principle and exemplary devotion to his people, a victim of evil times but sure of his eventual vindication. (Rating: emotive 2.)

Four U.S. New-Left Populists. C. Wright Mills is explicitly concerned to be a shepherd of thoughts not men. (Rating: instructive 2.)

In his text, Carl Oglesby disavows the role of teacher for that of moralist, proposing a grand choice between "corporatism or Humanism," and appealing to those who make the choice of virtue to "help us build." There is no effort to sketch the architecture of the non-corporate world which is a-building. (Rating: emotive 2.)

Newfield and Greenfield call Robert Kennedy "an earthy enemy of war, hunger, and crime," who assembled the kind of heterogenous following they envision at the triumph of populism. The description of Kennedy fits the image projected by the authors of this *Manifesto* as well, though a cerebral reader may note a tiny bit of opportunism in the rather facile style of this romp through the ruins of a high civilization. (Rating: emotive 2.)

Senator McGovern is the champion of the ordinary man against "the establishment center," whose personnel are not ordinary. His acceptance speech says nothing a weary and bibulous delegate in Florida, or a schoolchild, could not easily follow. The deep rhetoric is *just* below the surface, like that of U.S.-American wire-service journalism, which seems not to contain any of the individuality of mind one would suppose must lie behind. (Rating: emotive 2.)

Four Norwegian Populists. The PAG writers all come across as genuine midwives of their peaceful revolution. They are not 'bolshy' but temper a thorough critique of Labour's achievements and programmes with the rhetoric of reason. "The battle to get common goods prioritied over private consumption means that one raises demands which, in the long run, may be system-destructive" (1972: 167). This is not inflammatory stuff and does not project a sense of need for strong leadership. The rhetoric demands and exhibits intelligence, but also projects moderation by example. (Rating: instructive 1.)

Ottar Brox is perhaps less modest. He seems prepared to lead. His texts, taken together, carry the message that inspired intelligence, backed by social research, is wanted to prevent a national decline towards which the current regime has allowed itself to drift. Brox argues that social change must come through changing thought and action at the grass-roots level, clearly envisioning a decentralized leadership and a "de-heroized revolution." The function of such leadership is to "disclose and pinpoint concrete limitations on the development of working people," and to show how the way can be cleared (1972: 102). (Rating: instructive 2.)

Björn Unneberg's modesty is more convincing. He comes across as teacher-counsellor rather than politician. At the same time, he finds himself qualified to write such a book as this on the grounds of what he knows (*qua* sociologist) as well as where he stands (*qua* citizen). He writes both of "springs of information we shall drink from" and of learning as an "implement" (1971: 75). (Rating: balanced 0.)

Finn Gustavsen seems unable to rise in his rhetoric upon any sort of pedestal. In his warning against student domination he manages not to put students down, and in waving off Maoism he does not discredit Mao. In support of pacific tactics in today's Norway, he cites both Che and Mao to good effect. Along with the other Norwegian populists, he projects reluctance to lead; but he makes explicit the standard by which he rates his own leadership of his party: the pertinent qualities are always insight into events, not purity of intentions, and intellectual flexibility, not the merit of accumulating seniority. (Rating: instructive 2.)

Conclusions

The separate ratings sum up as shown in Table 1.

Although no claim can be made for the infallibility of this test, its general finding is obvious: populist rhetoric in the U.S. is predominantly emotive whereas its Norwegian counterpart is instructive. The exceptions to this trend are Unneberg, the Christian and Folk high school spokesman, whose rhetoric was found less consistently instructive than that of his Norwegian colleagues; and C. Wright Mills, a non-conforming academic.

Let us consider first the possibility that the Norwegians, like Mills, are addressing a more sophisticated audience than the others—and adapting accordingly. Gustavsen and Brox speak to the wide public of an active politician, whereas in America at least Nye, Norris and Newfield/Greenfield address select audiences. We should therefore expect (on the ground of audience-selection) more similarity than we have found between the two cultures. The source of the difference seems to lie deeper, in the strategic situation of the populist in Norway and the U.S. Institutionally, the Norwegian populist enjoys—with his system of

TABLE 1

Ratings of Populist Rhetoric

	Emotive			Instructive		
	2	1	0	1	2	
U.S. New Deal						
I: identity/programme	1	2		1		
II: grace/enlightenment	4					
III: exemplary/astute	2	1	1			
	7	3	1	1	0	(12)
U.S. New Left						
I: identity/programme	3				1	
II: grace/enlightenment	3				1	
III: exemplary/astute	3				1	
	9	0	0	0	3	(12)
Sum U.S.	16	3	1	1	3	(24)
Norwegians						
I: identity/programme				1	3	
II: grace/enlightenment		1			3	
III: exemplary/astute			1	1	2	
Sum Norway	0	1	1	2	8	(12)

proportional representation—a context which grants him time to build a movement. And, culturally, in Norway there is, relative to the U.S. context, a bias towards instructive rhetoric. In U.S. politics, a new party or movement must virtually capture the highest prize, the presidency, its first time out; otherwise a loose coalition can be expected to fall apart before the next election, under raiding and harassment by better-established party interests. We do not have to assume that Senator McGovern was incapable of clear thinking. We can understand the confusion of his campaign: he would have been looking for shortcuts to a popularity he could hardly have expected to win, in the time he was given, through the hard-headed argument of issues amounting to a firm reversal of established policy and all its premises. In contrast a splinter party in Norway, or a dissident leader, would have the use of Parliament as a forum for building a long-term following, thus having less need for stridency, histrionic techniques or dirty tricks. Differences in the political cultures of two nations are not ineffable—they have explanations. But my intention here has been to offer a modest measure of such a difference, not to trace its roots in history. It is more appropriate for me to ask what the foregoing exercise tells us about the politics of populism.

As my title suggests, I set out to explore the pertinence of a Norwegian proverb to politics: "Weaklings wax bigger with words." There is a special sense in which Senator McGovern, close as he was to the presidency of a vast system of power, must have felt weaker than Stortingsmann Finn Gustavsen, pilot of a small nation's smallest parliamentary party. This is the sense in which strength always derives from the confidence of genuine *intention*. When Senator McGovern contemplated the ground of his support and the massive institutional array lined up against him, could he really expect to implement, *if he won*, the sweeping and idealistic reforms which made up his "dream"? I think the quality of his rhetoric shows he had no such firm expectation, just as Senator Norris's soft-pedalling retrospect on his fight for miners' rights reflects *his* faltering confidence in a kind of populist militancy in which, in 1932, he must have believed with passion. Looking back from a cushioned present, he cannot even summon the intentions by which he once was driven.

Politics in its very essence is promissory, and that is what justifies the careful study of its rhetoric, through which the intentions of powerful persons and movements must be judged. In the U.S. arena the one uninfringeable rule is pragmatism. It means that political promises are short-lived, forever being thrown back into the hopper for reassortment into new forms of the perennial compromise which, though called a party platform, professes no sort of ideology at all.

Norway stands at the opposite end of this scale of hardness, where parties sometimes dare not adapt to change, fearing loss of a brittle ideological identity. Populism has an easier way initially in the softer system, but it is likely to have a more lasting influence in the system which demands more of it.

The rhetoric of a movement is, by and large, the evidence by which historians will judge it, and rightly so. When we use the deliberative and hortative language of a labour movement, of an enthusiastic sect, or of a party in or out of power to judge its authenticity, we stand outside any intended audience, asking what kind of compact was formed between speaker and crowd, writer and audience. The rhetoric of Captain Swing (Hobsbawm and Rudé 1969) was direct enough—burning hayricks carry a message of desperate conviction. This is the 'rhetoric of action,' not words, but it is no misnomer, for the purpose of rhetoric is to state what logic cannot—the quality of human intention. Yet in a harder sense, rhetoric cannot exceed logic. When your situation says you have puffed yourself up with false hope, the rhetoric you find will probably betray your weakness to others, if not to yourself.

Notes

1. The Norwegian proverb is *Umagen er i ordom størst.*
2. Natives of the United States of America call themselves "Americans" and their land "America"—a designation other Americans may find confusing.
3. I find one major ambiguity in available typologies, which I trace to the binary logic controlling our use of *rhetoric.* Aristotle rose above this in his conceptualization of virtues as grouped triadically with vices—one vice, as it were, to the left and one to the right of the strait path. Torrid, temperate and frigid constitute such a triad; applied to rhetoric, the schema calls for a third term, opposite to "emotive" (as "instructive" really is not). Consider:

emotive	instructive	discursive
(cardiac)	(balanced)	(cerebral)

It may be worth considering that Bailey's hedging hyphenation "pseudo-cerebral" may be standing in for the virtuous norm of all deliberative rhetoric, *per* Aristotle. Then it would be our latter-day denigration of rhetoric (which we associate with demagoguery and bad sermons) that accounts for our denying a rhetorical dimension to the discourses of science, so carefully done in the language of "cerebration." This is also a tongue with the most sanguinary stylistic rules and which, in short, celebrates itself in vinegar as surely as Bryan's prose does in oil.

Rhetoric of Race

6

The Art of Enoch Powell: The Rhetorical Structure of a Speech on Immigration

DAVID LLOYD-JONES

Introductory Remarks

Of all Powell's newsworthy utterances, the one that caused the greatest furore was made in 1968 in Birmingham, the heartland of British industry. It was the one that alluded to "the river Tiber foaming with much blood," and the one that still serves to identify him as the demon or the prophet of the contemporary British political scene. Taken from the "rivers of blood" speech, as it is popularly known, the phrase became the media's automatic means of identifying Powell. In a speech on immigration eight years later, Powell emphasized his point of view by repeating another phrase from the Birmingham speech: watching the flow of immigration was "like watching a nation busily engaged in heaping up its own funeral pyre."[1]

Such esoteric and literary images characterize the style that has helped Powell to establish his authority over a vast audience[2] despite his apparently weak base in the political structure. In the 1960s, restlessness over immigration was reflected in the acts that limited immigration, introduced by the Conservative Government in 1962 and by the Labour Government in 1964. Powell's bid to capitalize on this state of affairs was seen by political commentators as his attempt to create a public following during the time his party was in the relative freedom of opposition, and in 1965 when he placed third, after Maudling and Heath, in the leadership contest within the Conservative party. Having alienated himself from his former ministerial colleagues over the immigration issue and eventually from his party by refusing to support it on the Common Market issue (and by his ultimate recommendation to vote Labour in 1974), Powell sustained his image before the electorate

through his ability to express clearly and cogently his stand on controversial issues. His ability to command public respect despite the
unorthodoxy of his political ventures, together with the freedom left to
his admirers and followers to make their own interpretations of his
statements, cast Powell in the mould of a charismatic leader.

Whatever his motivations, and despite what appear to be considerable tactical blunders in his political career, he is listened to, and
admired or execrated. For notwithstanding the different interpretations
of his motives and intentions, he appears to have a coherent attitude to
the various problems that beset Britain—whether they concern
economic or racial issues, or the matter of nationhood (the definition of
a political identity in relation to the past and to other political communities). He has formulated a set of responses which he articulates
effectively to illuminate any situation or issue.

It seems worthwhile therefore to try to analyse his persuasive skill
by reference to the most notorious of his speeches on one of the most
contentious topics, a topic he has made his own by largely defining the
terms of the debate. Powell is an outstanding example of the politician
as prophet, the depicter of situations in terms that are both generally
acceptable and sufficiently novel as to lead the public towards a new
understanding of its problems. As he sees it, the politician's service "is
analogous to the functions of the medicine man in a primitive society: it
is to dramatise and personalise the abstract and impersonal forces by
which man's life is governed, and to create the comfortable illusion that
they can be manipulated by the practitioner" (Powell 1969: 151). Bring-
ing this sceptical irony nearer home, he says that "it is little enough that
politicians can achieve, but at least they can talk. And if from blindness
or lack of courage they fail to find the words to speak what the mass of
people want to hear expressed then they betray the one trust which is
reposed in them" (p. 166). At his most effective the statesman becomes
the myth-maker. Historical myths, which are the main source of
political ideologies, are defined by Powell as "a pattern which men
weave out of the materials of the past. The moment a fact enters into
history it becomes mythical, because it has been taken and fitted into its
place in a set of ordered relationships which is the creation of the human
mind and not otherwise present in nature" (p. 246).

Statesmen, like charismatic personalities in general, can perform
these feats of conceptual and perceptual readjustment successfully
because their reputation is such that people are willing to trust them and
be guided by them. In the analysis of rhetorical technique, what should
be noticed first is how the orator presents himself to his audience: what
elements of an existing reputation he chooses to emphasize by way of
establishing his identity with the particular audience and his authority

*Enoch Powell Delivering a Speech on
Immigration, 1976 (Courtesy of London Daily Express)*

to deal with a particular theme. In considering the exposition of this
theme or message, the student of rhetoric remembers that the logic of a
piece of political persuasion will not, as Aristotle showed, be of the same
type as that of a philosophical or scientific demonstration. Rhetorical or
persuasive arguments concerned with forming perceptions and altering
opinions rely on the enthymeme rather than on the rigour of the full
syllogism (cf. Chapter 2). The orator does not need to spell out the
logical connections of the propositions, but instead plays upon the
attitudes, values and prejudices shared by the audience. In general, their
feelings rather than their reasoned justification are the audience's source
of self-reference, though a good persuader helps to provide
rationalizations that appear to be respectable justifications for the
opinions he urges them to formulate.

In order to elicit a gut reaction rather than intellectual assent, the
rhetorician appeals to the emotions. He tries to activate the feelings by

which the principles of religion, politics and all ethical behaviour are normally nourished. Such sentiments are the marrow of the skeletal beliefs that motivate our behaviour. Without this rich source of associations, generated by time, chance and culture, the rational abstraction of a corpus of coherent principles and policies would have little force. A rational ordering of impressions and experience into a logically consistent set of points of view is a rare phenomenon, as public opinion surveys repeatedly show. In the eighteenth century, David Hume succinctly summarized the findings of social psychology: "Custom is man's second nature." Or, as that skilled strategist and politician, the Duke of Wellington put it: "Second nature? It's ten times nature!" One of the greatest rhetoricians, Edmund Burke, rephrased the matter: prejudice is the politician's purchase or point of leverage. We rely upon the habitual responses acquired by education and convention, rather than upon the frighteningly isolated projections of individual theorizing, when it is necessary to react with an immediate judgement and speedy action.

The skilful orator must know how to evoke from this obscure subconscious stratum the images, metaphors and reactions appropriate to the character of his message and the intention of his persuasion. For many effective orators, this artistry is probably the result of empathy rather than a rationally calculated matching of means to ends. Powell's background as a professor of classics, as a distinguished linguist, poet and admirer of A. E. Housman indicates, however, a high degree of self-conscious artistry. He may be compared to a composer who consciously combines the elements of a musical idiom to create effects. Perhaps his rival in populist 'pulling-power,' the Reverend Ian Paisley, belongs to those orators who spontaneously warble their native wood-notes wild.

The musical and poetic analogies here are apt because the analysis of rhetoric is like the appreciation of an artistic composition. Enjoyment of music, a picture or a performance, can appear spontaneous because art is to conceal art, and the artist has so orchestrated the elements appropriate to the field as to appeal to the cultural and emotional conditioning of the audience. But the intelligentsia, at least, finds that aesthetic appreciation of what is being done, and how, increases the sum of pleasure, or enhances its quality. The critique so developed can also be employed fruitfully in the extension of the art itself.

The student of political behaviour similarly becomes aware of the arts of leadership and the potentialities of his public material when he engages in rhetorical analysis. The aims of this analysis, however, are not scientific in the sense of leading to certain knowledge; and the terms used are not the immediately impressive language of quantification—though word counts can be helpful indicators of style and content. The results are not formulated as generalizations, hypotheses or laws. The aims are to enlighten understanding in order to aid judgement; the terms are drawn from the rich technical vocabulary of a discipline that for centuries was central to the educational process. In order not to be too esoteric, I have reduced them here to the most common concepts of logic and the criteria of fallacy, casuistry and sophistry. General aesthetic canons of theme, configuration or structure, tone and finally taste are taken from contemporary critical vocabularies. An objective attempt to appreciate the coherence of an argument, policy or project may be a valid criterion for judgement; but the question of whether judgement of political matters can ever be—or should ever pretend to be—entirely objective or scientific is too contentious to be discussed here. In rhetorical analysis it is difficult to come to a final assessment of the success or failure of a persuasive activity without some estimation of the motives and intentions of the persuader, and this judgement must, in the end, be subjective.

Since rhetoric appeals to feelings and leads to action, its quality must be judged in terms of its ability to evoke an appropriate response. A scholar unacquainted with the culture or the situation of a particular orator-audience relationship might be able to detect certain patterns of language and behaviour in operation, but would still be unable to appreciate the orator's skill, or understand the causes of the audience's response. He would not get the 'meaning' of the event and could hardly pass a sound judgement on it. Collections of famous orations from the past are today almost as unread as the technical handbooks of the art of rhetoric with which they were contemporaneous. A highly informed historical imagination is necessary to appreciate the first; as for the second, what is the use of a cook book when the ingredients for the recipes are no longer at hand? Today we undertake similar projects bearing in mind the current ingredients of political controversy and the radical changes in the frameworks for action—which likens the enterprise to catering to the pressure cooker and infra-red grill rather than the old baking oven!

The analysis of this particular speech is undertaken in the belief that despite the lapse of more than a decade, its ingredients are available to and 'analysable' by anyone familiar with contemporary British political culture—if not that of most societies in highly industrialized post-colonial situations. The common experience of a tension-ridden society, where 'race' as well as 'class' are the usual components of the perceived situation, should excuse my lack of analysis of the audience's prejudices and perceptions. As an effective rhetorician, Powell is undoubtedly sensitive to what will, in his own word, "reverberate" (1969: 242). Wallman considers this aspect of the phenomenon of Powellism in the next chapter. The continuing concern of politicians and the media with such a personality as Powell and with his view of the immigrant, or racial problem, indicates that a discussion of racialism as he defines it here is still relevant. The speech, also characteristic of Powell's style, is individual enough for us to expect to find similarities in his expository and evocative methods, whether yesterday, today or tomorrow, and whether his topic be financial profligacy, political delusions at home or abroad, or the basic question of national identity.

The Speech[3]

1* The supreme function of statesmanship is to provide against preventable evils. In seeking to do so, it encounters obstacles which are deeply rooted in human nature. One is that by the very order of things such evils are not demonstrable until they have occurred: at each stage in their onset there is room for doubt and for dispute whether they be real or imaginary. By the same token, they attract little attention in comparison with current troubles, which are both indisputable and pressing. Hence the besetting temptation of all politics to concern itself with the immediate present at the expense of the future. Above all, people are
10 disposed to mistake predicting troubles for causing troubles and even for desiring troubles: "If only," they love to think, "if only people wouldn't talk about it, it probably wouldn't happen." Perhaps this habit goes back to the primitive belief that the word and the thing, the name and the object, are identical. At all events, the discussion of future grave but, with effort now, avoidable evils is the most unpopular and at the same time the most necessary occupation for the politician. Those who knowingly shirk it, deserve, and not infrequently receive, the curses of those who come after.

2 A week or two ago I fell into conversation with a constituent, a middle-aged, quite ordinary working man employed in one of our nationalised industries. After a sentence or two about the weather, he suddenly said: "If I had the money to go, I wouldn't stay in this country." I made some deprecatory reply, to the effect that even this government wouldn't last for ever; but he took no notice, and continued: "I have three children, all of them been through grammar school and two of them married now, with family. I shan't be satisfied till I have seen them all settled overseas. In this country in 15 or 20 years time the black
10 man will have the whip hand over the white man."
3 I can already hear the chorus of execration. How dare I say such a horrible thing? How dare I stir up trouble and inflame feelings by repeating such a conversation? The answer is that I do not have the right

* Boldface numbers are paragraph numbers; lightface numbers are line numbers.

not to do so. Here is a decent, ordinary fellow-Englishman, who in broad daylight in my own town says to me, his Member of Parliament, that this country will not be worth living in for his children. I simply do not have the right to shrug my shoulders and think about something else. What he is saying, thousands and hundreds of thousands are saying and thinking—not throughout Great Britain, perhaps, but in the areas that are already undergoing the total transformation to which there is no   10 parallel in a thousand years of English history.

A MATTER OF NUMBERS

In 15 or 20 years, on present trends, there will be in this country 3½   4 million Commonwealth immigrants and their descendants. That is not my figure. That is the official figure given to Parliament by the spokesman of the Registrar General's office. There is no comparable official figure for the year 2000; but it must be in the region of five to seven million, approximately one-tenth of the whole population, and approaching that of greater London. Of course, it will not be evenly distributed from Margate to Aberystwyth and from Penzance to Aberdeen. Whole areas, towns and parts of towns across England will be occupied by different sections of the immigrant and immigrant-   10 descended population.

As time goes on, the proportion of this total who are immigrant   5 descendants, those born in England, who arrived here by exactly the same route as the rest of us, will rapidly increase. Already by 1985 those born here would constitute the majority. It is this fact above all which creates the extreme urgency of action now, of just that kind of action which is hardest for politicians to take, action where the difficulties lie in the present but the evils to be prevented or minimised lie several parliaments ahead.

The natural and rational first question for a nation confronted by   6 such a prospect is to ask: "how can its dimensions be reduced?" Granted it be not wholly preventable, can it be limited, bearing in mind that numbers are of the essence. The significance and consequences of an alien element introduced into a country or population are profoundly different according to whether that element is one per cent or 10 per cent. The answers to the simple and rational question are equally simple and rational: by stopping, or virtually stopping, further inflow, and by promoting the maximum outflow. Both answers are part of official policy of the Conservative Party.   10

It almost passes belief that at this moment 20 or 30 additional   7 immigrant children are arriving from overseas in Wolverhampton alone every week—and that means 15 or 20 additional families a decade or two hence. Those whom the gods wish to destroy, they first make mad. We

94   *David Lloyd-Jones*

must be mad, literally mad, as a nation to be permitting the annual
inflow of some 50,000 dependents, who are for the most part the material
of the future growth of the immigrant-descended population. It is like
watching a nation busily engaged in heaping up its own funeral pyre. So
insane are we that we actually permit unmarried persons to immigrate
10   for the purpose of founding a family with spouses and fiances whom
they have never seen. Let no one suppose that the flow of dependents will
automatically tail off. On the contrary, even at the present admission
rate of only 5,000 a year by voucher, there is sufficient for a further 25,000
dependents per annum *ad infinitum*, without taking into account the
huge reservoir of existing relations in this country—and I am making no
allowance at all for fraudulent entry. In these circumstances nothing
will suffice but that the total inflow for settlement should be reduced at
once to negligible proportions, and that the necessary legislative and
administrative measures be taken without delay. I stress the words "for
20   settlement." This has nothing to do with the entry of Commonwealth
citizens, any more than of aliens, into this country, for the purposes of
study or of improving their qualifications, like (for instance) the Commonwealth doctors who, to the advantage of their own countries, have
enabled our hospital service to be expanded faster than would otherwise
have been possible. These are not, and never have been, immigrants.

8   I turn to re-emigration. If all immigration ended tomorrow, the rate
of growth of the immigrant and immigrant-descended population
would be substantially reduced, but the prospective size of this element
in the population would still leave the basic character of the national
danger unaffected. This can only be tackled while a considerable
proportion of the total still comprises persons who entered this country
during the last 10 years or so. Hence the urgency of implementing now
the second element of the Conservative Party's policy: the encouragement of re-emigration. Nobody can make an estimate of the numbers
10   which, with generous grants and assistance, would choose either to
return to their countries of origin or to go to other countries anxious to
receive the manpower and the skills they represent. Nobody knows,
because no such policy has yet been attempted. I can only say that, even
at present, immigrants in my own constituency from time to time come
to me, asking if I can find them assistance to return home. If such a
policy were adopted and pursued with the determination which the
gravity of the alternative justifies, the resultant outflow could ap-
preciably alter the prospects for the future.

9   It can be no part of any policy that existing families should be kept
divided; but there are two directions in which families can be reunited,
and if our former and present immigration laws have brought about the
division of families, albeit voluntary or semi-voluntary, we ought to be

prepared to arrange for them to be reunited in their countries of origin. In short, suspension of immigration and encouragement of re-emigration hang together, logically and humanly, as two aspects of the same approach.

The third element of the Conservative Party's policy is that all who   10
are in this country as citizens should be equal before the law and that there shall be no discrimination or difference made between them by public authority. As Mr. Heath has put it, we will have no "first-class citizens" and "second-class citizens." This does not mean that the immigrant and his descendants should be elevated into a privileged or special class or that the citizen should be denied his right to discriminate in the management of his own affairs between one fellow-citizen and another or that he should be subjected to inquisition as to his reasons and motives for behaving in one lawful manner rather than another.   10

DISCRIMINATION: AGAINST WHOM?

There could be no grosser misconception of the realities than is enter-   11
tained by those who vociferously demand legislation as they call it "against discrimination," whether they be leader-writers of the same kidney and sometimes on the same newspapers which year after year in the 1930s tried to blind this country to the rising peril which confronted it, or archbishops who live in palaces, faring delicately, with the bedclothes pulled right up over their heads. They have got it exactly and diametrically wrong. The discrimination and the deprivation, the sense of alarm and of resentment, lies not with the immigrant population but with those among whom they have come and are still coming. This is   10
why to enact legislation of the kind before Parliament at this moment is to risk throwing a match on to gunpowder. The kindest thing that can be said about those who propose and support it is that they know not what they do.

Nothing is more misleading than comparison between the Com-   12
monwealth immigrant in Britain and the American negro. The negro population of the United States, which was already in existence before the United States became a nation, started literally as slaves and were later given the franchise and other rights of citizenship, to the exercise of which they have only gradually and still incompletely come. The Commonwealth immigrant came to Britain as a full citizen, to a country which knew no discrimination between one citizen and another, and he entered instantly into the possession of the rights of every citizen, from the vote to free treatment under the National Health Service. Whatever   10
drawbacks attended the immigrants—and they were drawbacks which did not, and do not, make admission into Britain by hook or by crook appear less than desirable—arose not from the law or from public policy

or from administration but from those personal circumstances and accidents which cause, and always will cause, the fortunes and experience of one man to be different from another's.

13   But while to the immigrant entry to this country was admission to privileges and opportunities eagerly sought, the impact upon the existing population was very different. For reasons which they could not comprehend, and in pursuance of a decision by default, on which they were never consulted, they found themselves made strangers in their own country. They found their wives unable to obtain hospital beds in childbirth, their children unable to obtain school places, their homes and neighbourhoods changed beyond recognition, their plans and prospects for the future defeated; at work they found that employers
10   hesitated to apply to the immigrant worker the standards of discipline and competence required of the native-born worker; they began to hear, as time went by, more and more voices which told them that they were now the unwanted. On top of this, they now learn that a one-way privilege is to be established by Act of Parliament: a law, which cannot, and is not intended to, operate to protect them or redress their grievances, is to be enacted to give the stranger, the disgruntled and the *agent provocateur* the power to pillory them for their private actions.

FEAR FOR THE FUTURE

14   In the hundreds upon hundreds of letters I received when I last spoke on this subject two or three months ago, there was one striking feature which was largely new and which I find ominous. All Members of Parliament are used to the typical anonymous correspondent; but what surprised and alarmed me was the high proportion of ordinary decent, sensible people, writing a rational and often well-educated letter, who believed that they had to omit their address because it was dangerous to have committed themselves to paper to a Member of Parliament agreeing with the views I had expressed, and that they would risk either
10   penalties or reprisals if they were known to have done so. The sense of being a persecuted minority which is growing among ordinary English people in the areas of the country affected is something that those without direct experience can hardly imagine. I am going to allow just one of those hundreds of people to speak for me. She did give her name and address, which I have detached from the letter which I am about to read. She was writing from Northumberland about something which is happening at this moment in my own constituency.

15   "Eight years ago in a respectable street in Wolverhampton a house was sold to a negro. Now only one white (a woman old-age pensioner) lives there. This is her story. She lost her husband and both her sons in the war. So she turned her seven-roomed house, her only asset, into a

boarding house. She worked hard and did well, paid off her mortgage and began to put something by for her old age. Then the immigrants moved in. With growing fear, she saw one house after another taken over. The quiet street became a place of noise and confusion. Regretfully, her white tenants moved out.

"The day after the last one left, she was awakened at 7 a.m. by two negroes who wanted to use her phone to contact their employer. When she refused, as she would have refused any stranger at such an hour, she was abused and feared she would have been attacked but for the chain on her door. Immigrant families have tried to rent rooms in her house, but she always refused. Her little store of money went, and after paying her rates, she has less than £2 per week. She went to apply for a rate reduction and was seen by a young girl, who on hearing she had a seven-roomed house, suggested she should let part of it. When she said the only people she could get were negroes, the girl said 'racial prejudice won't get you anywhere in this country.' So she went home.   16   10

"The telephone is her lifeline. Her family pay the bill, and help her out as best they can. Immigrants have offered to buy her house—at a price which the prospective landlord would be able to recover from his tenants in weeks, or at most a few months. She is becoming afraid to go out. Windows are broken. She finds excreta pushed through her letter-box. When she goes to the shops, she is followed by children, charming, wide-grinning piccaninnies. They cannot speak English, but one word they know, 'Racialist,' they chant. When the new Race Relations Bill is passed, this woman is convinced she will go to prison. And is she so wrong? I begin to wonder."   17   10

The other dangerous delusion from which those who are willfully or otherwise blind to realities suffer, is summed up in the word "integration." To be integrated into a population means to become for all practical purposes indistinguishable from its other members. Now, at all times, where there are marked physical differences, especially of colour, integration is difficult though, over a period, not impossible. There are among the Commonwealth immigrants who have come to live here in the last 15 years or so, many thousands whose wish and purpose is to be integrated and whose every thought and endeavour is bent in that direction. But to imagine that such a thing enters the heads of a great and growing majority of immigrants and their descendants is a ludicrous misconception, and a dangerous one to boot.   18   10

COMMUNALISM

We are on the verge here of a change. Hitherto it has been force of circumstance and of background which has rendered the very idea of integration inaccessible to the greater part of the immigrant   19

population—that they never conceived or intended such a thing, and
that their numbers and physical concentration meant the pressures
towards integration which normally bear upon any small minority did
not operate. Now we are seeing the growth of positive forces acting
against integration, of vested interests in the preservation and
sharpening of racial and religious differences, with a view to the exercise
10   of actual domination, first over fellow-immigrants and then over the rest
of the population. The cloud no bigger than a man's hand, that can so
rapidly overcast the sky, has been visible recently in Wolverhampton
and has shown signs of spreading quickly. The words I am about to use,
verbatim as they appeared in the local press of 17 February [1968], are not
mine, but those of a Labour Member of Parliament who is a Minister in
the Government. "The Sikh community's campaign to maintain
customs inappropriate in Britain is much to be regretted. Working in
Britain, particularly in the public services, they should be prepared to
accept the terms and conditions of their employment. To claim special
20   communal rights (or should one say rites?) leads to a dangerous
fragmentation within society. This communalism is a canker; whether
practised by one colour or another it is to be strongly condemned." All
credit to John Stonehouse for having had the insight to perceive that,
and the courage to say it.

20   For these dangerous and divisive elements the legislation proposed
in the Race Relations Bill is the very pabulum they need to flourish.
Here is the means of showing that the immigrant communities can
organise to consolidate their members, to agitate and campaign against
their fellow-citizens, and to overawe and dominate the rest with the legal
weapons which the ignorant and the ill-informed have provided. As I
look ahead, I am filled with foreboding. Like the Roman, I seem to see
"the River Tiber foaming with much blood." That tragic and
intractable phenomenon which we watch with horror on the other side
10   of the Atlantic but which there is interwoven with the history and
existence of the States itself, is coming upon us here by our own volition
and our own neglect. Indeed, it has all but come. In numerical terms, it
will be of American proportions long before the end of the century. Only
resolute and urgent action will avert it even now. Whether there will be
the public will to demand and obtain that action, I do not know. All I
know is that to see, and not to speak, would be the great betrayal.

Analysis of the Speech

The orator must establish his authority in order to communicate to his
audience. The reputation that Powell can assume is that of a

professional politician, and so he begins his speech with an enthymemic   1:1*
redefinition in terms of statesmanship; that is to say, instead of spelling
out his credentials (probably anyhow alluded to by the chairman
introducing Powell to the audience), he assumes that his listeners will
want him to address himself to 'higher' questions than mere 'party'
politics and personalities. The shorthand indication of this enthymeme
is his use of the word "statesmanship." At once the tone of the occasion is
elevated and the audience's expectations are raised to the considerations
of some momentous theme.

  Powell immediately draws a contrast between the comfortable
elements of depth, certainty, primitive belief, and the non-demonstrable   1:13
hypothesis of a future evil. He makes the logical distinction between   1:4
predicting and causing, and follows this with an apparent disjunction   1:10-11
between *unpopular* but *necessary*. The repetition of disjunctive
formulae culminates in the moral contrasts between the basic reactions
of shirking and cursing.   1:17

  Still in the first paragraph, Powell oscillates between the heroic
notion of statesmanship and the pithiest anglo-saxon language, thus
setting up an exciting tension in his audience that is heightened by the
disjunctions. But in the second paragraph, he suddenly switches into the
conversational mode for a narrative exposition of his topic. The tone   2:1
and tension are thus lowered once full attention has been secured and a
state of expectancy engendered. He depicts himself in conversation with
a representative constituent—thus recasting himself in the role of political mouthpiece rather than prophetic statesman. It is in the form of
reported speech that a vivid image is introduced: "the black man will   2:10
have the whip hand over the white man." Powell often uses the notion of
an M.P. as representative in order to perform a ventriloquist's function.
This mode is continued as he objectifies the responses of his audience: 3:1
the chorus of execration. He thereby takes the sting away from their
actual feelings onto himself as the violator of a taboo.

  Then he responds in terms of his duties as a representative, an M.P.
of "decent, ordinary fellow-Englishmen." Under this acceptable cover,   3:4
he states the proposition of a "total transformation" of our culture. This   3:10
claim is backed up by an appeal to authoritative intellectual arguments.
The first one is that of numbers, already introduced in the minor themes
of "hundreds of thousands are saying and thinking" and "a thousand   3:8-9
years," and now made a major theme with the apparently precise
number of years and immigrants (note that emotive black men have now   4:1-2
been 'scientifically' recategorized).

  Powell has often been accused of fallacious inferences in this

---

* Paragraph 1, line 1 of the speech.

statistical domain, but the running battle over the correctness of official figures and their subsequent interpretation have certainly kept his
4:4   opponents on their guard. For his immediate rhetorical purpose here, official figures and authoritative institutions impress the audience, and
4:5   the speculative extrapolation is disguised by a forceful "must." These
4:8-9   difficult abstractions are concretized in the image "whole areas, towns and parts of towns . . . will be occupied." The mathematical argument is obscure enough for a lagging listener to mistake the claim
5:3-4   that "by 1985 those born here would constitute the majority," and to conclude that Powell refers to the whole population, rather than the
5:4-5   immigrant section of it, especially in view of the statement: "this fact above all . . . creates the extreme urgency of action now."

To the preceding authority of his own official role and functions, and the panoply of official figures, Powell now brings the authority of logic. One of the peculiar marks of his style is the apparent use of procedures not normal to political discourse. He uses the rather formal, simplistic juxtapositions of an apparent syllogistic style to dramatize an argument. But this 'professional' style, with its associations of reasonableness and objectivity, holds authority for many and draws on his past reputation. Typical of the actual caricature of the logical mode,
6:1   however, is his conflation of "natural" and "rational." Terms such as
6:4-5   "essence," "significance," "consequence" and "element" have an academic ring to them. Even "alien" has connotations of official, if not biblical, language that serve to reclassify the topic as respectable. By the
6:7   end of this stage of the argument, "simple" has replaced "natural." The logical mode is retained to assert an equivalence between question and answer, so that by the third reiteration we are presented with "simple and rational" answers. The form of the answer is almost an algebraic
6:8-9   equation: stop inflow, promote outflow.

Such a logical solution to the problem is bolstered by a fourth
6:10   authoritative appeal—to the official policy of the Conservative Party. The generality of the argument is made vivid by examples taken from his
7:2   own constituency. Again this is an enthymemic reminder of his authority as the link between official policy and grass-roots experience. It might prove restrictive to spell this claim out to the national audience, but it rings responsive bells before the immediate audience. It is, however, hardly more than a grace note, because attention is at once shifted from this source of authority for his general argument to that
7:4   final authority with which his reputation is closely associated—classical learning. This background of learning strengthens Powell's image as a politician of intellectual rectitude, similar to that of the great nineteenth-century parliamentary figures, such as Gladstone, of whom

the middle class today know little except that they ruled justly, efficiently and inexpensively. The popular value to be had for Powell from these classical associations is that of the respect accorded to an authority in an arcane area.

The suicidal image of "a nation busily engaged in heaping up its   7:8
own funeral pyre" has been prepared for by a tag from our school days,
which usefully serves the further purpose of opening up a counter-point
sub-theme of classical order and which conjures up madness on the one   7:5
hand and chaos on the other. The synthesis of this little argument comes
in the joining of the classical and the measureless in "ad infinitum."   7:14
The association of pyres with suttee, and hence Macaulay's juggernaut
of Hindoo wives, may be rather too sophisticated for most of the
audience, but such covert literary resonances help to explain the
fascination of Powell's style for people not usually attuned to popular
rhetoric. The association here coheres with the obvious concern of his
argument with families and dependents.   7:10

The notion of the "fraudulent entry" of dependents introduces a   7:16
new (and sixth) type of authority—that of the law, itself historically
associated with the classical world. "The necessary legislative and   7:18-19
administrative measures" puts his proposals for action in the framework
which, there is no reason to doubt, is the one he sees as appropriate. A
legalistic point is also made to distinguish between the immigrants that
are settlers and others, such as students and doctors. This rider, in   7:20-23
addition to showing the sweet reasonableness of his argument, serves the
covert purpose of justifying his own policy as Minister of Health, which
otherwise appears inconsistent with his present priorities. It is, of
course, correct to say that these groups (students and doctors) "are not,   7:25-26
and never have been, immigrants." But to an audience aroused by the
picture so far painted, it might seem a casuistry, insofar as they note it at
all in their flow of feeling. Its function at the time of speaking must be to
strengthen Powell's style of 'scientific' definitions, and hence the
presumption of general accuracy when it comes to predictions.

The argument has now settled on policy, on what is to be done. The
incisiveness of Powell's style, where complex matters are concerned, is in
itself admirably persuasive. The policy of controlling, if not completely
stopping, immigration was relatively uncontroversial since both parties
were already committed to some form of it.[4] The policy of re-emigration   8:1
or repatriation—sometimes envisaged as deportation—was much more
controversial.[5] But the first measure leaves "the basic character of the   8:4-5
national danger unaffected," he asserts. The need for a more positive
policy is suggested by the use of terms that imply a will to overcome:
"tackle" and "implement." One is from a physical, popular vocabulary;   8:5,7

the other, from an intellectual and administrative sphere. These metaphors buttress the argument for the urgency of the second element of party policy. But then the humane aspect of this policy is quickly
8:10   displayed. "Generous grants and assistance," the needs of the
8:14   underdeveloped countries, and actual requests from "immigrants in my
9:1   own constituency" are added to a plea against keeping families divided. This particular inhumanity is ascribed to the existing legal situation, and the packet of arguments and policies are presented as "hang[ing]
9:7   together, logically and humanly."

The legalistic theme and authority now becomes dominant and is linked to the third element of Conservative policy: that of equality and
10:3   non-discrimination between citizens. The leader's reputation is invoked for support. Then the small print of this normally acceptable principle is spelled out. Logically, of course, it implies no special concern for, or
10:6   protection of, the immigrant and recognizes the right of private individuals to discriminate in private matters. The image of being
10:9   "subjected to [an] inquisition" on personal and private matters nicely turns the argument from a decently defensive one into a familiar radical Tory attack on the encroachment of the state on the liberties of citizens.

The modulation at this point in the speech from the defensive to the offensive is strengthened by the introduction of a philosophical
11:1   argument about the "misconception of . . . realities." To those familiar with Powell's speeches this will be recognized as one of his fundamental themes. He sees the chief job of a statesman as the formulation of a world view for his audience. The harsh realities of life are clothed in myths, of a more or less poetic nature, whose purpose is aesthetic and moral. These myths are the stuff of civilization, or of a national culture. Their celebration by public figures, such as priests and politicians, is the way values are affirmed and meaning is given to society's activities. But such ideological articulations of a 'truth' for a people are always in danger of becoming out of touch with manifold reality and hence mere delusions. When they no longer explain or take account of ever-changing reality, they lead to delusions or misconceptions that can only blind a people to necessities and lead to disaster.

In this case the deluders are those arguing in favour of the Race Relations Bill introduced into Parliament on 8 April 1968. This political prescription arises from general delusions about the tolerance of human societies (expressed in the socialist slogans of equality and fraternity) and more particularly from the current delusion of a "Commonwealth" citizenship, a disastrous entail from Britain's imperial past. Powell does not spell this out here for three reasons. Firstly, it would be already clear to most of his audience on the eve of a

Race Relations debate in Parliament that the enthymeme here presupposes this subject. Secondly, it would be tactically undesirable to advertise his opponents' policy proposal to those as yet unaware of the Bill. Thirdly, a fair exposition of the antagonistic position might draw attention to it and attract some who are at present reacting out of habitual prejudice along stock party-lines of allegiance. In this particular case, the arguments for egalitarian social treatment of minorities might appeal to the common sentiment of justice; and the notion of a common destiny, and hence responsibility, arising from the imperial past, could certainly appeal to Tories and complicate Powell's implicit undermining of these arguments.

By thus obscuring one of the premises of his argument, Powell also contributes effectively to the sense of muddle and distortion that is cunningly associated with the symbol, "legislation as they call it 'against discrimination.' " The agents to which he chooses to ascribe this "misconception of realities" are the "vociferous" media groups (another familiar bugbear of Powell's) and do-gooders. The first are linked with the truism of policy failure in the 1930s. The "rising peril" at that time was fascism, but in our subconscious the metaphors of 'rising sun' and the 'yellow peril' are not too far from exotic blackmen. Then it was the cry of appeasement; now it is "against discrimination." Powell is on tricky ground here: he is committed to being against "public" discrimination, yet is now trying to argue that the real evil in the situation is that private citizens are being discriminated against by public authorities because of their colour prejudice.

11:3

11:5

10:4
10:8–10

Perhaps in order to distract attention from these subtleties, he chooses to ridicule the second group. They are personified—as a relief from the abstractions of public and private discrimination—as privileged, antiquated and "faring delicately." This archaic phrase emphasizes, by contrast, the humorous image of archbishops "with the bedclothes pulled right up over their heads." This flash of comic metaphor is nicely placed, about half-way through the speech. It relaxes the tension built up during his closely reasoned deployment of arguments and authorities. His very 'logical' reasoning seems to be parodied and the argument for delusion (or perhaps nightmare?) strengthened by "They have got it exactly and diametrically wrong."

11:6
11:6–7

11:7–8

The audience now has its critical guard down and is drawn by the bond of shared laughter to identify with the orator as he recapitulates the major theme—what has hitherto been only a minor one: that it is not the immigrant but the rest who are discriminated against, deprived, alarmed and resentful. The Race Relations legislation risks "throwing a match on to gunpowder." The simile is apt because of its associations with the

11:9–10

11:12

parliament and another minority in the seventeenth century. It is followed by a phrase derived from the Psalms and applied to the last words of Christ. The provenance will probably escape the audience, but not its familiar tragic tone.

11:13–14

The general theme of misconceptions is sustained as Powell turns from the areas of myth and history to that of "misleading comparisons." Reiteration of the almost taboo term "negro" is calculated to rivet attention on this new stage of the argument, whose coherence with the previous steps would otherwise require tortuous and tedious explication and probably raise doubts in the listeners' minds. The first comparison, between Commonwealth immigrants and negroes, serves to emphasize how gradual and incomplete has been the enfranchisement of the slaves. The second comparison emphasizes that despite every public assistance our immigrants nevertheless suffer from personal difficulties. An impression of inability as being a natural trait of coloured people seems to be conveyed. These comparisons climax in the contrast between the "privileges and opportunities eagerly sought" by the immigrant and the "impact" upon those who thereby "found themselves made strangers in their own country."

12:1
12:2

12:4–6
12:7–15

13:2
13:5–6

The helpless plight of the majority is emphasized by Powell's use of the familiar political dichotomy between them (the authorities) and us. To increase the sense of powerlessness and ineffectiveness *we/us* now becomes *them*, a helpless mass who rely for a voice on the ventriloquism of their spokesman, Powell. This dramatic new perspective on the situation is sustained by making the authorities (normally *them* versus us) become wholly impersonal "voices," or an Act of Parliament. The lack of personal communication between these 'powers-that-be' and the wronged indigenous population is characterized by Powell's use of the syntactical form of the passive voice, indicating that the Kafka-like situation of oppression is experienced without being understood.

13:3–14

13:12

Non-comprehension, "decision by default," "never consulted," "homes and neighbourhoods changed beyond recognition," "defeated," even (the immediate authorities) their "employers hesitated"—the catalogue of alienation builds up until "more and more voices . . . told them that they were now the unwanted." The jigsaw of social deprivation is re-applied, piece by piece, to the "native-born," who thus appear in the condition of slavery previously associated with the negro. "They now learn that a one-way privilege is to be established . . . a law which cannot, and is not intended to, . . . protect them. . . ." The impersonal, complex expression, "is to be enacted," completes the sense of 'our' existential impotence.

13:3–5
13:6–10

13:12–13

13:11

13:13–15

13:16

The final example of the misleading comparisons that Powell has

manipulated to create a topsy-turvy situation is the recognized justice of
law and its perverted caricature, which does not "protect . . . or   13:15
redress . . . grievances" but gives "the power to pillory them for their   13:17
private actions" to a nasty crew, the enumeration of whom culminates in
that type of sneak who can only be described by a foreign term!

The picture of alienated non-persons is now deployed to legitimate
the use of anonymity. He recalls the numbers theme to authorize his   14:4
example of how fear is making "ordinary decent, sensible, . . .   14:5-6
rational . . . and often well-educated" people seek anonymity; he
touches on another source of authority, the medical, by speaking of "the
areas . . . affected" as though they were subject to a contagious disease   14:12
(his own reputation is tenuously associated with this type of popular
authority by virtue of his former cabinet post); finally, the authority of
direct experience is invoked and contrasted with imagination: this   14:13-14
inclines our respect towards the former—which we all acknowledge as
sovereign—and awakens our resolve to exercise the latter as Powell pulls   15
out a quotation from his mail bag.

The ventriloquist's role is now reversed as he reads the   14:13-16
Northumberland lady's letter. From a rhetorical point of view, it is
intriguing to note how this example is framed in obfuscation. The lady
was not anonymous, but now is. She may have been in Wolverhampton,
but now is not. She reports something that began eight years ago, but is,
Powell says, "happening at this moment in my own constituency."   14:17
Such fuzzy framing must help to draw attention away from the
credentials and to the vivid language of the letter. The pathos of the   15:3-6
message activates the deepest emotions of the audience. It is a
masterpiece of middle-class clichés: this war-widow, come down in the
world, but paying off her mortgage and managing to save, has an   16:2,6
indomitable will, shown by her refusals to deal with immigrants, for
which she suffers abuse from both negroes and a "young girl"   16:8
bureaucrat. It is from this example of 'them' that "racial prejudice" at   16:10
last emerges in the speech. The context is likely to evoke maximum
sympathy for that prejudice: an oasis of quiet, white respectability in a   15:8
waste of black confusion. A telephone is the widow's tenuous lifeline,   17:1
maintained by loyal but distant relatives. They are distant in blood as
well as space—since she lost her nearest and dearest in the war—so that   17:2
the hint that blood calls to blood is conveyed. The family's helping "as
best they can" appeals to the most basic nexus of solidarity for the British
working class, and helps to broaden the appeal of what otherwise might
be too narrow a middle-class stereotype. Our everyday anxieties are
focused on this frightened woman, imprisoned in her home, faced with
acting against her will or being exploited on the sale of her property.

17:5   Excreta—taboo of taboos—replaces the mail. At a deep level, where the
term "meaning" is perhaps inappropriate, the feelings of isolation and
alienation seem here to be associated with anal functions in a typically
Freudian way. Such obscure suggestions juxtaposed with the explicit
imagery of fear and outrage are powerfully disturbing. This shocking
picture is followed by the contrast between the paternalistic image of
17:7   "charming, wide-grinning piccaninnies" and their hateful chant. It is
so vivid (and so reminiscent of Mr. Powell's own artistry) that one
almost forgets the implausibility of the widow's being convicted under
17:9   the Race Relations Bill. Her convictions, the rhetorical question and the
doubt, serve to zoom the focus out of the picture and back to the
framework of uncertainties.

    If this letter really did originate in Northumberland, Mr. Powell
must have seized on it as wrought by one as skilful in rhetoric as he is. If
this 'letter' is an example of sleight-of-hand, of conscious deception, it
has to be classed under the ancient rhetorical criterion of sophistry. At
least, by using this form, he is able to express the most outrageous
fantasies, without necessarily being held to endorse them or to be
responsible for them.

    With the audience still awash with sympathy, indignation and
shock, Powell energetically elevates the argument by returning to his
philosophical theme of dangerous delusions. The juxtaposition of what
18:1   the widow "wonders" and "the other dangerous delusion" makes one
wonder whether Powell is encouraging his audience to infer that the
good lady may also have suffered from delusions (and perhaps that the
whole letter is an illusion, a rhetorical conjuring trick?). Be that as it
18:3–6   may, Powell turns our attention firmly to his analysis of the concept of
integration, and this is done in his best logical style. Underlying his
argument is the theme of will and wilfulness—another of Powell's main
18:8–9   components of political psychology. By considering the "many
thousands whose wish and purpose is to be integrated," he shows his
justice and impartiality, re-establishing a tone lost during the
anonymous-letter section. A further purpose here is to emphasize the
18:10   difference between this type of admirable (though often misguided)
endeavour of the political will—to create a new environment by legal
19:8   means—and the other political will—to entrench the 'vested interests' of
another type of political culture. The 'mores' of this alternative society
19:21   are expressed in the term "communalism"—whose similarity to the
bogey word "communism" is sufficient to deter a more careful analysis
of its content. To support this important argument, he evokes a
19:15,23   bipartisan authority by quoting a Labour minister.

    This final argument about a new form of positive, political danger
18:11–12   is carefully prepared. Integrationist policy is belittled as ludicrous and

stigmatized as dangerous. The frighteningly physical image of "the verge . . . of a change" is followed by the metaphysical notion of "force of circumstance." The rational possibility of willing change is ruled out because "background . . . has rendered the very idea of integration inaccessible" to immigrants. What they "never conceived or intended" would, at any rate, have been contradicted by the facts of "numbers and physical concentration." To these negative propositions is added the "growth of positive forces acting against integration," "vested interests" and the "sharpening of racial and religious differences," leading to "the exercise of actual domination first over fellow-immigrants and then over the rest of the population." The populist mythology of sinister interests and a conspiracy theory here seem to be rearing their ugly heads, though Powell only suggests this by his quotation from Mr. Stonehouse on the Sikh claim to "special communal rights" which leads to "a dangerous fragmentation . . . a canker." 19:1 19:1-2 19:2-3 19:4-5 19:8-11 19:19-21

The previous attack on the Race Relations Bill is linked with this incipient threat. From such "pabulum" these dangerous and divisive elements draw the "means" as communities to "organise and to consolidate" legal weapons in order "to agitate . . . against their fellow-citizens . . . to overawe and dominate the rest." This is a sketch of the scenario which Powell would develop with greater plausibility in the situation of Ulster politics. In that more crucial context, however, he has preferred to emphasize his solution, which was embodied in the will for unity and nationhood to overcome such cultural and communal divisions. 20:2 20:2-5

Overt references to religion have begun to occur by this point in the speech and are strengthened by the metaphor of "the cloud," which is an image of doom from the Old Testament. By such means Powell resumes his prophetic mantle. The famous Tiber quotation reminds us of the other source of ancient authority and wisdom, the classical world, and is actually culled from Shakespeare's *Julius Caesar*—perhaps another subliminal clue to his own conception of his future political role? The imperative of immediate urgent action is highlighted by this momentary reference to history. The one contemporary comparison with the American racial situation, with which his audience is familiar from the media, is now repeated and linked to the classical past, so that it has meaning and significance in terms of tragedy. This is not just a loose exclamation, but a precise notion of the relation between will and necessity that justifies Cassandra-like "horror" at the idea that a properly "tragic and intractable" situation is being reproduced "here by our own volition and our own neglect." 19:9,20 19:11 20:8 20:10-11 20:3-6 20:8 20:9 20:11-12

Misguided will and want of action: the immediate persuasive

20:15   purport of this speech is to reform and strengthen the will and thus encourage appropriate action. The action he refers to is not that of fascist thuggery or mob disorder, but the coordinated activity that results from the concentration of political will upon the institutions that define a community's priorities and mores. A major theme of the speech has been the improper manipulation of the law and alternatively, how

20:5   proper use can be made of the law. In Powell's brief peroration the theme is not repeated because it is the understood part of this last enthymeme. Its assumption allows Powell to concentrate on the urgent and dramatic imagery of will, and on the possibilities of choice and decision that are left as the responsibility of the audience. After the prophecy, the

20:14   religious mode and the glimpse of tragic fate, Powell reminds the audience that a political will can be mobilized.[6] He stresses the power of political will to mould a sense of national identity by putting the facts into a particular perceptual perspective and by suggesting appropriate institutional arrangements for channelling such interests and values— particularly a sovereign parliament. His basic political conviction is thus cleverly embroidered into the grammar and syntax of the

20:14-15 penultimate sentence, and finally, is linked to his function as prophetic statesman. And so Powell brings us full circle to the first theme in his speech, and ends on the ambiguous note that an abnegation of will would have positively immoral implications.

Summary

The structure of the speech is remarkably symmetrical. Having established his claim to be listened to by the subtle support of various

2   types of authority, Powell presents the problem of his country in a straightforward narrative form. To curb immigration, he proposes three

6:8-9   official policies: stopping the influx, repatriation and the equal treatment of citizens. Various logical arguments are developed in the discussion of these proposals. The central portion of the speech is

11   skilfully modulated into a humorous interlude, during which officialdom is denied the correct perception of reality.

Ridicule is the normal reaction to behaviour that springs from 'unreal' presuppositions—whether it is that of a poor lunatic or a fearsome power (as Churchill's rhetoric against Nazism showed). Here the Race Relations Bill, which is the immediate occasion for the speech, is the central topic, though it is not actually named until paragraph 17. Its causes and effects are related to the delusions arising from misbegotten perceptions of the real situation and the real interests of a

homogeneous community. These misconceptions entail subsequently   12
perverted forms of logic—mainly inversions of common-sense experience and false comparisons. The first effect of these absurdities is to   14
drive a dispirited and dispersed people into anonymity (Powell's
example is the anonymous letter whose pathos and shock echo in a
different key the emotional moment of humour). The second effect is   19
revealed as the mobilization and arming of immigrant communities;
this emerges through a final comparison of the concepts of integration   18,19
and communalism, with the conclusion that one is impossible and the
other undesirable but probable, thanks to the race-relations-policy
proposals. To avert the likelihood of tragedy, Powell ends with an
invocation to action through the mobilization of the political will of the
majority.

The deep structure of parallel arguments can be presented schematically, as a mirror image, as shown in Figure 1. At the deepest level of
emotional response, the pattern is again symmetrical: at first, a challenge and expectation, surrounded by a sense of security, derived from
authorities and developed by reasonableness; then a break for humour is   11
followed by confusion at the rational level and pathos at the emotional.   15
The insecurity engendered by violence, wilfulness and future threat
reproduce the original state of expectancy, but it is now shadowed by
fear.

Beginning of Speech   *End of Speech*

Statesmanship (para. 1)   Options for action (para. 20)
The bases of authority to speak   The duty of prophecy (para. 20)
  (para. 1)   Predictions of consequences of
Narrative of the topic (para. 2)   policy options (para. 19)
Policy options (para. 6):   Policy options (para. 18–19):
  (a) Stop inflow   (a) Integration
  (b) Repatriation   (b) Mobilization of immigrant
                                                     communities
  (c) Legal enforcement of equal   (c) Implied reiteration of para.
      treatment   6(a) and 6(b)
Ridicule (para. 11)   Shock (para. 17)
Perceptions of reality (para.   The letter: 'concrete' evidence or
  11–12)   illusion? (para. 15–17)

Disruption and paralysis of indigenous population
(para. 13–14)

FIGURE 1

Structure of Powell's "Rivers of Blood" Speech

At each stage in the speech, the rational argument is encapsulated in
2:10   a colourful image. In the first section the "black man will have the whip
hand over the white." In the second, the widow's letter and the filth of
17:5   excreta present the pathos and the resentment felt by the silent majority.
20:8   In the final prophetic invocation the easily abridged metaphor, "rivers
of blood," sustains the tone of violence and catastrophe. The invocation
is open to two interpretations according to individual inclinations: a
20:15   possible optimistic but difficult mobilization of political will, or a
probable pessimistic turning to a messiah-like leader. Following the
logic of rhetoric, the possibility of this final enthymeme is not spelled
out; the audience has to draw its own conclusions.

Whereas the first half of the speech is about the rational political
11   solutions to the black problem (there is an urgent call to face realities,
but the discussion is rational), the second half is its mirror image. It is
about the white problem: the inability of our native population to be
realistic, responsible and free, in the sense of master of its fate. And the
topsy-turvy logic of this half culminates in the imminent possibility of
the black minority oppressing the native majority. According to
Wallman's analysis (Chapter 7), Powell's technique is to use com-
paratively straightforward 'signs,' whose meanings are conventional
and limited, in the first half of the speech. But in the second half, he
relies much more on symbolic content to orchestrate a varied set of non-
logical meanings. After the authoritative character of the first half, the
ambiguity of the second half is logically unsatisfactory, but its
psychological density makes it a rich field for the members of the
audience to make their own identifications and conclusions: they can
read various meanings from the message. Out of such a situation Powell
skilfully resumes his authoritative role, but now in the prophetic mode.

No doubt Powell himself would prefer the theoretically possible
outcome whereby political will is mobilized to turn aside the otherwise
18:4-10   inexorable results of the pressures of concentrated numbers. Indeed he
points to this goal in the passages on the importance of the political will,
20:3-6,13-15   which are amongst the most coherent in the puzzling density of the
second half of the speech. But the general tenor of this half, with its
attack on the political establishment and bureaucracy for being
10,11,12   unreasonable, illogical and deluded, has the effect of turning the
13,14   audience further away from accepted rational strategies, except insofar
2,3,8   as they have already been carefully related to Powell himself in the first
half. His originally stated orthodox claims to authority remain, but
his identification with the audience has been consolidated by his
sympathetic depiction of the dilemmas of 'us' against 'them'—'them'
being both the foreigners and the elites. He emerges as a charismatic
leader, distinct from his professional background and his party.

It is noteworthy that he makes nothing of the fact that the proposed legislation is a measure of a Labour Government. This, of course, is his immediate licence to attack the Bill, but he does not confine himself to defining the target of his critical argument in party terms. It seems that if the Race Relations Bill was the occasion for raising the immigration issue, and if the latter was the cause of the speech, then the purpose of the speech was to stake out Powell's claim to be the man of the hour. Certainly that was its most lasting effect. Once the shock of so respectable a political figure explosively breaching this taboo political topic had subsided, and before the utility of his work in thus placing the issue openly on the orthodox political agenda had become apparent to more cautious politicians, an immense popular authority was seen to have accrued to Powell.[7] This was a fitting reward for his courage and his craft.

14,20

But every political option carries its penalties as well as its promises. Whether Powell was aware of both must remain open for debate. The evidence of this and other speeches and activities leads one to think that he was; that instead of the role of successful politician measured in terms of office and administration, he consciously chose the role of prophet, and perhaps statesman.

1,20

Notes

1. In Egham, Surrey, 7 January 1976. The phrase has been frequently repeated, and the catch-phrase corrected, by Powell, on a BBC television programme on "Race" (12 September 1977).

2. After his dismissal from the Shadow Cabinet in 1968, he had a higher rating in the polls than his leader, Mr. Heath: see Foot (1969: 112). In 1970 he topped BBC's "World at One" Man-of-the-Year Poll: see Moorehead (1975:7). On the effects of his intervention in General Elections since 1970, see Johnson and Schoen (1976).

3. Text from Powell (1969: 213–19).

4. The Commonwealth Immigration Act, passed through Parliament 29 February/1 March 1968 by the Labour Government, had extended the work-voucher entry system of 1965 to apply also to the Kenyan Asians under threat of expulsion from Kenya. See Foot (1969: 111).

5. Though Powell had first advocated it in a speech in Birmingham (22 November 1965); see Powell (1969: 90).

6. This theme expresses his basic political conviction—whether on the racial problem, on Ulster or the various nationalist, separatist movements within the U.K., or in relation to the EEC.

7. For evidence see sources cited in note 2 above.

7

Refractions of Rhetoric: Evidence for the Meaning of 'Race' in England

SANDRA WALLMAN

Prologue

This exercise began as an attempt to account for the discrepancy between the local view of a particular local event and the interest taken in it by various media of the press. It evolved into a concern with the meanings put on 'race' or 'race difference' in England, and their relation to current political rhetoric.[1] My suspicion is that other public events interpreted in terms of 'race' would show similar patterns and make the same point.

The scenario (described in detail in Wallman 1975) is less sensational than other events and otherwise entirely ordinary: a short dilapidated street in inner London was designated for compulsory purchase and demolition by the borough authority. Such an act would, according to the formula, allow and entail the rehousing of the street's residents in new purpose-built, low-rent council accommodation within the borough—a benevolent if not admirable objective, in keeping with the tenets of the welfare state. But the residents, after one or two false starts, appealed against the compulsory purchase order, and a public enquiry into the case had to be held. After months of discussion and prevarication, against the judgement and advice of his local inspector, the Minister of the Environment revoked the order and (so) saved the street. The residents subsequently hoped to rehabilitate it themselves through some form of co-operative organization.

Over the period of fifteen months during which the case was in dispute, the street's expressed preoccupations centred on the threat of the local government's bulldozer and its implications for better or worse housing. Some residents were doubtful that the amenities scheduled to follow in the wake of demolition could or would materialize, and the majority were, at any rate, fiercely reluctant to be 'dispersed' into council accommodation.

Over the same period, the street had more than its share of coverage in the press. It was given heroic mention in local (south London) and national newspapers of a wide range of relationship and political stance, in the official publication of the Race Relations Board (*Equals*), and, apparently by diffusion, in four of South Africa's most widely circulated newspapers.[2]

But its significance in virtually all these reports had little to do with the desperate shortage of housing in inner London or with the central or local government housing policy. Even the appealing little-guys-against-the-big-guys dimension of the battle failed to catch the collective eye of the media. The street's news value lay only in the "harmonious" cohabitation of its "racially mixed" population; indeed, it became widely and popularly known as "Harmony Street." Most reporters were strongly in favour of the street precisely *because* it was polyglot; a handful were, for substantially the same reason, just as strongly against it. The minority 'intelligent press' contented itself with a careful reporting of both sides of the 'story.' No one showed much interest in the way the community itself defined the issues, or in what it was trying to do about them. It was interesting only because of the way its members looked—because of their 'race.'

The discrepancy between 'real life' and the reporting of it lay exactly here: in the context of the residents' appeal against compulsory purchase and demolition, 'racial' difference or discrimination did not figure at all. In the wider context, in which the matter was reported in the press and (presumably) found interesting by the public, 'race' was the crux. This is not unusual. Whereas it may be observed that 'race' (that is to say, racial difference) is read more often as a source of conflict than of harmony, and that these reports may constitute more or less subtle and responsible efforts to redress the balance (see Evans 1976), there is no doubt that 'race' makes the story either way. 'Race' is news.

Introduction

This chapter offers an analysis of the symbolic values put on race in Britain and of the way in which they reflect, refract, contradict or determine the imagery of national political rhetoric.

Although racial rhetoric in England has become the hallmark of the (now) Unionist member for Ulster, and is invariably associated with his name, this is not a study of Enoch Powell as a political 'big man.' Powell is not in power; nor, I think, is he seeking it. More important, there is no market for 'big men' in English politics at this time: the top politicians are neither flamboyantly big nor personally powerful. They are, it is said, almost impossible to caricature. So is Powell. But he gets a big man's press in opening and then provoking public discussion of immigration, nationhood, English values—and racial issues. He does nothing about these issues: he is concerned not with planning or the execution of plans, but with ideology, and so can afford to be, *has* to be, grandiloquent (see Bailey 1969; Parkin 1975). It may be that the role of image-maker/symbol-manipulator/rhetorician in England is functionally equivalent to the role of big man in a smaller, less industrialized community. Certainly there is a difference in political need: developing systems are still dealing with "primordial problems" of solidarity and power and are in need of "authority focus." In highly developed (over-developed?) systems, "primordial sentiments are less a problem than are confusion, irresponsibility, withdrawal and cynicism" (Apter 1964: 22)—in which case the spinner of meanings will wield the greater clout.

This is not a study of Enoch Powell, but an effort to understand the reactions of his audience.[3] What meanings does he spin? And for whom? His rhetoric reverberates in all corners of the orthodox and unorthodox political scenes. Voters are said to change lifelong political allegiances unknowing of the fact—or at least unwilling to admit—that "their vote was influenced by a man almost universally adjudged a pariah" (Johnson and Schoen 1976). Apparently one does not have to admire a man's rhetoric in order to be influenced by it. The same rhetoric is used to justify extra-parliamentary attitudes and activities of political interest groups fiercely opposed to each other. It is implicated in the resurgence of the extreme right-wing National Front, from which Powell openly dissociates himself, and in the shift of its explicit focus from anti-Semitic to anti-black (Walker 1977). On the same bandwagon, the extreme left now sports a militant pro-black (and so, racist) mode that has yet to show any helpful relevance to the minorities it purports to champion. On the contrary. Since 'race' is regularly made the focus of a confrontation between right and left, Powellist rhetoric may be said to have provoked—or at least to have allowed—the harassment of minorities and violence in the streets. It has also allowed 'ordinary' people to express 'ordinary' views on the subject in the pages of some newspapers (as in the letters to *The Guardian*). On the whole, reasoned and reasonable discussion is not prominent. When it does occur, it is as likely to debate the pros and cons of Powell and the ins and outs of Powellist rhetoric as the circumstances that give each of them credence.[4] Even

116   *Sandra Wallman*

positive (but still racial) discrimination of the 'bending-over-backwards'
kind tends to be justified on the grounds that *his* view, *his* effect must be
countered. Equally, any unrealistic insistence, such as the one foisted on
Harmony Street, that all is well and that *racial* brotherhood and co-
operation are everywhere, can be attributed, by refraction, to the same
stimulus.

Given the strength of the extremes, any self-styled centre has little
option but to hold. Just as a poll, taken soon after the Notting Hill race
riots, showed a general tendency to underrate hostile views (Patterson
1963: 148), so the veneer of caution now characteristic of official reactions to 'race relations' indicates both that the country is nervous and
that opinion is fragmented. In the present climate, any official action on
'race' will be resented by someone: it is therefore politically prudent to
do, or to appear to do, as little as possible.

These effects all spring more or less directly from Powell's having
said aloud and respectably things that previously were not, and could
not, be said by any but the lunatic fringe (Edgar 1974). *"Whatever his
motivations, and despite what appear to be considerable tactical
blunders in his political career, he is listened to, and admired or
execrated. For . . . he appears to have a coherent attitude to the various
problems that beset Britain—whether they concern economic or racial
issues, or the matter of nationhood (the definition of a political identity
in relation to the past and to other political communities). He has
formulated a set of responses which he articulates effectively to
illuminate any situation or issue"* (Lloyd-Jones's chapter in this
volume; emphasis added).

Powell's rhetoric, however, is distinct from the effects it is used to
justify. He expresses strong views on all the current big issues. He is
fiercely pro-NATO and just as fiercely anti-EEC—not because they have
different memberships and entail different alliances, but because they
have different kinds of jurisdiction over the English: the one increases
English sovereignty whereas the other diminishes it. Similarly he is
against development aid abroad and the welfare state at home: morally
speaking, handouts are not the job of government; economically
speaking, they are a disaster. His arguments are based on full knowledge
of these various issues, which he tries to relay in terms appropriate to the
immediate audience on each occasion. His delivery is consistently
didactic, 'donnish' and fiery—but only to the degree that is appropriate
to an Englishman; it is never hysterical. The concession to his
immediate audience occurs in syntax and metaphor. Whenever he
adjudges a little-educated audience to be without expertise in the
economic and political technicalities of inflation, the Common Market,

Ulster, and the like, he alludes to these issues only indirectly and rhetorically, offering instead more familiar topics to the man-in-the-street—immigrants, cities, government waste—topics in which every elector thinks he has expertise. Now that inflation is discussed by everybody, Powell may feel, not without some justification, that he has done his educational job for the public and has made the necessary identifications, for even when he is not talking about race, he has the attention of the English audience.

Although 'race' accounts for only a small part of the content of Powell's speeches and although the word itself rarely appears, it is with 'race' that he is popularly associated. Powellism has come to mean racism willy-nilly. The refractions of Powellist rhetoric therefore say more about England than they do about Powell, and Powell's *intentions* are quite beside the point. This paper attempts to assess how and to what degree the processes that extend and sustain Powell's peculiar reputation relate to the meaning of 'race' in England. The prominence given to 'race' in interpretations of rhetorical or political events is itself significant, but it is the range of meaning given to 'race' and so to racial rhetoric that needs explaining.

Four reasons for this range of meaning suggest themselves: (1) There is some failure in the racial rhetoric itself: it confuses more than it instructs. (2) The meaning of 'race,' the dominant theme of the rhetoric, is not clear or not consistent in the culture. (3) The meaning of 'race' is clear enough, but it is refracted by the media through which it is transmitted. (4) The transmitted meaning of 'race' is unambiguous, but its value varies with the structural position of the audience: it is refracted by the logic of differentiation in England.

These possibilities are represented in Figure 1 as steps in a single communication sequence. The whole process is necessarily contained within a cultural frame or context that determines both the messages sent and the symbols appropriate to their sending. In a setting with more direct means of communication and/or a more homogeneous and less confused audience (one less thirsty for meanings?), the extent of refraction of the rhetoric and the range of meanings taken from it would be reduced. The two refractive panels would then look quite different and might not pertain at all. (Their complicating effect is probably characteristic of 'developed' as opposed to 'traditional' rhetorical systems such as those in Bloch 1975.) The feedback to Powell, which necessarily completes the circuit, is shown in the figure, but is not germane to this analysis. I am not competent to deal with particular effects of the media on the message communicated; they have been monitored by others (see Evans 1976; Husband 1975; and McLuhan

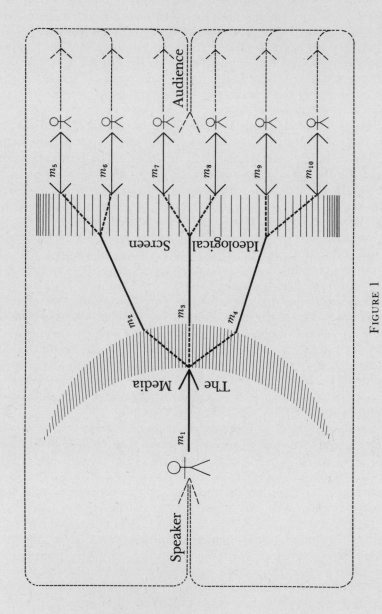

FIGURE 1

Refractions of the Rhetorical Message (m)

1965), and are referred to only indirectly and parenthetically in the sections that follow. The first section sets out the features of rhetoric most relevant to the present theme; the second relates anthropological theories of symbolism to the symbol 'race' in the English context; and the third attempts to analyse the audience in such a way as to account for differences and shifts in its interpretation of the symbol 'race.'

Rhetoric

According to Burke (1969a), successful rhetoric involves the expert manipulation of "signs" (Aristotle called them "topics") appropriate to the occasion, and according to the rules of rhetorical thumb. But the meaning of a sign is not invariable: "The same rhetorical act could vary in its effectiveness [effect?] according to shifts in the situation and in the attitude of audiences" (*ibid*.: 62). Successful rhetoric therefore involves also the accurate assessment of the context in which the signs are to be used. This is hard to do in a complex, technologically advanced setting. "The extraordinary heterogeneity of modern life and the ubiquitous press and media coverage of rhetorical events make it difficult to specify and limit the appeal to an audience which will respond in the terms wished." The strictly commercial rhetorician (that is, the advertiser) may have the possibility of carving out an audience of customers defined on the basis of income (p. 64), but few political messages are so straightforward.

Neither the complexity nor the alteration of sign or situation alters the formal rules. These hinge on identification, opposition and climax. Most obviously, the use of appropriate imagery associates the desired event or praiseworthy person with things good, and the unwanted outcome or group with things bad. Similarly, skilful imagery can transform an adversary's argument by turning it on its head, can exaggerate his inconsistencies, and can make nonsense of his case by pushing it *ad absurdum*.

The ordinary language expert can achieve this transformation to some extent, but the master of political rhetoric does more. By association of images he identifies himself with his audience and his audience with himself (it helps, says Burke, if he really feels that way!), and then rouses in it a sense of "collaborative expectancy" such that "once you grasp the trend of the form, it invites participation regardless of the subject matter" (p. 58). The effect is created by a number of prescribed rhetorical devices, two of which are especially interesting. In one device, a passage is built about a set of oppositions. In the second, the passage reaches a climax of disaster or triumph by building logically, formally and obviously one step at a time. In both cases, regardless of doubts about the proposition that comprises the *content* of the passage, "by the time you arrive at the second of three stages you sense how it is destined to develop and, on the level of purely formal assent, you . . . collaborate to round out the symmetry by spontaneously willing its completion and perfection as an utterance" (p. 59). You feel, in effect, as though you thought of it yourself.

Both these devices are familiar in Powellist rhetoric. The first makes boundaries by exclusion and is ideally suited to anti-immigrant or proto-racist persuasion; the second is a clear paradigm for the doomcry of the so-called "rivers of blood" peroration, discussed by Lloyd-Jones in Chapter 6. But it is the obverse of the boundary coin that is pertinent here. The more narrowly 'they' (the others) are defined and the more clearly 'they' are visualized, the stronger the sense of 'us' evoked. The 'they' of Powellist rhetoric are only incidentally black immigrants. Blacks are significant only insofar as they are, like the Court Jews of another era, the pawns of an international freemasonry of elites, cosmopolites, media men, and bureaucratic minions. Unlike the Jews in proto-Nazi and Nazi Germany, however, blacks hold few key positions in English society, few goodies that anyone else wants.[5] English racial rhetoric uses 'them' accordingly. 'They' and their arrival are associated with, rather than being the cause of, our decline. 'They' are the indication that things are not perfect—or not as perfect as we like to believe they once were—and are linked with our losses in exactly the way the classical rhetoricians intended.

'We,' in opposition to 'they,' are, of course, the real and true people. 'We' are powerless in this case not because 'they' are powerful but because we have lost our political will, our common purpose, our sense of 'us.' Powell's 1968 speech, the benchmark of English racial rhetoric, is a threnody for just this sense of 'us'—'our' identity, 'our' integrity, 'our' nationhood, 'our' self-sufficiency, all of which were once glorious, but are now jeopardized or lost.

These losses are not sheer words, invented for the sake of oratory. England's political and economic position is at present markedly less supreme than it was in the days of the empire and economic growth. (The fact that different groups in the society experience these losses differently is taken up below.) Powell has taken upon himself what he describes as the responsibilities of a statesman. As Lloyd-Jones points out in Chapter 6, Powell considers himself not a persuader but a "ventriloquist," the articulate voice of the powerless and a "myth-maker," weaving patterns out of the materials of the past. Myth used in this way should be distinguished from the 'delusion' of myth-out-of-date, of which empire, commonwealth citizenship and open immigration are prime and closely linked examples.

This facet of political rhetoric fits nicely into anthropological frames. Myths provide charters for, and explanations of, the present in terms of the past and the eternal values of the past. Their structures may be universal, but the content of each is specific to the cultural setting in which, and of which, it makes sense. The structure (and the telling?) of a myth holds the attention of the audience just as the form of rhetoric is designed to carry the audience through propositions to which it might not normally subscribe. Whether assent at the formal level entails assent to the proposition(s) as doctrine depends on factors extrinsic to it. These are nowhere precisely defined. Burke considers "the psychosis of nationalism" a sufficient condition of total acceptance (1969a: 59), but it is not clear what the evidence for such a psychosis would be. Although there is no doubt that Powellist rhetorical forms are true to prototype, they do not tell us much about the current English political scene. Perhaps the topic of the rhetoric will tell us more.

Symbols

If rhetoric is language manipulated in order to persuade, then rhetoric is the persuasive use of symbols, and racial rhetoric is built on manipulations of the symbolic value of 'race.' Whereas Burke uses the notions *topic, image, sign* and *symbol* interchangeably, the distinction sometimes drawn between sign and symbol is particularly useful to the understanding of 'race.' A sign (or signal) is just an abstraction of, or an alternative to, something else—the object it stands for. A symbol, on the other hand, "stands for a complex set of emotional and intellectual dispositions" (Firth 1973: 228), "for more than itself. . . . To it are assigned meanings of a complex kind of which the individual is unconscious or only partly conscious" (*ibid.*: 225). The point to be taken is that a symbol contains a store of meanings and so offers scope for interpretation. The value of a symbol inheres to some degree in the uncertainty of its meaning—although too much meaning, like electronic noise, may clog communication altogether.

There are now many meanings inherent in the notion 'race' in England. It is being treated, therefore, as a symbol. In other settings and at other times 'race' is, or has been, a sign to the extent that it signified a specific caste, cultural or geographic affiliation (Banton 1977). But not in England. Not any more. 'Race' is no longer just another way of classifying human types. Even in situations that appear to be about colour or phenotype, race stands "for more than itself." The superficial physical differences on which racial typologies are based today bear no certain relation to the social characteristics of individuals or to their general social performance. Any expectation to the contrary is, of course, what racial prejudice is about. But the fact that these physical modes are not socially meaningful *signs* does not prevent their being used in some contexts as if they were: "Symbols are not signs [but] people [may] pretend they are in order to use them for their own ends" (Creyghton n.d.).

It is important to notice that when colour is taken to be a sign, it is not inevitably a bad sign, either within or across so-called racial boundaries (Wallman 1978); and that there are situations or events in which colour has no relevance for the participants, and so is not for them a sign or a symbol of anything (cf. Wallman 1974; Dawes 1974: 178). Obvious as this possibility may seem, it is commonly disallowed by the framework of serious academic analysis (see, for example, Critcher 1975).

There are, however, circumstances in which the meaning assigned to colour is apparently so precise that the extent of unacceptability or of danger seems to vary directly with the degree of pigmentation. The careful landlady asks of a self-confessed African who has phoned to enquire about renting a room: "Are you dark? Or very light?" (Soyinka 1974: 152).[6] But we must be cautious; in cases like this, the basis of unacceptability and the source of the danger associated with colour are ambiguous. The meaning of colour is a great deal less specific than it may appear. The landlady is probably more afraid of what her neighbour would construe of her having a black tenant than she is of his skin colour as such. His colour is not, in effect, just an abstraction of something else. It has meanings of which the landlady is "unconscious or only partly conscious" (Firth 1973: 225). Her worry is not about the degree of pigmentation, but rather about a whole chain of items and events that is associated with colour. Colour, the sign, has in effect become 'race,' the symbol.

'Race' in England is now not a sign (of one thing) but a symbol (of many things). It is a store of multiplex and often conflicting meanings. As such it offers so much scope for interpretation that the most competent rhetorician is hard put to reconcile inconsistencies and to resolve— or to use—ambiguities in ways that will establish meanings. Communication about 'race' is regularly impeded by 'noise.' Nevertheless, some precise symbolic associations have been established. It is not clear whether racial rhetoric has caused these associations to be established or has only exploited existing chains of meaning, but some amount of feedback in both directions is likely (Figure 1).

Whatever its origins, the symbolic sequence most characteristic of Powellist rhetoric is the association of 'race' with 'them': 'them' with blacks; blacks with immigration. The identification of black with immigrant is now indeed so close that all black people in England must be immigrants and all immigrants must be black. Any person who has either of these characteristics is interpreted as also having the other. If demonstrably he does not, then he falls *hors de categorie* since white immigrants and black natives are impossible concepts (Wallman 1978).[7]

Once the association of 'race' with immigration is made, the symbolic steps to imputing scarcity, crowding, unemployment, and urban violence to blacks are a matter of simple logic. By the same logic, anyone who speaks *for* blacks is also speaking *for* (open) immigration and urban decline. In the classical manner, the adversary's case is made absurd by the manipulation of his meaning. Thus Powell's rhetorical association of blacks with bureaucratic minions, state monopolies, communalists (*sic*), and student demonstrators entails their joint responsibility for—and even, absurdly, their advocacy of—urban blight and national decline. Together they constitute "the enemies within" (Lloyd-Jones's chapter in this volume; see also Johnson and Schoen 1976). The association is assisted by alliteration—blacks and blight, bulldozers, bolshies, and bureaucrats—a device that Powell does not have to point out himself: the commercial media are quick to spot and use a catchy mnemonic, even if they deny its general inference.

So much for the dissemination of the racial rhetorical message. But why the inversions of it? Why can the value of 'race' be shifted from 'boo' to 'hurrah' in the course of a single communication cycle? To some extent, the inversion is a direct result of the parent rhetoric. "Even as Aristotle [by his rules of rhetoric] is teaching one man how most effectively to make people say 'Yes,' he is teaching an opponent how to make them say just as forceful a 'No' " (Burke 1969a: 52). If the press coverage of our scenario uses racial rhetoric, or the refraction of rhetoric, then the linked exaggerations of harmony and diversity on which it is built can be understood as an effort to pull other meanings out of 'race,' and to forge contrary and more glowing associations.

But not every symbol is rhetorically so versatile. The fact that 'race' in England is invested with so many meanings, and sometimes contradictory meanings, gives it an importance in English culture similar to that of the "dominant symbol" abstracted by Turner from Ndembu ritual (1967). 'Race' in England is a rhetorical, not a ritual symbol, but it has all the properties of dominance. The first is *condensation*: 'race' serves as a shorthand reference to many things. The second is the *unification of disparate significata*: 'race' refers, or can refer, to different items that are "widely distributed over a range of phenomena . . . [but are] interconnected by analogous qualities or by association in fact or thought." The third property of a dominant symbol, and perhaps the most instructive for understanding 'race,' is the *polarization of meaning* between "sensory and ideological poles" (Turner 1967: 28).

The *sensory pole* tends towards the crude or base, involving "those significata that may be expected to arouse desires and feelings" (*ibid.*). In the Ndembu case, these are bluntly physiological: blood, milk, semen, faeces. In ours, they are occasionally so (Lloyd-Jones's chapter in this volume) but often less openly base. Our culture is notoriously reluctant to recognize bodily functions and we rarely speak of them except to shock (as did Powell). The base *significata* of 'race' in our society are political and economic instead of physiological, but they are as much concerned with our vital 'bases': our jobs, housing, personal status, and, inevitably, sexual competence and competition.

These vital bases are the "raw energies of conflict." They are "domesticated into the service of the social order" (Turner 1967: 39) at the opposite, *ideological pole*. Ideological interpretations of the same dominant symbol will "tend to stress the harmonious and cohesive aspects of social relationships" (*ibid.*: 33). Thus harmony, brotherhood, co-operation, community, and, implicitly, fair play are also *significata* of 'race' (Figure 2), used as such by the media and, of course, by Powell. They too are concepts by which we define ourselves. Unlike those pertaining to the base and negative pole, however, they are concepts by which we would wish to be defined by others—not only now, but historically, eternally and mythically. A contrast in time perspective may be a necessary polarization of meaning in dominant political symbols. The difference allows us to associate, and to move between, the things that preoccupy us now (us-as-we-are) and the things that we *ought* to stand for (us-as-we-would-like-to-be); this allowance gives our political identity its necessary resilience.[8]

Contrasting sets of meaning are not stored in a single symbol without hazard. Values pertaining to opposite poles will sometimes stand in contrast or contradiction to each other. So it can be with 'race.' The crude pairing of meanings in Figure 2 below suggests associations of this kind: to increase immigration controls is to diminish fair play; to enhance fair play is to open immigration. These conflicts of meaning are normal and necessary to the survival of any value system (Gellner 1973), and they certainly extend the range and dominance of any par-

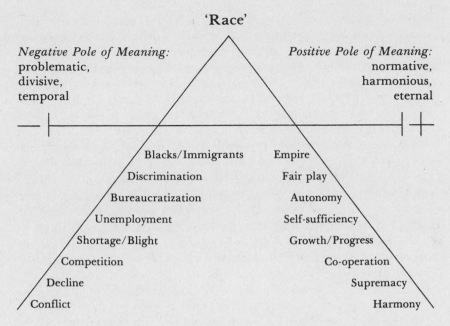

FIGURE 2

Meanings Contained in the Symbol 'Race'

ticular symbol. The bind of incompatible meanings need not impair the commitment of participants. The participant in a ritual process "tends to regard as axiomatic and primary [all] the ideals, values and norms that are overtly expressed" (Turner 1967: 28), and to select from them according to the exigencies of structure or situation. Similarly, the task of political rhetoric is to package the various meanings of political symbols in such a way as to mask or minimize any zero-sum relation between them and still allow the participant to select, or to feel that he is selecting, the meaning appropriate to himself.

With regard to such a view, *The American Dilemma* (Myrdal 1962) must be the classic example: a system that defined itself both by norms of racial tolerance and equality as well as by the subjugation and humiliation of its black citizens could (and did) maintain remarkably static 'race relations' for a remarkably long time precisely because participants in it, black as well as white, could switch between poles of meaning to reconcile inconsistencies in the system itself. The line between symbolic richness and political double think is today more clearly drawn in America than it is in England on this issue, but the process through symbolic into structural change (and back) is still obscure (Kuper 1974).

It may be that dominant symbols such as 'race' bear so fundamental a relation to the sense of 'us'—both sensory and ideological, base and normative—that they evoke strong, immediate and largely unthinking responses. These symbols can be readily expressed in the form of slogans. They neither demand nor permit critical discussion by those who feel them, know them to be existentially crucial. They are commonplaces. Political rhetoric involving these symbols does not lend itself to reasonable debate or to rational argument (cf. Bailey 1969); on the contrary, it may actually serve to throw dust in the eyes, to detract or distract from real needs or issues. Just as liberal rhetoric of the colonial era has been caricatured as: "When the people say they're hungry, offer them Freedom," so the rhetoric surrounding the fight against the compulsory purchase and demolition of an inner London street can be caricatured as: "When the people demand housing, talk to them of Harmony." In both cases, there is a more or less deliberate deflection from the base and conflicting pole of meaning to the normative, unifying and undebatable pole. Being more formal and more ambiguous than the practical details of political action, the move to the normative pole, like the appeal to traditional authority, pre-empts political division (Bloch 1975: 28). Who would dispute the value of motherhood or apple pie?

All political rhetoric requires the manipulation of commonplace symbols, and runs the risk of backfire or backlash when the symbols are not read as intended. This is true of even so simple and successful a slogan as "black is beautiful." At a particular phase in its political career, the slogan was interpreted by some young blacks in the United States to mean that they need make no effort to study, work, improve their chances or otherwise prepare themselves for 'a better future.' Like a symbolic cargo, their beauty/status/power/achievement was coming; they had only to sit and wait for the prizes. In so doing, they inverted the slogan's meaning from active to passive, drawing from it values quite opposite to those it had been expected to enhance[9] (see Kuper 1974: 83–109).

The central point is that a symbol has many potential meanings and will be selectively interpreted. The richer and more complex a symbol's store of essential values, the more dominant its symbolic role; and the more dominant the symbol, the greater its rhetorical potential. Meanings are selected from it at each stage in the communication sequence, first by the orator or politician, then by the media or mediator of the message, then by the audience receiving it (see Figure 1 above). Shifts in topic or context account for some part of the meaning selected and for a good part of its effect, and the good rhetorician manipulates this variability to make the symbolic associations appropriate to getting a particular message across to a particular audience.

At least, he tries to. In classical times, the audience could be expected to vary its responses only with setting and occasion—just as it is said to do in contemporary pre-industrial/traditional political systems (Wallman 1968; Bloch 1975). In those days, too, the rhetorician would have had no need to worry about the form in which his message would be transmitted or diffused. In the modern world, by contrast, neither the form of message nor the audience response can be taken for granted. The modern rhetorician's message might be refracted or distorted on its way to his audience ("the medium is the message" is a great slogan of our time; McLuhan 1965), and his audience is ideologically much more slippery than its ancient counterpart.

Any modern example of unanimous response relates, in fact, to the "primordial" issue of national/cultural/group survival said to be a problem only for "developing" (and so not yet 'modern'?) societies (Apter 1964: 22). But this particular anxiety varies not with development as much as with the extent to which the group's identity or survival is threatened (Geertz 1964: 72; and more generally Homans 1968). Churchill and Hitler, each in his own context, met the need for "authority focus," which 'big men' are designated to provide. Each "formulated accurately the mood of his countrymen and, formulating it, mobilized it by making it a public possession, a social fact, rather than a set of disconnected, unrealized private emotions" (Geertz, *loc. cit.*). Each, in other terms, achieved the conversion of (multiple) private symbols into a (singular) public analogue (cf. Firth 1973).

It may be that the key to success for modern rhetoricians lies simply in persuading diverse interest groups that they suffer a common threat, just as the commercial advertiser raises the possibilities of ostracism and decay to unify us in our need for a particular kind of toothpaste. The case under discussion in this essay is not as gross, but can nevertheless be understood as an effort to focus the separate anxieties of various interest groups around a recognizably collective issue. This issue is, I am suggesting, the threat of a decline in, or loss of, the proper sense of 'us.'

Crudely put, therefore, successful 'racial' rhetoric would entail persuading everyone in England that being overrun by black immigrants was the only or primary threat to their common and collective well-being, the only or primary cause of national and personal malaise. The rhetoric is successful to the extent that this meaning is one of the many stored in the symbol 'race.' All the 'enemies within' are wrapped in the same symbolic package and can be drawn by some people in some situations. But not by everyone, and not all the time. If 'race' *is* a collective issue, it is not always the same issue.

The inconsistency or "transitoriness" of symbolic meanings "is due not to the fact that [any one meaning is] wholly alien to people living under other conditions [in the same culture], but that [particular meanings] are *more persuasive* with people living under one particular set of circumstances" than another (Burke 1969a: 62–63; author's emphasis). The media and the contexts in which meanings operate do not therefore account for all the refractions of 'racial' rhetoric. We also need to know how and to what degree the structural position of the audience affects its interpretation of 'race.'

Differentiation

With respect to dominant symbols in general, "each participant has his own structural perspective . . . [and] is likely to be governed in his actions by a number of interests, purposes and sentiments, dependent upon his specific position, which impair his understanding of the total situation" (Turner 1967: 28). Similarly, regarding the symbol 'race,' the English do not respond alike. Their various perspectives of it have been filtered through, or refracted by, an ideological screen of the kind described by Turner (and represented in Figure 1). What logic of position governs their separate responses?

It is important to establish that it is not only Powellites who respond to Powellist rhetoric, and not only 'racists' who respond to 'race.' Much of the 'noise' transmitted by, or refracted from, Powellist rhetoric is made by those who denounce what they take to be the Powellist message. The crude version of this message is as summarized above: blacks and/or immigrants, being irrevocably alien to our values and our country, are the cause of every personal and national frustration. Those persons whose actions or expressed attitudes can be explained by this reasoning are those who will popularly be labelled "racist."

'Racists' are not disproportionately of any one class (Johnson and Schoen 1976). Nor do the national daily newspapers, each with its class-specific or sub-class-specific readership, line up tidily along any racist/non-racist line, whatever their expressed sympathies or antipathies towards Powell himself (cf. Evans 1976).

The support of the major political parties is also not clearly differentiated on the 'race' issue. Both Labour and Conservative parties have openly denounced Powell on one occasion or another and have spent some part of their collective energies rejecting (some) inferences of Powellist rhetoric. But each party is inevitably accused by the other of 'racist' stances. Certainly each has been embarrassed by the movement of voters into and out of its ranks for 'racial' reasons; it is said to be Powellist rhetoric that won "the Tory white racists" over to Labour, at the same time causing the Tories to lose a few black votes (Labour being "the immigrant's party"), but still accountable for the narrow margin that kept Wilson in office in 1974 (Johnson and Schoen 1976).

Nor are the minority parties clearly differentiated by the 'race' issue, although their political reputations are more crucially related to race and so are more fiercely debated. For example, following the publication of Johnson and Schoen's article, a correspondent to *New Society* from Manchester University's Department of Government insisted on the "interchangeability . . . for floating and disillusioned voters" of the Liberal and National Front parties. He further objected to the equation of Powellism with racism implied in the article (5 August 1976). One of the authors then replied, saying that they "had been at pains to show a Powell effect independent of that issue," and went so far as to claim that, "by early 1975 anti-EEC attitudes were a better indicator [of Powellist sympathies] than racial attitudes" (19 August 1976).

Exchanges of this sort are indicative of the ambiguity of the 'race' issue. The various changes in English voting patterns and political attitudes should be understood as part of a general psephological to-ing and fro-ing rather than as a 'racist' upsurge, in the crude sense of the term. The changes are remarkable because England is (or has been) a country of never-changing party affiliations (Crewe *et al.* 1977). The changes are the effect of widespread disaffection with the way things are: 'racist' but only if 'race' is given a much expanded meaning. In this latter sense, "anti-EEC attitudes" and "racial attitudes" are part of the same package (Figure 2 above).

I have argued that 'race' in England is rarely about straightforward *signs* of phenotypical difference, but represents a range of separate and symbolically associated items; that these items are associated as *significata* of the loss of, or the threat to, a generalized sense of 'us'; and that the dominance of 'race' in our political discourse will be clearest in contexts in which these losses are most marked. Again, it is not necessarily only the individuals who are in closest competition with blacks and who therefore stand to lose to blacks who will be most 'racist.' 'Race' in England covers so much more than white/black interactions that it need not be about white/black interactions at all. Certainly it is not only about the losses suffered by either group (whites or blacks) at the hands of the other.

Some of the losses signified by 'race' are the whole nation's losses, specifically the loss of imperial and economic supremacy, and the erosion of associated 'eternals' by which 'we' are or wish to be defined

(Figure 2: positive pole). Other losses affect particular groups or sectors of the nation. Times are hard for (almost) everybody, but there is no doubt that some parts of the country and some members of the population have been hit harder than others. Inner-city areas in London and the Midlands have suffered the accumulated blight of bad housing, too few jobs and bureaucratic over-management more acutely than smaller, greener, less congested settlements (Rex and Moore 1967). And since the beginning of urban decline has coincided, or appears to have coincided, with the arrival of significant numbers of black immigrants in these areas, the identification of blacks and/or immigrants with the various indices of blight and shortage follows readily (Figure 2: negative pole). Similarly, those whose claim to particular reserves of skill or occupation is no longer legitimate, or is not recognized as legitimate, have suffered particular losses. This is true of, for example, dockers (Hill 1976), miners (Rodger's chapter in this volume), small shopkeepers (Aldrich n.d.), civil and ex-colonial bureaucrats (Flett 1979; Edgar 1974), and skilled industrial workers. In the last category, support for 'racist' views has been found to increase with industrial skill (Miles and Phisaklea 1978). The fact that these views are rarely translated into political action suggests that the English dilemma with regard to 'race' is no less paralyzing than its American prototype: the symbolic bind of opposite and contradictory values in a single notion allows lots of talk in reasonable moral comfort, but it tends to inhibit innovative action of any kind.

Whether various losses affect nation or sector or individual, they are felt, in some form, by everybody. This is partly, of course, because they are the same losses; whatever happens in any one corner of the polity reverberates in all others. But the unification of all these losses is no less important an achievement of racial rhetoric. The symbol 'race' serves not only to unify all of 'us' by association with losses suffered by some of us, but also to blur the distinction between the various *kinds* of loss covered by 'race.' At least three different levels are at issue. The simplest is loss against what one previously had—a loss usually described as 'real' deprivation. More complex but no less galling is loss against what others have—or 'relative' deprivation. Most complex is loss against what one expected or felt entitled to have—a loss against aspiration or entitlement. This last could be most painful of all. It carries with it not only nameless disappointment, but an irresistible sense of shame (Wallman 1977: 13–14; see also Marris 1974 *passim*).

The confusion of these levels of loss is easily achieved. Urban conditions and living standards in much of England have actually improved since 1945, that is, in the period of her imperial decline. But they are widely felt to have deteriorated and are cited as evidence that 'we' are less well off than before. In fact, the English are today worse off *relative* to North Americans and continental Europeans, whose equal or better they could once claim to be; and they are less well off, both collectively and individually, than they expected to be by this time.

All of these losses are conflated and represented by 'race' (Figure 2), and they are experienced as a generalized loss of national and personal significance. But, whereas the association of loss with 'race' is peculiar to the English scene, the sense of loss in the face of change is more widespread. Apter (1964: 30–39) has proposed a model of stratification that puts the present extent of these losses into historical perspective. Although designed for the United States, his model provides a logic of differentiation which begins to account for refractions of racial rhetoric wrought by the political audience in England (Figure 1). It is not a class model, but post-industrial and post-Marxist.[10] Stratification occurs (still) according to relative power and status, and power and status are (still) measured in terms of access to, and control over, productive resources. But four fundamental changes are observed: (1) status is continually shifting, and both downward and upward mobility are feasible and frequent; (2) scientific acumen has displaced land/ labour/capital as the most highly valued of productive resources. This means (3) that ownership of the means of production counts for less in the political-economic process than personal significance to it—that is, the significance of the work a person does. Most crucially, (4) the ideal of the post-industrial system is that status, power and significance should be distributed on the basis of personal ability: *from* each according to his ability and *to* each according to his ability. In these ideal terms, a man gets what he is worth, not what he needs.

Whether this is the way it is matters less than the effect of the expectation. "Boundless hope [of the industrial revolution?] becomes tempered with the realisation of the limits of one's abilities. This realisation causes considerable bitterness against the system, if only because the alternative to alienation is self-hatred. Modern societies harbour large proportions of people with extraordinary degrees of self-hatred and self-doubt" (Apter, *op. cit.*: 33), against which they can only defend themselves with new and post-industrial ideologies. Accordingly, they find themselves belonging to either of two strata: the meritocratic *establishment* and the *disestablished*. The latter is subdivided into those who are functionally still useful, but with lower status than before, and the [functionally] superfluous (*ibid.*). Each derives its power differently: "the establishment . . . from expertise . . . ; the middle from electional [electoral?] strength; and the

bottom from the threat of local violence." Each of these groups has
different foci of identity and solidarity, and (we may suppose) perceives
its own advantage or loss in different terms. Accordingly, in England
each will take a different meaning from Powellist rhetoric.

The establishment increasingly derives its identity from the
satisfaction—that is, the significance—of work. Its reference group is
widely recruited across national/cultural/racial boundaries. None of
these attributes, as such, is relevant to scientific/technological/ad-
ministrative acumen. 'Race' within the meritocratic elite is not a
political issue; on the one hand, racial conflict, urban decline,
immigration pressures—all the negative elements in racial rhetoric—
constitute items to be reported, problems to be solved, grist for the mill of
ability; on the other hand, the positive stuff of English-ness is of
minimal relevance to those who must be anational to the extent that they
are identified by the work they do (Wallman 1979).

The identity of the second rank, the disestablished-but-still-useful,
was with business and work; they focused on churches, voluntary
associations, trade and craft guilds, and so on. Business and work
became increasingly unsatisfactory because they became less and less
powerful, especially *vis-à-vis* the establishment. The relation of this
group to the establishment is ambivalent: it seeks to undermine it but
wants to get its children into it. Similarly, it is squeezed from below,
bearing the brunt of the pressure from, and anxious to prevent, the rise of
those in the "functionally superfluous" stratum.

The most characteristic feature of the middle stratum is the loss of
past foci of power and identity, the loss of security and significance
provided by the values of the past. This may entail for its members "an
increase in the significance of patriotic organizations associated with the
radical right" and a compensatory effort "to link local with national
[organizations] which would make the disestablished powerful" (Apter
1964: 34). The recent increase in membership of the National Front is
drawn partly from this category (Kosmin and Grizzard 1974). The
increase clearly responds to the Powellist equation of 'race' with
immigration and of immigration with foreign takeover, as well as the
loss of English strength and mores (Figure 2: negative pole). Members of
the same category, in an upward phase of the status shift, or the same
members in a more promising context, could be those who argue that the
accommodation of *all* commonwealth citizens is itself evidence that the
past survives untarnished (Figure 2: positive pole).

The third and bottom rank is disestablished to the extent of being
"functionally superfluous" (and does not therefore include the skilled or
employable working class). Its members (according to Apter) feel no

solidarity and have few permanent foci of identity. They are preoccupied with their own poverty, both real and relative, and "in an affluent society, with escape . . . [Their] behaviour is divided between apathy and hysteria" (1964: 34). It takes no great leap of the imagination to recognize in this description the disaffected young of all colours. There are no jobs for them, or they do not want the jobs offered. Given the options, their reluctance to work is entirely predictable. "In a culture where the worth of a man is measured by how far he has gotten [will get?], the unskilled labourer or service worker, despite the pieties that may be uttered . . . about the dignity of labour, knows that he has not gotten [will not get?] very far. . . . One of the things wrong with a working class job is simply that it is working class . . ." (Weiss and Riesman 1966: 583).

Petty crime and (not always petty) violence are efforts to escape from apathy and boredom. They are not mounted as deliberate attacks on the system. Both the crime and the violence tend to be indiscriminate, seldom directed against any specific category of others. But the rationale and the world view of blacks as well as whites in this group tend to be racist in the narrow sense: 'they' are used to reassert 'our' significance. Each will find some comfort in attributing his lack of advance to the presence and the machinations of his racially opposite number. The symbolic equation of 'race' with competition for jobs, houses and opportunity is tailor-made for the "functionally superfluous." Indeed, they use, or are said to use, the negative associations of 'race' (Figure 2) more or less directly to explain what they do (Phillips 1976; Willis 1976; see also Seabrook 1976).

Summary Conclusions

1. In a post-imperial, post-industrial, no longer powerful era, we cannot define ourselves the way we used to. There is, as there was in the thirties, a demand for new meanings and ideologies that will explain and justify the way we are now. So, pressing a political need is ideally suited to the abilities and ambitions of the creative rhetorician.

2. The rhetorical task is twofold: to assist in the understanding of new and still shifting circumstances, and to reaffirm 'our' identity in relation to 'our' essential political values. To be successful, therefore, the rhetoric will need to associate a range of meanings from good to bad, 'boo' to 'hurrah,' present to past, temporal to eternal. And to an important extent the power of a rhetorical symbol will inhere in the contradictions it embodies.

3. 'Race' in England is a powerful rhetorical symbol. It is powerful because it counts for everybody, and because it counts in so many different ways. For both reasons it is malleable to the making of almost any political point.

4. This proliferation of messages is both an achievement of the rhetorician and a potential that waits to be exploited by him, but it is never entirely within his control. The media refract its messages, and the audience takes from them the meanings it wants or needs.

5. The greater the range and contradiction of values stored in a symbol, or in the rhetoric built on that symbol, the less likely it is to persuade to political action. Just as bombast gets in the way of policy or planning and tends to be used by politicians who do not expect to be called to account (Bailey 1969; Parkin 1975), so a rich range of meanings associated with 'race' impedes the making of practical political decisions about real 'race' issues.

6. The more differentiated the audience in relation to the symbols of the rhetoric, the more variously the message will be interpreted and the further its meaning may move from the one intended by the rhetorician.

7. The meaning(s) taken from 'race' reveal as much about the political audience as they do about the symbol itself. As much explanation of the present meaning of 'race' inheres in the present social structure as in legacies of the colonial past; and the refractions of meaning ascribed to 'racial' rhetoric may be useful indicators of present ideological and social trends.

8. Whether the meanings ascribed to 'race' affect or are affected by the realities of power difference and racial hierarchy remains problematic (Kuper 1974; Banton 1977). Certainly 'race' will not be consistently interpreted as long as its significance varies with the political realities of the rhetorical audience. If, on the contrary, the meaning of 'race' were to jell across English society so that it signified *only* difference, or *only* hierarchy, we could be sure that relations between racially distinct populations in England would be crucially different, and that the notion 'race' would lose its rhetorical potential.

9. If rhetoric is speech designed to persuade to a particular view, then rhetoric can become successful only by establishing a single meaning for its dominant symbol, and so depriving it of its rhetorical clout. This process may restrict the political life of rhetorical topics even if the context in which they are used is not significantly changed.

10. There is more to rhetoric than motive, form, content or context. None of these can constitute more than a partial explanation of the meanings given to, or taken from, 'race' and 'racial' rhetoric in

England. The rhetoric, the symbol and the audience may in combination throw off meanings no one intended, and produce effects no one would have dared to expect.

Epilogue

The extremes of meaning carried by the symbol 'race' are thrown into relief by contrasting the positive newspaper coverage of the Harmony Street story (Figure 3) against the negative coverage of similar events occurring in the same city and sometimes in the same local area, throughout the same period of time (Figure 4). The case of Harmony Street can therefore be used to illustrate the scope and the limitations of the rhetorical effect.

The real tale of Harmony Street was a tale of housing standards and

FIGURE 3

Racial Rhetoric: Positive Refractions

FIGURE 4

Racial Rhetoric: Negative Refractions

shortages, bureaucratic inefficiencies and a profligate local government. It was also a tale of people who rather liked living where they were—because they were used to it, because it was near their place of work, because they had friends or relatives nearby, because they had heard that the borough council did not have the money to rehouse them, or because they were not convinced that milk and honey would flow to them even if it did. The case of Harmony Street was the case of a battle against compulsory purchase, demolition and relocation. The cultural and phenotypic variety of Harmony Street residents had no bearing on the story for the people who participated in it. But as the news media reported it, Harmony Street was about 'race.' Nothing else was interesting, nothing else was news. Why?

Let us return to the rhetorical process (Figure 1). An astute politician knows that the diffuse political notions of his culture will serve the purpose of cohesion if they can be synthesized and made available to the political audience. If, besides being astute, he is skilled in the art of rhetoric, the politician will be able to group the notions around a central theme and articulate them in some appropriately persuasive form. The choice of a central or centralizing theme is crucial. It must be striking enough to attract the collective attention, and yet be sufficiently variable in meaning to cover a range of separate, and not necessarily, compatible needs and notions; that is, it must be dominant.

So it is with 'race' in England. Whether its dominance is a cause or an effect of racial rhetoric, 'race' now strikes and holds the collective attention. It is not a simple sign; it is a total symbolic package (Figure 2). The meaning of 'race' can be negative or positive, but it is always viscerally important. At its negative pole it encompasses present losses and anxieties—the things that threaten 'us' as a people—in a single explanatory frame. At its positive pole it affirms or reaffirms the traditions and values of the past—the things that enhance 'us' as a people. Because we cannot fail to be attentive to both poles, 'race,' either way, is *news*.

It follows that a news item can be made 'racial' by reference to the standards and values by which a people defines itself (compare Figure 3 with Figure 2: positive pole), or by reference to the erosion of those standards and values (compare Figure 4 with Figure 2: negative pole). By the same logic, a public event is about 'race' if it pertains to either theme. The news items photographed in Figures 3 and 4 are all, in this sense, 'racial' items. Further, as the rhetorical process is analysed, the items are evidence of successful racial rhetoric: a wide range of political issues has been overlaid and integrated by a generalized 'racial' gloss.

But if political rhetoric is designed to "persuade to action or opinion," its message must get through to the political audience in an operational and unambiguous form. Where there is evidence of a clear split between positive and negative poles of meaning, like that shown in the press coverage of ordinary public events over a limited period of time, there is evidence that the message is refractive, ambiguous. By the rule of rhetorical paradox, it is inevitable that this be the outcome. The same set of events can be interpreted in quite opposite ways because the main message contains quite opposite meanings. The values reflected in Figures 3 and 4 are contradictory but not mutually exclusive because 'race' represents both poles.

Although this ambiguity is an essential feature of powerful rhetorical symbols, it puts important limits on the control that even an expert rhetorician can have over his own rhetorical effect. The political audience cannot act collectively on what he says because his message involves many issues, many values. If it did not, the audience would not have listened to him in the first place. Contradictions at the level of meaning are no problem. But constrained by contradictions at the level of action—whether action to 'deal with' poor housing or to 'deal with' immigrants—the only sensible course is to affirm the main message and to do nothing. Power relations are unaltered, economic problems unsolved, and the rhetorical effect is bombast willy-nilly.

Notes

1. This analysis was first presented in 1976. It applies substantially but not exactly to the English political scene at the start of the 1980s. The use of "England" and "English" is deliberately maintained throughout. I do not know whether the observations made apply to other countries in Britain.

2. *The Star* (Johannesburg), 21 October 1975; *The Rand Daily Mail* (Johannesburg), 27 October 1975; *The Argus* (Cape Town), 22 October 1975; *The Cape Times* (Cape Town), 22 October 1975. These reports were themselves reported in the English press.

3. It has been assisted by discussion about Powell with Lloyd-Jones and by his intricate analysis (in this volume) of the form and content of Powell's 1968 speech.

4. See Bernard Levin in *The Times*, 27 May 1976, and Ronald Butt in *The Times*, 10 June 1976.

5. I am grateful to Dr. Barry Kosmin, Research Director of the Board of Deputies of British Jews, for reminding me of this analogy and of its limitations.

6. A different black writer reports quite another response to the same confession made to a prospective landlady over the phone in Paris: "I am sorry Monsieur, but there can be no reduction for [colour]. *Le prix est fixé*" (Braithwaite 1973: 95).

7. Pursuing the comparison with France, I should note that the terminology used there in connection with non-white residents carries the opposite inference: those listed or referred to as immigrants (*immigrés*) are those from southern Europe and from the Maghreb—many of whom return occasionally or permanently to their places of origin. Black (West) Africans, whatever their status or expressed intention, are never *immigrés* in the official statistics or in journalistic reference. Contrary to English usage, in France a black man may be an immigrant, but an immigrant cannot be black. It was suggested to me by Dr. Daniel du Coppet of the *Centre Nationale des Récherches Scientifiques* in Paris that this implies either that blacks may be thought of as not wanting to stay, or that they may not be wanted to stay. The difference in symbolic association and its relation to legal rights of citizenship and nationality in Britain and France could do with thorough comparative study.

8. The development of personal, as opposed to national, identity with regard to 'race' was analysed by Dr. Peter Weinreich and associates at the SSRC Research Unit in Ethnic Relations at the University of Bristol.

9. This symbolic unintended consequence was observed at first hand by Mr. Lanny Berry, and will be elaborated in his doctoral thesis in anthropology for the University of California, Berkeley. I am happy to acknowledge his insight here.

10. I am indebted to Professor Milton Santos, of Columbia University (New York) and the University of São Paulo, for introducing me to this useful concept. It is not explicit in the Apter paper cited.

Campaign Rhetoric

8

Cousin and the Gros Chiens: The Limits of Cajun Political Rhetoric

GERALD L. GOLD

> The voters of Louisiana prized oratory as an art, judged it with professional interest, and evaluated a candidate almost solely by how he handled himself on the platform.
>
> T. Harry Williams,
> *Huey Long* (1970: 279)

The objective of this essay is to assess the role of political communication and, in particular, of metaphor in the speeches of Cajun local-level politicians in southwestern Louisiana. Of primary interest is the effect on political metaphor of social and cultural constraints, the most pertinent of which is a strong moral consensus and an egalitarianism that approaches the ideal of *communitas* (Turner 1969: 96). Another constraint crucial to this analysis is that the Cajuns of this region cannot read or write French, their dominant mother tongue (English is the language taught in schools).[1] Therefore, French has become essentially an oral language, the one in which politicians choose to communicate to their publics.

Politics, in such a closely knit arena, is just as affected by moral sanctions and by reciprocal obligations as any other social activity. Specifically, we may ask whether the medium, the performance of a political speech rather than its content, can become the message? Also, to what extent do these political campaigns reflect 'real politics' rather than specific and 'traditional' courses of action (Bloch 1975: 16)? That is, in a situation of total involvement of a community in a political campaign, are the rewards restricted to winning office, or is there a more subtle and intangible compensation for participation? A final issue which I shall touch on briefly is the extent to which Cajun political rhetoric provides an understanding of minority group politics and of the revival of a French identity in Louisiana.

To answer these questions, I must first turn to a short description of the political arena in the Great Southwestern Prairie of Louisiana, focusing on the first 1975 Democratic Primary election in the small town of Cajun Prairie in St. Gabriel Parish.[2] Singled out for analysis are a series of radio speeches broadcast by Lurlin Lafleur, one of five candidates competing for a district seat on the St. Gabriel Parish Police Jury. The discussion that follows is based on transcriptions of these speeches and on interviews with the incumbent, Ronald Aucoin, and with other participants in the election.

The Political Arena in Cajun Prairie

The everyday life of the adult population of Cajun Prairie is still carried on largely in Cajun French, and a wide range of Cajun institutions and customs are taken for granted despite the overwhelming presence of an Anglo-Southern population several miles north of the town limits. Like many other French-speaking prairie towns of southwestern Louisiana, Cajun Prairie swelled in size after the post–World War II transformation from tenant-cropping of cotton to mechanized production of rice, together with the movement of much of the labour force from outlying farms to the towns. There the migrants became wage labourers, operators of small businesses, offshore oil workers or welfare recipients. Two aspects of this migration are of immediate relevance to local and regional politics: the abandonment of a rural settlement pattern based almost exclusively on small communities or "coves" (*anses*) of farmers and sharecroppers;[3] and the rise of a new stratum of self-employed shopkeepers and craftsmen, a group that grew beyond what a town of several thousand could normally support.

Virtually everyone in Cajun Prairie, whatever his trade, has been a sharecropper (in cotton) in one of the rural coves. Contemporary kinship and friendship ties, fundamental loyalties that have economic, social and political significance, often have their origins in the farm communities and in places of resettlement. Certainly the dominant local values of egalitarianism and humility, the experience of past misery, and the symbols of a common French-speaking Cajun culture[4] are found throughout the Southwestern Prairie. This pre-industrial experience is incorporated into a vibrant oral tradition of stories and songs, which constitutes an essential part of what Cajun politicians communicate in their rhetoric.

Cajun Prairie has been a political entity only since 1910. Even then, politics in Louisiana was still firmly in the hands of planters and merchants who had "captured the Democratic Party and treated the Louisiana version of the 'solid South' as if it were a closed corporation. . . . the Democratic Party had a clear field in Louisiana Politics" (Howard 1971: 193). A direct consequence of Louisiana's segregationist voter-registration laws[5] was that landless and illiterate whites were kept marginal to state politics; many of these voters were Francophones living in the geographically isolated parishes of the Gulf Coast (*ibid*.: 189). Throughout Louisiana, party politics were limited to the Democratic party primary, and the regional factions contesting the nominations: the local "courthouse ring," and the "out ring" waiting to defeat it (Williams 1970: 134). Since many candidates cannot get a clear majority in the first primary because of a large slate of candidates, most local and state seats are contested in two primaries, the first occurring in early November and the second in early December.

Since the early days, electoral candidates in Cajun Prairie have had a chance to test the political 'wind' by giving public speeches on the town's main street during the annual Armistice Day celebrations (*l'onze de Novembre*). The roster includes both the aspirants to and incumbents of local seats, such as those of the police jury, justice-of-the-peace and school board; of parish seats such as those of the sheriff and assessor; and of state or national offices (representatives, senator, governor, and others). Local political bosses, representing the two dominant factions in municipal politics, are among the many who savour the fiery rhetoric and scout for candidates in, what seems to be, a political free-for-all.

One of the most hotly contested offices, and the only one of immediate interest to us is that of police juror. The political rewards that accrue to a successful candidate of the police jury include the control over road maintenance and drainage in his district, and the power to hire and fire road crews. In practice, the distribution of patronage may be so complete that road-grading machinery and gravel are stored close to the police juror's home, and employees check in with their boss every day. In addition to the road work, the police jury acts as a parish (county) council, voting on buildings and new facilities for the parish, such as the court house in a neighbouring town. It follows that landowners with extensive frontage, builders and most businessmen and professionals— those whom the average Cajun calls *gros chiens* (big dogs)—have a strong interest in whom they elect for police jury. But so does the small farmer, who needs his entrance graded, his ditches cleared of shrubbery, and his private lands terraced with parish machinery.[6]

These interests have been represented by two factions, one of which had been controlled by the owner of the town's largest cotton mill. The second faction had been controlled by a country doctor (now deceased), whose sons now operate Cajun Prairie's hospital and also have extensive land interests. These doctors work in close association with another physician, who is the town's mayor and a dominant force in town politics.

Until recently whole families delivered all their votes, through a family patriarch, to the leader of one or the other of the two factions. Voting patterns were rigidly repeated, and if a small number of voters shifted from one patron (*gros chien*) to another, this could affect the results of an election. In the election that concerns us, only the doctors' faction retained its former leadership, and a new opposing faction was formed under the leadership of a young lawyer. Each faction makes its own allies with the courthouse rings in the county seat. Faction leaders depend on these allies to finance much of the local campaign by supporting certain candidates running for state and national offices.

Voter and candidate allegiances shift shortly before the primaries, when candidates are busy getting together a "ticket" of other men to run for office. At the same time, each ticket will make its bargain with one or other of the factions and their leaders. The factions will then finance the political campaigns of their candidates: pay for political suppers, buy votes, especially the re-enfranchised black vote, and co-ordinate the distribution of posters and election cards.[7] Kinship and friendship considerations frequently lead voters to split their ticket, supporting candidates from both factions.

On election day, "lieutenants" on both sides offer some voters "transportation money" to the polls; many of these and other electors are 'assisted' in their voting on the grounds of illiteracy.[8] Candidates or their agents will accompany a voter to the curtain of the polling booth under the watchful eyes of their opponents and their lieutenants. It may seem that voting has little effect on the outcome as only a few incumbents are defeated. However, since several are voted out of office in every election, all incumbents have little choice but to seek some reaffirmation of the voters' support, and much of this is accomplished through their style of communication.

Thus, the most important aspect of a campaign is the political speech-making—in particular for new candidates who cannot rely on a previous record in office or on handing out political prestations. The speeches are almost all in French and highly rhetorical; most are made at political suppers, to which all candidates are frequently invited, especially when they are sponsored by a general-store owner or by a restaurateur. It would be unthinkable for a candidate to refuse an invitation to speak, even when the affair is sponsored by the opposition faction. For if any of his supporters or would-be supporters noticed his absence, it might be taken as a sign of disinterest.

In the past thirty years, the radio has been an important medium of campaign rhetoric. Although radio speeches are but an extension of the political supper, they can be more vicious and flamboyant, given the absence of opponents in the recording studio. Even the state-level and national-level candidates will make French-language political 'spot' broadcasts on radio, sometimes using broadcasters to make their speeches. The same speeches are repeated for a week or longer as many families leave their radio tuned to the county station, which has extensive Cajun-language broadcasts sponsored by local merchants. Opponents monitor each other's oratory so that they can prepare effective replies. Significantly, the town or parish elite, the *gros chiens*, rarely speak in public for the candidates whom they back financially.

The first effective use of French-language radio in Louisiana politics took place at the national rather than the local level. In the 1930s and 1940s, Dudley Leblanc made extensive use of French-language radio broadcasts, which helped earn him the electoral support of southern Louisiana in a bid for state and national office. His deliberate selection of strong ethnic metaphors corresponded with the opening of this region to massive outside influences and state intervention.

> For many of the listeners, especially those who spoke only French, this was one of their few links with the outside world. Many of them could neither read nor understand the English language, especially in the 1930s and 1940s, and they trusted Dudley to keep them posted on the major news events . . . his style was informal; his tone of voice was conversational; his words were often mispronounced; he coughed while on the air. But he sounded sure of himself and he had great credibility among his regular listeners. He was one of them and his radio style projected that image. (Angers 1977: 47.)

Today, the use of French and of French-language radio in political campaigning has survived in the Southwestern Prairie, although according to our data on generational linguistic assimilation in Cajun Prairie, French may become less important than other symbols of "Cajun-ness" in future election campaigns.

THE 1975 PRIMARY

In his campaign for the office of police jury in 1975, Lurlin Lafleur broadcast seven speeches, each fifteen minutes in duration and each repeated every day for a week. As these were recorded by a home listener, they serve as documents for studying the changes in political language during the campaign. I also interviewed the incumbent, Aucoin, and met with Guidry, a third challenger, who is barely mentioned in the Lafleur radio talks. I learned from relatively non-involved third parties that Lafleur and Guidry were both promised support from the doctors' faction, and the incumbent Aucoin (or "Police Jury," as Lafleur calls him on the radio) was supported by the second and newer faction.

In his speeches, Lafleur first establishes his equality with the listeners (he was a Cajun, a local, and not a *gros chien*) and presents his kith and kin as credentials. He then builds on a series of metaphors, beginning with the egalitarian past of the poor sharecropper, then moving to indirect attacks on "Police Jury" and his alleged contacts with dishonest outsiders. By the fourth speech, Lafleur is offering prestations to the voters and more direct personal attacks on Police Jury. Metaphor is all but replaced with metonym in the sixth speech, and in the seventh, Lafleur begins with a direct personal attack on the social *persona* of Police Jury.

In planning his radio speeches, a candidate must consider the continuity of his rhetoric and the timing of his metaphors. Working from only a few sketch notes (in English!), he seeks balance in his metaphors, using a strategy that will slowly bring listeners to his way of thinking and keep them there. He is mediating the political world for his listeners (Paine 1976), and by formalizing his argument into known and predictable metaphors, he reduces the specificity of events, ruling out disagreement with his major points (Bloch 1975: 15–16). In leading his followers towards his conclusion, an error in timing, a metaphor out of place, could seriously flaw the argument.

Both candidates and voters confirm the importance in political rhetoric of denying or minimizing local differences in wealth and status. Conflicts are approached by skirting the issue, first with metaphor and then with less disguised metonymic innuendo, rather than by direct accusations.[9] In this way the candidate seeks reaffirmation from his supporters (*gros chiens* included), while not offending or threatening potential supporters who are often kinsmen and associates of opposition candidates. For example, to accuse an opponent of being supported by *gros chiens* would not be an insult. Factions and their backers are well known, and all the candidates have influential supporters. But to actually name someone, or to invade the closed doors of family intimacy would be breaking the rules of the game. Therefore, candidates only make such moves in the last week of the campaign, especially if they feel it might make a difference in a close race. The social sanctions for failing are unpleasant for persons who cannot afford to cut off contacts with an entire family. Lafleur uses such a strategy at the end of his campaign and convincingly shows, by its failure, that the rhetoric *is* the message.

Campaign Rhetoric*

WEEK 1: I'M A CAJUN LIKE YOU; POLICE JURY IS A NICHOIS

Lafleur begins his first speech with a recording of *Jolie Blon'*, a Cajun tune that is regarded in the Southwestern Prairie as one of the most traditional. The recording allows time for those already listening to call their kin, their godmother (*nanaine*) and their friends.

After the music, Lafleur narrates an incident from his sharecropping childhood. The moral lies in a game of Tarzan that he played while his father's precious fuel leaked into a gulley. His father's biting reprimand shows him to be a humble man who, unlike Police Jury (Aucoin), knows when he has gone too far in ignoring his responsibilities. The metaphor is built up slowly with meticulous detail, beginning with his childhood experience and ending with his opponent's folly. Both parts of the metaphor are given equal weight and elaboration, and the same key words are repeated to emphasize the point of the story.

> "Lurlin, what are you doing boy?"
>
> "But Dad, I'm just playing Tarzan . . ." [swinging on a wire cable]. I then showed him how I played Tarzan. I jumped over the river, I was that happy. . . .
>
> "Look, while I was gone, gas leaked out over there. . . . I worked hard for that gas—it's leaking into that ditch and you never noticed it."
>
> Well, right there and then, my friends, I saw that something was wrong. I realized that I had made a little error somewhere. . . .
>
> "Dear boy, you have no business playing Tarzan if you are not more observant than that." He took his knife out of his pocket, *got up on his tiptoes. He cut my cable.*

His own childhood experience exposed, Lafleur brings the metaphor to bear on his opponent.

* The English translations are my own. Emphasis, where shown, is my addition.

> And now, my friends, your present man in Police Jury, *he is playing Tarzan
> there. He is just playing Police Jury.* He goes out on the road. He doesn't feel
> the holes in the road. He doesn't see a hole in the road. He doesn't see water
> in the ditches. He doesn't see your beans being scorched. . . . At the
> crossroads, one cannot see if someone is coming. He doesn't see nothing.
> He's just on his way out there. He's playing Police Jury. . . .

The metaphor is strengthened by a comparison of Police Jury with a fat
lady at the circus who is full of air.

> Well your Police Jury . . . is making you promises . . . but he is full of
> air as well. . . . You know what you got to do? . . . You have to do like
> Dad did with me when I was playing Tarzan. *You have to get up on your
> tip-toes and then cut that cable.*

Lafleur closes his first characterization of the effectiveness of Police
Jury but still without impugning his reputation. He chooses the
familiar rural metaphor of the *nichois* (nest egg).

> The hen has an instinct that if you take all the eggs out from inside her nest,
> she is going to stop laying. She might think that the snakes are taking them
> or the muskrats or something. Then she changes the place of her nest. But
> when you place a *nichois* in there, you're sure that the hen will always lay in
> that same nest.
>   And that's what your Police Jury does. I call him a *nichois.* He's the one
> who wants to continue keeping your taxes, letting them fall into his own
> nest. He wants to eat your eggs. . . . It's time that you remove the *nichois*
> and you start to have eggs for yourself, to have roads for yourself, and
> drainage . . . and black top. You need all these things.

To finish his speech and support his own reputational claims,
Lafleur gives some character references, "not necessarily people who are
going to vote for me." In fact, so much is said about the good character
and reputation of his referees that a listener would not think of con-
sulting them.

> . . . there is Monsieur Olivier Fuselier and his wife, who live near Gary
> Fontenot's shop there in Eunice. Olivier makes *mais tendre* [sweet corn] so
> good, as good as you have ever put your teeth into. And such good
> people. . . . Chat with Olivier and his wife, and ask about me while you
> are there.
>   . . . Miguel Fontenot works here in the village. . . . He collects trash
> and trees and all sorts of things. He's been doing that for 15 years. *Nearly all
> of you from Cajun Prairie know Miguel. There's no doubt about that.* Every

month when he came to my station, we had a good ice cream. Miguel started to work at the time that the deceased Ozème was there. . . . Ask Miguel what kind of man I am.

WEEK 2: I NEVER QUIT (*Je ne lâche pas la patate*)

Lafleur begins his second speech with his family tree: the names of his parents and grandparents and in which "cove" they once lived. The two communities cited, Bayou Croche and l'Anse Gris, correspond to the district that Lafleur is contesting, and serve to remind those who could potentially be counted as family where their obligations lie.

Lafleur then lays the groundwork for the rhetoric that follows, hinting that he will reply to charges that his opponents have made about him in their (neighbourhood) speeches. He also may be revealing that the wealthy *gros chiens* who were allegedly supporting him are also backing another horse.[10] "There are a few *gros chiens* who are playing dirty politics. They're ready to play politics on both sides of the fence." He likens those *gros chiens* to a nest of wasps who are out to sting him once again, "to make me withdraw from the race." (Lafleur had lost two previous elections.)

Having established common kith among his listeners and caught their sympathy, Lafleur begins another tale of *communitas*, which begins with his poverty as a fledgling country grocer after leaving his father's farm (in 1954).[11] He confides to his listeners that this is something "I have never talked about," and he urges them to decide if he is the type of man who would ever withdraw from the race.[12]

My wife and my children began eating black beans three times a day, week after week. We had a *hâle* [country butcher shop] back then, and during those terrible times, we sold a lot of baloney. People used to bring their lunches with them when they went to work, so you couldn't sell the small ends of baloney. It was broken and dry. . . . But we took the ends, cut them up into little squares and put them into our beans. . . . I was determined to make it on my own. We told no one because we didn't want Mom and Dad to know.

When his mother and father finally invited them to dinner, he instructed the children not to mention anything about beans. Even before anything was served, his youngest began to wail, repeatedly screaming, "I don't want beans."

I got up and I looked around the table. There were tears in everyone's eyes. Except for the little girl. She was busy eating huge gourmet mouthfuls as if she had never eaten before. . . . Mom started to bring us food in the afternoons. . . . Dad said that it was almost a sin to throw out all that good food. But I knew what they were doing, yes. But I never said anything.

My Mom and Dad are dead now. And the thing that I regret the most is that I never thanked them for that. If they were still around I would like to tell them how very much I appreciated what they did for us and our children.

Lafleur completes this metaphor with a Cajun folk saying: "My friends, you know why I can tell this story? Because I want you to know that I am not the kind of man *qui lâche la patate juste parce qu'elle est chaude*! ['who drops the potato just because it's hot!']. I've never been a quitter and I'm not going to quit!" The finishing touch is also a folk metaphor (*brasseur de mauvais oeuf*) that recounts the vain egg-making efforts of a disgruntled country-wife to show that no matter what he, Lafleur, said or did, his adversaries would find something wrong with it. Again Lafleur assures the voters that he *is* a winner and that they should vote for him so that he can make it into the second "race" (primary).

Lafleur invites his listeners to come hear him speak with his two opponents, and share in fifty pounds of tripe stew (*bouilli*)[13] that he will cook at a country store three miles west of the village. The invitation is followed by a first promise:

> They've got to stop saying that we can't have black top [paved road]. . . . I'm going to say to you that for what it costs to maintain a road over four years, we can make black tops. We're going to black-top all the gravel roads. We'll go into the south subdivision, we'll take all those roads there that have no black top. We'll black-top all of that. We'll take the driveways of the people in the village, we'll black-top all of that. . . .

To remind his listeners that he's the kind of man who can do this, he adds a second list of references.

WEEK 3: FROM METAPHOR TO CONFRONTATION (*La saison des cocodries*)

The third week of speeches begins on a very defensive note: Lafleur notes that his candidates have ridiculed his black-top platform, and he replies with more character references (people living on gravel roads), going into considerable detail about their roles as classmates, clients and crawfish growers. He then plays on the metaphor of seasons. For the first time, Police Jury's moral character is openly questioned.

> My friends, what I wanted to talk to you about today is seasons. You know that there is a season for almost everything. There is a season for you to

plant. There is a season for you to plow. There is a season for you to bring in the harvest. . . . But the season that I would like to talk to you about today is the season for *cocodries* [alligators].

If you kill a *cocodrie*, they'll give you 5 years in the penitentiary. Not one *cocodrie* is in danger! Just a couple of years ago, they told us that it has come to the point that if you went hand-line fishing, and you put your foot over the side of the boat, you would step on a *cocodrie*. . . . There were no *cocodries* and now there are an awful lot.

Well, your Police Jury is like this matter of the *cocodrie*. . . . Two or three weeks ago, but before that, two or three years ago, he said he didn't have any gravel. There was no way to buy gravel. . . . But today gravel is in season. It's open season on it. . . . It's not whether you have any gravel, it's how many trips of gravel you want. Well my friends, take the gravel that I want to give you. Haven't you been needing it for four years? . . . We'll take that same gravel and make black tops with it.

Reaching out of *communitas* towards the forces that threaten it, Lafleur uses wealthy and dangerous outsiders and *gros chiens* (an internal disequilibrating force) to show where Aucoin has really spent the Police Jury budget. In doing so, he again appeals to his neighbours to consider him as a social equal who has their interests in mind. He turns to the new camp ground, which Police Jury built instead of roads:

Sure, you couldn't have any gravel. *But he took good care of the strangers*, well looked-after, well-arranged, that. Tell me something, how many hours a day do you spend at Crooked Creek, fishing or barbecuing? You don't spend one hour a day there, eh? But you spend the better part of your day on your little gravel roads, letting your head swelter at the wheel of your truck or car. It was against the law to put down gravel. There was none. But to give it to strangers—there!

Then the new courthouse comes under attack:

Those guys like the gros chiens better than you. Oh they do nothing, they talk, but no fooling, they like the *gros chiens* better. He [Police Jury] couldn't give you trees to put in your ditches. . . . But he goes to the parish seat and builds a courthouse that is not even in his own district. He gives that to the *gros chiens* so that everything will be nice. And me—I'm happy for them, *I'm not against the gros chiens . . . but certainly I like you as much as he likes the gros chiens.*

Finally, he reminds the listeners of a new prison built by Police Jury.

I know that many good people make mistakes. . . . If you get caught you go to prison. Maybe you will go if you shoot [a duck] 5 or 10 minutes before the season opens. . . . So when I tell you this, it's because I want you to know I am not seeking to abuse the people in prison. . . . When he came to do the driveway before your home, he couldn't do your entry because it was against the law. *But he took your money and he put it into a* prison down there, a *hotel for the criminals.* All air-conditioned. Fixed-up. Number one.

The boundaries of *communitas* are now crossed and the circumlocution of metaphor gives way to metonym: Police Jury, collaborator with the *gros chiens.* "He has not given a piastre for you: he has given it to the strangers, he gives it to the *gros chiens.* He gives it to the criminals."

In a less constrained arena than Cajun Prairie, three weeks before an election, such an accusation could be a strategic bridge to a new series of district attacks on the *persona* of Police Jury. However, Lafleur chooses to retreat into the morally acceptable idiom of kinship.

WEEK 4: COUSIN LURLIN

A very real factor influencing a candidate's success in Cajun Prairie is that each candidate's kin are unlikely to vote for the opposition. Thus, although the family vote, mentioned earlier, is no longer delivered to the *gros chiens,* it was not in Lafleur's favour that Aucoin and Guidry, the other serious challenger, had large and influential families with kin ties that criss-crossed the electoral district. Moreover, Aucoin could count on the support of the families of his nine permanent employees. I know of at least several persons who voted for Aucoin because of a brother or a cousin in his road crew, even though these voters thought that Lafleur, Guidry or one of the other two candidates might be equally suitable for the job.

Aware of these family ties, Lafleur opens his fourth week of radio speeches with an appeal to *all voters* to consider him as a cousin, a ploy made famous by the most successful Cajun radio campaigner, "Coozan Dud" Leblanc (Angers 1977: 47). Lafleur begins thus:

In the past few weeks I have been observing that everyone likes to vote for their kin. . . . That's why *I tried to calculate a way in which I could be related to you.* You know that if a politician, even if he has but a little thread small enough to pass through the eye of a needle, if there is some distant relative, he wants this relative. They're like brothers. . . .
Well I've been figuring who would be my kinsmen and I discovered that it's everyone who talks French. *I'm a Cajun, you know. Everyone who talks French—we are all like cousins.* Because you speak French and I speak French, that makes us first cousins. And if you talk English, then *I am the*

cousin of those who talk English as well, because I speak English. And if you talk English and French, well then we are double-cousins, you understand. So don't forget that, my friends, when you go vote. Vote for your "Tit coozan," Lurlin Lafleur.

These ethno-linguistic credentials may appear to be gratuitous. After all, he is speaking in Cajun French and his opponents are all Cajuns and Francophones. However, this whole segment of the speech is a deliberate attempt to seek a value concensus with all the candidates. Lafleur is asking his listeners to concur with a succession of statements in which "you are drawn to the form, not in your capacity as a partisan, but because of some 'universal' appeal in it" (Burke 1969a: 58). This strategy becomes apparent as the empathy with his audience becomes a warning against a sympathy vote for Police Jury.

Lafleur takes advantage of rumours that Aucoin is using the appeal of his large family as a cover-up for real campaign issues. In fact, the incumbent was vulnerable on this point, as his campaign literature displayed a family portrait of Aucoin and his wife with all nine of their children. It is not surprising that Lafleur should try to devalue his opponent's trump card by following his kinship appeal with praise for the Aucoin family: "a good family man. I don't think that this man does anything wrong . . . a pretty little wife . . . their children are *vaillant* . . . well brought up. They work with their *poupa* . . . *couldn't ask for a better family than that.*"

Lafleur then builds his Brutus-like praise into metonym that accentuates alleged misdemeanours of a man who does as he pleases. First, he qualifies his initial judgement: "He's not got a grip on what's going on, and he is a little bit of a liar. But that doesn't mean that a man cannot be a good man. *Good men can tell little lies.*"

Concluding his fourth speech, Lafleur promises l'Anse Gris, Aucoin's own neighbourhood, a junkyard that they have allegedly been seeking for some time. Referring to Aucoin's ever-present notebook, he says: "*I* have all my brains with me when I get up in the morning. I don't have to go back to the house to get a little notebook to see what I figured out yesterday."

WEEK 5: "BLACK-TOP" LAFLEUR

In the fifth week, Lafleur continues by seeking yet another familiar Cajun idiom of intimacy: the practice of giving kin and friends colourful and unsolicited nicknames (*tit noms*). The *tit nom* is employed as a metonym that encompasses Lafleur's political promises. The listener is asked to accept the new label as the measure of the man. There are no more credentials or personal experiences. The candidate is at his peak of confidence.

> I was walking with one of my good friends this week and he told me . . . "Lurlin, if you win this office and if you make all these black tops, I'm going to give you the *tit nom* of Black-top."

It is "Black-top" Lafleur who then paints a comical and exaggerated metaphor of Aucoin's roadways as a setting for a Tarzan movie, with alligators, snakes, crawfish, and macaques swinging from the trees in the ditches. "When a man goes out on the road after a rain, he can lean down with his net to catch himself a plate of crawfish right there on the highway. He doesn't even have to take chances and cut his feet on the glass bottles in the ditches." "Black-top" has the "prescription" to cure the problems of Police Jury's paradise. Police Jury is compared with a plumber who gives a doctor a prescription to fix his leaking sink: "Two trips of gravel every four years and if the roads and drains are not healed, well, four years later he'll give you another load of gravel to try to cure the matter."

To show that Police Jury would not black-top the countryside Lafleur turns to the image of a man who reluctantly installed a large horn instead of an adequate boiler in his boat. He found that every time he had to use the horn (Lafleur groans) in dense fog, the boiler lost all its power. "Well, your Police Jury is like that. He is just a big horn, but he does nothing. There's too much profit in it for him" [a direct attack on Aucoin's honesty].

Lafleur, as "Black-top," then drives his metonym in like a wedge. *His* workers would willingly pave everyone's driveway, working seven days a week, with emergency vehicles providing meals and relief. Throughout Cajun Prairie this part of the speech was interpreted as a threat to dismiss Aucoin's road workers, at least one of whom redoubled his campaign efforts for his boss.

As if to justify a turn to more vitriolic rhetoric, and to counter criticism he had already received for having said too much, Lafleur explains that his passion for politics is natural. "Me, what I like best is to go out and politick and chat with everyone, rather than fish or hunt."

The listener's suspicion that Lafleur may have overextended the acceptable boundaries of Cajun political rhetoric in his neighbourhood supper talks, as well as on the radio, is confirmed by the failure of his last two speeches.

WEEK 6: A TIME TO BE SERIOUS

In the sixth week it is apparent that Lafleur has doubts about making it
to the second primary. He veers away from intricate parables and makes
a direct attack on Police Jury. He asks for the compassion of his public to
give him a chance in the second primary (first, he needs to deny Police
Jury a majority in the first primary).

> The matter has become serious. . . . Every candidate who is running [says
> he] will be in the second race. . . . I'm the only one who is not sure of being
> in the second race. So vote for me the first time, and then you can always vote
> for your friend in the second race.

The metonym of black-top is carried over into a simple metaphoric
and metonymic analogy with Lafleur's expertise in retreading tires.

> Every time a man asks me my opinion about this matter [retreading] I tell
> him the same thing. *If you have a new tire . . . that has given you good
> service, it's worth retreading.* But if you have a new tire that has not given
> you service, you're just going to waste your money with a retread.
> The Police Jury you have in office at this time, *you put him in new* four
> years ago; *he's not given you service.* You got nothing from him. *It does not
> pay to retread*, my friends. . . . He will think that you have re-elected him
> because he has done a good job. But he'll only give you the same old thing.

Victory or defeat, Lafleur invites his listeners to an election-eve
party in two restaurants operated by members of his organizing committee. In a statement that casts more doubt on his own confidence in
winning, he warns his listeners to "bring a handkerchief, for in case of a
defeat everyone must have a handkerchief so that we can cry together."
The latter is a metonymic reference to the Cajun *gumbo des babins*
("loser's" gumbo), the election-evening party of Cajun Prairie's
political losers who meet with their supporters to commiserate with
gumbo and whiskey. The fact that Lafleur now sees himself as a *babin* is
crystal clear in the seventh speech, which did more to damage his own
reputation than to defeat Police Jury.

WEEK 7: RHETORIC WITHOUT RULES?

Candidates can say virtually anything during the last week of elec-
tioneering, but in the small world of Cajun Prairie, it is to the candidate's advantage to keep good relations with his opponents after the
election. There are too many cross-cutting relationships to encourage

clude Police Jury as a legitimate member of the local political arena (he is cast as an enemy of insiders, whose interests could only be defended by Lafleur were he to be elected). There could have been a post-election price for this transgression; Aucoin, a highly respected man and perhaps one of the most honest members of the police jury, found the attack to be beyond the realm of political licence. However, there was nothing in Lafleur's rhetorical *style* that would have prevented him from speaking out again in the next election. He would have had to choose a weaker opponent and a better issue. In fact, a year later, Lafleur, as an advocate rather than as a candidate, delivered another series of radio and public speeches that favoured the most powerful municipal political faction, the faction that was seeking public money to purchase the doctors' hospital. But this raises the questions of whether Lafleur was seeking public affirmation and a possible victory, and of whether he had a good chance of winning Police Jury's job. The 1975 primary was Lafleur's third unsuccessful attempt to be elected and he may have already achieved the reputation of a loser who puts on a good performance at election time—a perennial candidate.

Election victories in Cajun Prairie depend largely on a candidate's "ticket," the alliance of candidates and their monied backers. (The election itself is only the culmination of the political process.) In this respect, Aucoin was fortunate in having the support of a state senatorial candidate who is a native son of Cajun Prairie, whereas his opponents, who had the support of the doctors' faction, were backing an out-of-town political friend who was unable to carry as many Cajun Prairie voters as the native son. Guidry, a third candidate in the first primary, also had considerable support. Both Lafleur and Guidry are Baptists in a staunchly Catholic community; however, it is uncertain what influence this fact had on voting behaviour.[15] More important is that the Cajun public recognizes that elections can have formal winners and moral victors, the latter excelling in electoral performance without ever taking office. The moral victor is the kind of candidate who can 'float' his rhetoric at the beginning of the race and then ground it in a controlled manner to score his points and make his parables. The elegance of this operation is what makes a good politician—whether or not he actually wins. The timing and content of Lafleur's rhetoric have been shown to be unsuccessful both in winning a moral victory and in getting himself elected.

Thus it would be an error to depict the political arena solely in terms of power politics. As I have insisted at the outset of this paper, Cajun elections are games that involve the entire adult community as players. As total phenomena, they keep the candidates occupied with a game that they can play in their own cultural idiom. The public use of French, and the extraordinary allocation of time and resources by candidates who have little chance of winning, are no different, qualitatively, from the cycle of elaborate suppers and festive events that are part of the lives of most families in Cajun Prairie.[16] It is not coincidental that the most active and most boisterous part of the joint local and national campaign is the local contest—carried out in Cajun French. Regional interests are protected through local control of parish politics, and local candidates can be elected on the coat-tails of persons seeking higher stakes in Baton Rouge and in Washington.

This is not politics with a dialectic of party ideologies. Local politicians in the Prairies are expected to make use of the symbols of their "Cajun-ness" and of the metaphors that express, however indirectly, their unity against outsiders. This is a regional limit of an ethnic boundary that includes even the *gros chiens* as fellow Cajuns.[17]

The mediators of this boundary and those who benefit explicitly by its existence are bilingual merchants, tradesmen and farmers between thirty and fifty years of age, men like Lurlin Lafleur and Ronald Aucoin who have chosen to make their living in Cajun Prairie. For them, French is the more restricted idiom of two possible behavioural "codes" (Cajun and American), both of which are situationally deployed. In this restricted economic and political realm, cultural idioms are essential in dealing with networks of kith, kin and clients. Whereas the same bilinguals may open festivals (such as Mardi Gras) and dances to outsiders, the election is a closed affair, carried out best in Cajun French and within the boundaries of the group. The voter, in his commitment to listen, and to give or deny approbation, is implicitly also defending his own group boundaries. Locals, in this context, speak for outsiders, mediating their message and translating it into the acceptable language of the Cajun political arena. Essential to this mediation, and to the political game that locals cherish, is a highly developed politics of speaking.

Notes

1. Only a small percentage of those over forty have more than a few years of primary school education, and those over fifty are frequently illiterate. At the time of writing, a weekly English-language newspaper provided basic news coverage. Some by-lines and an occasional article are printed in French.

2. Place names and the names of local-level politicians are pseudonyms. This phase of research in Cajun Prairie was carried out with a grant from the

162   *Gerald L. Gold*

Wenner-Gren Foundation for Anthropological Research. Subsequent research (1976–77), including a survey of 200 households, was sponsored by the Canada Council. For their helpful comments, my thanks to Paul Leventhal, Lili-Vaillancourt Larouche, Robert Paine, Eric Waddell, Barry Ancelet, my colleagues at York University, the participants of the ISER colloquium held at St. John's, and the politicians and voters of Cajun Prairie who read the first draft of this paper.

3. At least until the Second World War, there were few important status differences between most property owners (*le bourgeois*) and those who worked shares (*travail à la part*). Mechanization and conversion to rice production brought about a concentration of holdings and an imbalance in economic power within, what was, an egalitarian society.

4. Politicians will use Cajun French in their speeches even if they cannot speak it well, or even if they have to have their mother or a radio announcer speak for them. Cultural appeals, such as one man's call for a *coup de main* (co-operative labour), attempt to recreate family intimacy of the old days.

5. Governed by the state constitution of 1898, these laws reversed an anti-Jim Crow tendency in Louisiana (Woodward 1960: 42) and were designed explicitly to limit the effective participation of blacks in post-reconstruction politics.

6. The police juror can legally grade any private lands that are included in the public drainage areas. In practice, resources are limited and deployed at the discretion of the office-holder.

7. These are small cards with the photograph, brief campaign message and voting-machine numbers of a candidate. Some merchants arrange the stacks of cards in a way so as to represent their "ticket" near their cash registers, but most distribute all cards, fearful of losing clients.

8. The practice has been for a candidate's "lieutenants" to conclude the bargain before election day, when the voter gives a slip of paper to the condidate's poll commissioner to indicate that he has honoured his debt. A substantial proportion of voters over forty-five are registered as illiterate.

9. I realize that metaphor and metonym are not always distinct from one another. In this context, metonym is used for a direct transfer of meaning, and metaphor is reserved for more disguised and subtle comparisons.

10. I was told that the *gros chien* backers did this so as to ensure that the incumbent, Aucoin, would not win a majority in the first primary, or perhaps it was to minimize the risk in picking a winner for the second primary.

11. The early fifties saw the last large movement out of sharecropping and into the town of Cajun Prairie.

12. See note 10. Lafleur may be alluding to a possible 'front man' who could split the vote in the first primary.

13. A stew of beef tripe that is usually cooked by men at large suppers.

14. My thanks to Rex Clark, who brought this point to my attention.

15. About 10 percent of Cajun Prairie is Baptist and non-Catholic. Although Baptists frequently form separate social networks from Catholics,

there are many exceptions (including Lafleur). Religion has never been an explicit political issue.

16. Preliminary analysis of household data indicates the existence of a distinctive Cajun lifestyle that corresponds with high French language use.

17. The bilingual group and the situational aspect of ethnic boundaries is the subject of a separate research report by Paul Leventhal.

9

Campaign Rhetoric in Bermuda: The Politics of Race and Religion

FRANK E. MANNING

In Bermuda, a circum-Caribbean British colony of 60,000 persons, politics is of consummate interest. The movement for decolonization and democratic reform developed later than in other imperial appendages, but has proceeded rapidly in the past decade, generating an intense sense of expectancy. The basis of political concern and action is race, tangibly represented in the primordial, persistent division between the three-fifths of the population who are black and the remainder who are white. Nowhere in the Caribbean does race hold a more paramount and fundamental importance than it does in Bermuda.[1]

This essay examines the campaign rhetoric of black Bermudians, in particular its conceptual relationship to their symbolic structure and ideology, its role in defining their cultural and political opposition to whites, and its practical effectiveness in winning intellectual agreement and electoral support. I begin with an account of the political background, move to an ethnography of campaign rhetoric, and conclude with a discussion of the cultural order in which rhetorical symbols convey meaning and instigate action.

Patronage, Partnership and Party Politics

Among its claims to uniqueness, Bermuda boasts the oldest Parliament in the British Commonwealth overseas, an assembly that has met since 1620. Yet for nearly three and a half centuries the actual form of government was one of oligarchy rather than democracy. Franchise rights were restricted to landholders, who voted in as many parishes as they owned property. Elections were spread out over three days, enabling the voters to travel between polling stations at a leisurely pace.

The architects and beneficiaries of this system were the landed gentry, an aristocracy of white families descended from the original seventeenth-century English settlers, and known colloquially for the past few generations as either "Front Street" (their commercial address) or "the Forty Thieves" (their acquisitive style). Seafarers until the 1870s, agricultural import-export agents from then until the 1920s, and now an interlocking establishment of merchants, bankers and corporate lawyers, the aristocracy have symbolized their position through the instruments of patronage: jobs, loans, credit, 'recallable' mortgages, charitable donations. Grateful clients have usually found them paternal and benevolent, whereas opponents have been economically destroyed and socially ostracized by them.

Blacks delivered their first challenge to this system through the Political Associations, parochial organizations of landholders, initially formed in the late nineteenth century. Their modest aim was to win one of the four parish seats in the House of Assembly—an objective gradually met in heavily black parishes, but only through the selection of candidates deemed acceptable to the aristocracy. The group of successful tradesmen, small shopkeepers and rising professionals, introduced to politics through the associations, were thus made fully aware of their client role, as well as of the fragility of their economic and political positions.

Aided by Bermuda's first labour union, the black movement accelerated on all fronts after World War II. Increased pressure for the removal of archaic voting restrictions in the early 1960s resulted in a temporary compromise that extended the vote to all adults but raised the minimum age from 21 to 25. In addition, property owners were compensated with an extra or 'plus' vote. The new political potential of blacks inspired the formation of the Progressive Labour party (PLP) three months before the general election in 1963. Despite the absence of a designated leader, the party elected six of its nine candidates, and won seats from both white aristocrats and conservative blacks who were sponsored by the Political Associations. With the plus vote scheduled to be phased out and the voting age returned to 21 in that session of Parliament, the fall of the *ancien régime* seemed a foregone conclusion.

What happened instead established the unique character of contemporary Bermudian politics. The aristocracy regained the offensive in 1964 by forming a coalition party with the growing white middle class and an influential segment of conservative, upwardly mobile blacks. Named the United Bermuda party (UBP), the coalition had an economic rationale. The rapid expansion of tourism since World War II, and the phenomenal growth of the international finance sector after 1960, had produced an economy that the aristocracy continued to dominate but no longer monopolized. The UBP was a pragmatic alliance of Bermuda's old and new money interests, brought together by their common stake in a buoyant but extremely fragile economy, and by their perception of a threat to that economy. The threat came from a party that favoured organized labour and that was susceptible to influences from both the black American movement, then in its most radical phase, and the West Indian drive for national independence. Terrified by the spectre of economic catastrophe, the UBP subdued racial and class divisions in a way that appeared, on the surface, to transcend the structural compartmentalization of Bermudian society.

Legislatively, the UBP co-opted the PLP's democratic reform proposals, leading the push for desegregation, free secondary education, and full and equal adult suffrage. On more controversial matters, it modified the PLP's positions, but nonetheless gradually implemented government-financed social services, and made a formal commitment to the Bermudianization of the work force. The strategy was aimed both at winning the marginal black vote and at the more subtle, but crucial, objective of forcing the PLP into a leftist position that would dramatize its radicalism and thereby enhance the solidarity of the UBP. The strategy worked. A serious split emerged early in the PLP's history between professionals and labour-union representatives, a rift in which labour gained the upper hand through its covert financial support of the party and commensurate influence. In the mid-sixties five of the six members of the parliamentary caucus either left or were expelled from the party, three to form a short-lived splinter party and two to come back with scars that never really healed. Other professionals—physicians, dentists, lawyers, teachers—also bolted from the party, in some cases joining the UBP and in others simply quitting politics.

A drift towards ideological radicalism developed later in the decade, primarily through the influence of an intellectual fringe that formulated a loose synthesis of American black power and concepts of revolutionary socialism imported from Africa and the Caribbean. Besides further alienating conservative professionals, this stance also disturbed the PLP's core of working-class supporters, whose political goals are immediate and mundane, and whose dream of advancement centres more on capitalist competition than socialist equality (Manning 1973: 87–147). The party's most enthusiastic constituency became the black street-gangs and para-military youth groups, whose brief florescence in the late sixties and early seventies contributed to two race riots and a spate of killings, including the assassinations of the governor and the police commissioner.

The polarity between the parties at this time can be summarized by their dominant personalities: Lois Browne of the PLP and Sir Henry Tucker of the UBP. Born in 1927 in East Pembroke, Bermuda's poorest and most heavily black area (Bermuda 1966), Lois Browne earned a law degree in England and returned to become Bermuda's first female barrister. She took an active role in the universal-suffrage movement and ran successfully on the PLP's first slate of candidates, topping the poll over two long-term incumbents: a white aristocrat, and a black supported by the parish Political Association. Of the original PLP parliamentary caucus, she alone remained loyal throughout the dissension period of the middle sixties. Re-elected three times, each time with increasing popular support, she served as opposition leader from 1968 to 1972, and again since 1976. Besides her involvement in the party, she has

Mrs. Lois Browne, Parliamentary Leader
of Bermuda's Progressive Labour Party
(Courtesy of Frank E. Manning)

become Bermuda's foremost defense lawyer—a role that keeps her in the public eye and endears her to blacks under 30, the group most frequently on trial for crimes against person and property (Bermuda 1974).

By contrast, Sir Henry "Jack" Tucker is an aristocrat of celebrated ancestry, Bermuda's foremost banker, a director of a dozen prominent local companies, and an extensive landholder. Born in 1903, he was first elected to the House of Assembly in the 1930s from Paget, Bermuda's wealthiest parish and his own home district. He pioneered the development of Bermuda as a tax haven, an achievement for which he was rewarded by being given about seventy-five directorships of international companies operating from Bermuda. He was the chief architect and initial leader of the UBP, persuading twenty-three of his twenty-nine independent parliamentary colleagues to join the party at its formation. He fully understood the patronage system and realized that the cohesion of the UBP required the wide distribution of not only cabinet posts and other political appointments, but also club memberships, company directorships and investment opportunities previously restricted to the traditional elite. He had the authority and economic leverage to procure this largesse from the business establishment, and the political sagacity to dispense it effectively. His dominance of the UBP is suggested by the party's unofficial name: "The House That Jack Built."

The irony of this contrast between the parties and their axial figures is that the UBP emerged as the more moral and humane group. Of course, this resulted in part from the UBP's greater influence over the media. But it also resulted from the skilful exploitation of their chief slogan and symbol: the "partnership" of the races, represented by a handshake in black and white and portrayed rhetorically as the harbinger of a new social order, which would replace segregation with integration, bigotry with tolerance, animosity with respect and trust. Conversely, the PLP was not only mono-racial in composition but increasingly race-oriented in its explicit ideology—an image that made it the scapegoat for the perpetuation of racial division. The commission of inquiry investigating the 1968 riot—which occurred only three weeks before the general election—observed that the UBP was seen as urging "fraternization for the colony's good." On the other hand, the PLP, through its black nationalism, was viewed as representing a "denunciation of the colony's status" (Wooding 1969: 69).

Given the commitment of many blacks to integration and to liberal social reforms of the type that the UBP had partially accepted, the outcome of the 1968 election was inevitable. The PLP polled only a third of the popular vote, winning ten of the forty seats in an expanded House of Assembly. The remaining thirty seats were won by UBP candidates, seven of whom were black. Bermuda thus became the only country in the Antilles with a black majority to return a predominantly white government in its first election under full and equal adult suffrage (Allen 1973: 122).

Four years later, in the election of 1972, that phenomenon was repeated with an identical distribution of parliamentary seats. The UBP now included nine blacks among its successful candidates. Surveys indicate that the UBP gained unanimous white support and more than a fifth of the black vote (Manning 1978: 36). On a constituency basis, the UBP won districts with voting populations as high as three-quarters black; no district less than four-fifths black returned a PLP candidate.

Coupled with the UBP's second landslide victory was the retirement of Sir Henry Tucker. To succeed him as premier, the party chose Bermuda's first black knight, a Guyanese-born lawyer. To inherit Tucker's constituency, a district more than nine-tenths white and the UBP's safest seat, it chose Bermuda's most successful black businessman. The racial partnership was again displayed.

Pre-empted and despondent, the PLP retreated from combat to reassess their position. A few party veterans quietly disengaged from politics to devote more attention to occupational careers. Others who remained active changed their views, generally concluding that racial militancy and revolutionary socialism were, after all, unsuitable for Bermuda. Concurrently, a group of culturally bourgeois professionals, mainly teachers, took enough interest in the party to seek seats on the policy-making central committee, and small businessmen became active at the parish level, grooming themselves as future candidates. Rapport was built with socially respectable black organizations, notably the churches and particularly the African Methodist Episcopal (AME) Church, the largest and most influential black denomination. Public relations were taken over by media and advertising specialists, who cultivated an image aimed at the black middle and upper classes.

The diminution of a militant black threat undercut the brokerage value of UBP blacks to their white colleagues, especially with regard to elevating a black to the party leadership. The blacks reacted by forming the Black Caucus, a pressure group that agitated for better educational and job-training programmes, financial assistance for aspiring black businessmen, and a moratorium on the granting of status (citizenship) to expatriates—positions long taken by the PLP. A report prepared in 1975, and leaked to the press five weeks before the 1976 election, rationalized these demands by solemnly cautioning UBP whites about the black public's militant unrest and growing support for the PLP. The solution, urged the report, was for UBP blacks to be seen receiving greater recognition and assurances of "meaningful participation" in the councils of power. Failure to heed the warning, and in particular, to integrate blacks into the upper echelons of the economy would result in a socialist upheaval of the type seen in Jamaica (Black Caucus, n.d.).

This brief synopsis highlights the interplay of race, patronage and ideology—the primary socio-cultural, economic and symbolic elements of Bermudian politics—within the organizational parameters of the party system. The party era began with UBP solidly united against the racial and ideological threat of the PLP, and it was therefore willing to assume a centrist position and to bestow patronage on its black supporters. In the short term, the PLP was goaded to move to the radical left, allowing the UBP to win two resounding electoral victories. In the long term, however, the PLP was enfeebled to the extent that the UBP's *raison d'être* was clouded. As the PLP rebuilt along more moderate and bourgeois lines, UBP blacks saw their bargaining position substantially diminished. They reacted by agitating for greater patronage, exposing the racial tensions in a party that had been presented for a decade as an exemplary "partnership."

These circumstances gave the PLP an unprecedented opportunity for electoral gains in 1976. But to realize such gains it needed at once to ridicule the UBP's exposed racism, to reduce its own vulnerability to charges of racism, and to coalesce a precarious constituency of working-class blacks, the traditional core of supporters, and the black bourgeoisie, who had gradually and timidly begun to return its support. The instrument for that task was political rhetoric.

The Rhetoric of Revivalism

The importance of speech behaviour in Afro-American and Afro-Caribbean societies has long impressed sensitive observers. Talk and "talk about talk" are major foci of cultural concern, as reflected in elaborate taxonomies of speech idioms (Kochman 1970: 145–62; Abrahams and Bauman 1971). Verbal abilities are highly esteemed and confer power and prestige on those who ably demonstrate them: preachers, politicians, comedians, broadcasters, entertainers of every description, and the "men of words" who hold sway in the male peer-group.

The stress on performance is perhaps the most striking quality of oral communication among blacks. Formal verbal presentations are clearly histrionic, and even ordinary conversations are easily and frequently raised to a high level of showmanship. Kochman (*loc. cit.*) concludes that black speech is generally expressive or expressive-directive; it is not simply a means of reporting information. Speech content is important, of course, but it is only one component of meaning. The form of speech is both meaningful in itself and affects the interpretation of what is actually said. The context of performance, form and content together establish a sense of dynamic rapport between speaker and audience, the foremost criterion by which speech events are evaluated within the culture.

PLP campaign rallies are popular speech events. In the three weeks of the 1976 parliamentary campaign, the party held nine rallies, as well as a victory meeting a few days after the election. Attendance averaged about three hundred persons, the capacity of most school and workmen's-club auditoriums. Just as at church services, there were usually another fifty persons milling around outside the building, listening through doors and windows, and occasionally venturing inside. By contrast, the UBP held only three rallies during the same period, two of which drew fewer than a hundred persons.

Like political and para-political movements throughout the Caribbean, the PLP has characteristically embellished its rhetoric with millenarian imagery. In the 1968 and 1972 campaigns, revolutionary socialism and Black Power were envisioned as the basis of a new order that would overturn a capitalist, colonial and racist system. The prevailing sentiment was not only secular, but rather explicitly anti-religious. Religion was depicted in Marxist terms, as an opiate against oppression, and therefore a deterrent to necessary militancy. The black churches were often attacked for failing to enlist in the political struggle and for becoming instruments of the patronage system. A few prominent party figures proclaimed themselves atheists, and in general, party activists shunned involvement in church groups.

In 1976, however, the vocabulary of secular radicalism was replaced by one of religion. The PLP maintained its ideological commitment to the planks it had supported for a decade: national independence, voting reforms, progressive taxation, Bermudianization of the work force, expanded social services, and so on. But it related these issues rhetorically to an apocalypse constructed from religious symbolism. The organizing metaphor likened the campaign to a crusade against social immorality, waged by a people whom God had chosen to remake and inherit Bermuda. Party leader Lois Browne, who spoke at seven of the nine meetings, typically used the metaphor as follows: "God doesn't mean for oppression to win. So ultimately we will win. We must rededicate ourselves to the task. We have faith, strength. Even if we don't win, we're going to go on. It's inevitable. We know we're going up and the others are coming down. We will claim the victory in 1980, or 1984, or whenever. It is God's work to so take us there. . . . The party wants to build idealism and restore it to our lives and politics. Our members are quality people. They are made in the image of God, and will represent you."

Biblical imagery, especially from the Old Testament, was extensively tapped. One candidate said that the campaign reminded him of "Climbing Jacob's Ladder," a familiar hymn about the mystical ladder that linked heaven and earth and represented the promise of redemption. "Like the people in the song," he said, "we are going higher, higher, higher." Another candidate used the Biblical dream archetype, relating his vision of the marginal parishes falling successively to the PLP: "I see Sandys. I see Warwick. I see Hamilton. And I see St. George. And the ugly head of the UBP is put down forever." As he called the names of the parishes there was a gathering crescendo of excitement and interpolation in the crowd. When he reached St. George, the critical twenty-first seat, one supporter yelled: "Go down, Moses. He's leading us to victory."

With the partisan opposition defined on moral terms, UBP blacks could be denounced as sinners rather than as "Uncle Toms," their more traditional stereotype. "They [UPB blacks] are clasping the hand that gives them money," charged Lois Browne at the opening campaign rally, "and I think God is going to strike them dead." At the post-election victory meeting, she used a converse religious image to congratulate the PLP's committed followers: "You have to be really baptized to be in the PLP. We don't have any lollipops to give away."

The form and style of performance at the rallies were based on the revivalist prototype. Rallies were opened with prayers and closed with benedictions and the singing of religio-political hymns, such as "We Shall Overcome." A well-known gospel singer was recruited as a candidate and called upon several times to render "Oh, Freedom," "Sometimes I Feel Like a Motherless Child," and other favourites. Her appearances usually came after the prayers and opening remarks but before the main speeches, the same place given to solo-singing in Pentecostal services.

A new and successful candidate borrowed a hallmark of preaching by keynoting his speech with a Biblical text: "Unless the Lord build a house, they labour in vain who build it." His theme was that the PLP's political philosophy carried out God's plan. By contrast, the UBP's efforts reflected materialism and man-made objectives.

As in black revivalism (cf. Manning 1977), entertainment and evangelism were frequently brought together, introducing an element of fun and consciously calling attention to virtuosity in oral performance. The obvious analogy between collections at rallies and offerings in church allowed Lois Browne to invoke the central metaphor of the campaign as a religious movement, and to comment humorously on the black custom of raising money for religion: "It's part of our heritage, our culture, to pass the bucket. At the Church of God [Bermuda's largest Pentecostal assembly], they say that one-tenth of what you have belongs to God. So give it to us now. We are his agents" [laughter].

Aside from the regular collections, there were calls for pledges at the first two meetings of the campaign, each of which raised about three thousand dollars. Lois Browne comically compared the pledging decision to the salvation experience: "You know, you wriggle around in your seat and you hope that you have another hoot before you get saved. And you sit there and you don't go up for prayer. I have a feeling that there's someone out there tonight who's going through that feeling. You want to make that pledge. But you just can't get the courage. Yes now. The woman out there has finally got the courage. Stand up."

The decision to pledge was likened to conversion, and the form of pledging to 'testimony': the admission, during church services, of personal religious experiences. The layman's opportunity to preach, testimony is often an entertaining and somewhat competitive exchange with the pastor. The political counterpart had similar characteristics:

PLEDGE DONOR [after making his own pledge and praising the PLP]: I'm going to pledge ten dollars from my father. And if you don't get it from him, I'll get it from him [laughter].

LOIS BROWNE [speaking first to recording secretary]: Ten dollars from _____, from his son. I'm going to leave it just like that, so I'll know what it is. And if I don't get it from him, I'm going to come looking for you [laughter]. Anybody else want to pledge for their fathers? You can pledge for your mothers, too [laughter].

After several other pledges were made in the same manner, Lois Browne noticed a young woman with a tape recorder: "Oh, you're taping it all down. I'm going to have to do something on the Flip Wilson show.[2] I know I missed my calling. I should have been an entertainer."

Audiences participated more spontaneously by interjecting speeches with shouts of agreement and encouragement, the form of response typically evoked by inspired preaching in revival services. The pattern evolved into a highly stylized choral dialogue at one early meeting, when deputy leader Frederick Wade introduced the campaign slogan: "Time for a Change. Send Jack a Message. Vote PLP." He urged the crowd to repeat the slogan, and soon had them chanting loudly and in unison. Continuing his speech, he used the slogan again after each major point: "Under the Westminster Model, it's either all power or no power. And that's why it's time for a change, send Jack a message, vote PLP. The UBP stay in power because of gerrymandered districts. There should be one member per district, and all districts should be equal in population. That's why it's time for a change, send Jack a message, vote PLP."

As the speech unfolded, it illustrated the familiar form of black oral expression, which Keil describes as "constant repetition coupled with small but striking deviations" (1966: 97). The speaker introduced a litany of grievances and proposals, each affirmed by the rhythmic refrain of the campaign slogan. At the end of the speech, the slogan was again chanted in cadence by the audience, with pauses for individuals to insert their own petitions. One woman followed "Time for a Change" with the comment, " 'Cause I'm tired of working. I want a pension."

PLP candidates made a concerted effort to associate themselves with religious ritual, the prototype of the rallies. As a group, they attended one or more churches every Sunday throughout the campaign—a rhetoric of action to support their verbal rhetoric. Speeches frequently made use of the black trope that Abrahams (1970: 164) calls the "intrusive I"—the intrusion of first-person pronouns into narrative in order to relate speaker to subject. Recalling her childhood exposure to religion, Lois Browne commented at one rally: "My dear grandmother brought me up in the Christian church. She sent me to two and sometimes three churches—St. Augustine's [Anglican], the Salvation Army, and the Holy Rollers [Pentecostal]—to make sure that I didn't become a heathen or an athiest."

The cultural, as well as chronological, climax of the campaign was the final rally on election eve, held outdoors at a racetrack before an estimated two thousand people. The adult choirs of the largest African Methodist Episcopal, and Pentecostal, assemblies appeared in their robes and mortarboards, introducing the program with a medley of gospel music. The starring role, however, was given to three black pastors. The candidates (aside from Lois Browne, who spoke briefly) merely sat on the stage and acknowledged introductions, much like invited dignitaries at special church programs.

The first pastor to speak was known for his friendship with the UBP and aversion to the PLP. He explained his presence as the audience suppressed laughter: "Mr. _____ [the rally organizer and a key party strategist] called me and said, 'You know, sometimes we tend to forget there's a God. We'd like you to come and remind us, and lead us in prayer.' As a minister of this parish and a member of the community, I could not say no." He then opened the meeting with a brief prayer, and left quickly for home on the grounds that he was coming down with the flu.

His two colleagues, both known as PLP sympathizers but previously inactive politically, offered no such apologies or explanations for their presence. They not only led the audience in prayer, but went on to attack the government with all the flamboyance and drama of hell-fire preaching. One of them, a Pentecostal, who had recently had the mortgage on his church revoked, began by joking about the racetrack setting. He then observed:

> Some horses are black, and some are white. It's the horses that endure to the end who will win. I have been praying and fasting that God will have his way in this election, and not a certain group of people. It's time God ruled this island. We know God uses men to do his work. It seems God is unsatisfied with the job that some folk have been doing. Tomorrow he might be satisfied to have the results a little different.

Later he debunked the partnership symbol:

> We've been hearing a lot lately about some kind of partnership. For so many years we never had this partnership. It's true we can look at our TV screens and see blacks shaking hands with whites. I'm not against it. God knows I'm not against it. But I like the real thing.

The Family

The PLP's symbolic alternative to the UBP's partnership became the family. Without abandoning the issues it traditionally preached, the PLP related them to their central theme: the strengthening of the family. In the platform, for example, the family was mentioned eight times. The following planks are representative:

> We view the steady deterioration of family life with alarm, and undertake to institute social and economic measures designed to strengthen the family unit, and particularly as it is affected by unemployment.
> Every form of encouragement and support will be given to persons engaged in various forms of agricultural production. . . . Home gardening encourages the strengthening of family units.
> A restructured, comprehensive social insurance programme will be

instituted. Additional resources will be directed towards the strengthening of family life.

Regulations will be instituted to ensure that TV and other forms of mass media are used to build and strengthen rather than destroy family life.

In order to cater to the full development of family life, there must be available a proper layout of roads and houses along with adequate provisions for cultural and recreational facilities to occupy leisure hours [PLP 1976].

Whereas the platform refers to the ideal type of family unit prescribed by the churches, the rhetoric of rallies often spoke to the victim and the sinner. For example, the popularity at rallies of the hymn "Sometimes I Feel Like a Motherless Child" attests to the chronic instability of the black family and the resulting sense of loneliness (Frazier 1964: 15–16). In a speech entitled "Restoring Humanity That Has Been Robbed," a physician, recruited as a new PLP candidate, addressed the subject of illegitimacy, the most stigmatized deviation from the ideal family and the status of about two-fifths of black births. "I don't accept the designation that some children are illegitimate. All children are legitimate because they are conceived in love. They must be loved the way only a mother can." He continued by relating the child's need for maternal care to the chief problem of single mothers: the necessity to work and therefore be away from their children: "One-fifth of a child's education occurs between the ages of four and six. Parents should read and sing to their children, and play with them. Mothers should be with their children, instead of working outside. The PLP will make this possible, because it is dedicated to the restoration of the family unit."

Interestingly, the physician was billed as a "family doctor," emphasizing the difference between himself and the incumbent, a white neurosurgeon. Although it was his first bid for office, he topped the poll over both the neurosurgeon and another long-term UBP incumbent.

The party encouraged the family structure in both words and action. PLP candidates were urged to bring their spouses and children to meetings and to seat them on stage. A determined effort was made by speakers to recognize husbands and wives together in the audience, and to comment on their political and matrimonial unity. A popular bumper sticker read, "Our whole family is voting PLP." When Lois Browne received a pledge from her cousin she commented: "Ten dollars from my cousin. You know, PLP support runs right through my family. I have only one cousin and one auntie in the UBP. I've got some swell cousins. She was on crutches the other day. She was the subject of a hit and run accident. She's still on crutches but she's here tonight and she's pledging. I wish I could reach out and touch you, and feel you." Her brief remarks at the final rally were more serious, coming after the stern admonitions of the preachers. Expounding on the "vital issue" faced by voters, she used the family to summarize the religious character of the campaign and the moral dichotomy between the parties. "It's the question of family life, the quality of life, and what's going to happen to Bermuda. We have taken on this issue as a means of saving Bermuda from degradation and corruption. We have tried to impart the true social meaning and truth of life. There are big gaps between PLP and UBP. It's not just money. It's a question of values, dignity, love, and brother-hood."

The following day, Bermudians gave the PLP 44 percent of the popular vote and fourteen of the forty seats in the House of Assembly— an increase over 1972 of six percentage points and four seats. Survey research (Manning 1978: 29–44) revealed that the gains came almost entirely from the black electorate, notably from those who previously supported the UBP, or who previously failed to vote. To appreciate the role of campaign rhetoric in this impressive shift, we must examine its range of meanings in relation to the symbolic structure of black society.

Salvation, Performance and Issues

Two themes dominate PLP rhetoric. The more explicit is religion, conveyed through three prominent and recurrent symbols: (1) a central metaphor that represents the campaign as a moral and millenarian crusade; (2) a performance orientation that likens the rallies to revival services in form, content and expressive style; (3) the family issue, used to summarize the moral purpose of PLP politics and the essential difference between the parties.

The vitality of revivalist Protestantism in Bermuda is striking. Preachers deliver terrifying sermons on street corners and outside workmen's clubs. Visiting evangelists regularly draw huge crowds to open-air rallies and tent meetings. Pastors roam the hospitals, urging patients to "get saved." Zealous laymen deliver tracts on the street and door-to-door. Local and imported religious broadcasts fill the air time on Sunday, and are also heard throughout the week. Sunday services take up two full pages of newspaper advertisements, and special services are given additional publicity through handbills, press releases and radio announcements. In sum, Bermuda illustrates what Cross (1950) called a "burned over district"—an area scorched by the fire of revivalism.

   The culture and constituency of revivalism in Bermuda are black, thus providing the second theme of PLP campaign rhetoric: racial identity. In previous campaigns, the PLP had ideologically rationalized and aggressively provoked racial confrontation. Race was relatively muted in 1976, but unequivocally if implicitly communicated through the distinctively black performance tropes of revivalism: the call-and-response exchange between speaker and spectators; a generally high level of oral, kinetic and emotional audience participation; histrionics as a means of emphasis and self-mockery; the interplay of entertainment and proselytization; a greater value on spontaneity than planned programming; and a preference for dramatic hyperbole rather than factual precision. Furthermore, in Bermuda the black identity of revivalism is social as well as symbolic; whites worship exclusively in the Catholic and classical Protestant assemblies, leaving the evangelical groups with congregations that are entirely black.

   The use of the revivalist idiom was therefore a way of 'speaking race' on a meta-level while 'speaking religion' on a more literal level. The observations of two native informants are insightful. One, a woman who ran unsuccessfully on the PLP ticket, suggested that the emphasis on religion was a way of building rapport by using a vocabulary that was familiar to and valued by blacks. In effect, the PLP was presenting itself as a party-of-the-people, conversant in an idiom that touches the deepest cultural sensitivities of its audience. The other informant, a male party-worker, commented: "We haven't really solved the race problem in Bermuda; we've simply absorbed it." To paraphrase, race was symbolically internalized by the PLP, protecting the party from charges of racism while retaining the appeal of a black identity.

   The cultural relationship between religion and race is symbolized in the familiar notion of "soul," defined by Hannerz (1970: 16) as an encapsulation of the black "national character." A religious style has become equated with race, and a racial identity has been distilled in a distinctively religious experience. Like the notion of soul, the PLP's family symbol brings together the religious and racial orders of meaning. Explicitly, the family summarized the moral purpose of the campaign. Implicitly, it stood in opposition to the partnership of the races—the UBP's chief symbol and slogan. Although the partnership has an idealistic dimension, its principal rationale—even in UBP rhetoric—is economic; it is claimed that harmonious integration is essential for the stability needed to attract tourists and international companies. By contrast, the family symbol represents a social unit that is 'natural' rather than instrumental. Above all, the family is mono-racial and therefore analogous to the PLP.

The significance of religion and race is further brought to light with reference to two classification schemes that structure the black Bermudian perception of thought and behaviour. The first scheme deals with salvation and sin, moral and metaphysical poles that are represented institutionally in the opposition between the two major arenas of black Bermudian social life, the church and the club (Manning 1973). Although verbalized as absolutes, salvation and sin are in fact linked by a continuum. With reference to adherents of the two major denominations, the rigid asceticism required of a Pentecostal tends to be compromised by an African Methodist, who will drink wine at a dinner party, wear sedate items of jewellery and attend the theatre, but nonetheless stay clear of clubs. Likewise, within clubs there are recognizable differences in lifestyle between those whose chief interests lie in sports and beneficial programs and those whose time is spent mainly at the bar and at entertainment productions.

The second classificatory scheme is a social hierarchy. Its poles are "respectability" and "reputation," opposing value systems discerned by Wilson (1969, 1973) in his seminal model of the symbolic order of Caribbean and circum-Caribbean societies. Respectability predicates stratification in terms of standards inherited from external metropolitan (that is, white) influences: the ideals of monogamous formal marriage, bourgeois sexual morality, the nuclear family, strict child-rearing practices, conformity to law, and the virtues of sobriety, discretion, responsibility, and self-improvement. Reputation, by contrast, is socially egalitarian and premissed on indigenous (that is, black) ideals of behaviour and demeanour: competitive and performance abilities, verbal fluency, sexual prowess and potency, swagger and "prettiness" (flashy clothes, ostentatious jewellery, an air of hedonism and the like).

Both salvation and respectability are overall ideals. Club-goers acknowledge their Christian status as "backsliders," and invariably hope to be "saved" at a later period in their lives (Manning 1973: 72–83). Similarly, the social pull of respectability is the basis of "crab antics," the native (and Wilson's) metaphor for the endless striving for upward mobility. At the same time, the cultural styles associated with sin and reputation are deemed situationally appropriate and valued in their own right. Abrahams and Bauman (1971) demonstrate this point in a discussion of Caribbean diglossia, the linguistic duality between "sense" (standard English, respectability) and "nonsense" (creole dialects, reputation); nonsense speech suffers social denigration, but it is considered fitting for informal occasions and widely admired when skilfully performed.

The two schemes of classification often coincide. Religious norms embody respectability, and much of what is judged sinful is also seen as reputation. Nonetheless, their reference to conceptually distinct (from the native viewpoint) orders of meaning (morality-metaphysics versus social hierarchy) suggests the perpendicular relationship seen in Figure 1. Moreover, the two orders of meaning vary with respect to each other. The salvation-sin opposition moves from the context of cosmology to ethos, corresponding to the progression from reputation to respectabili-

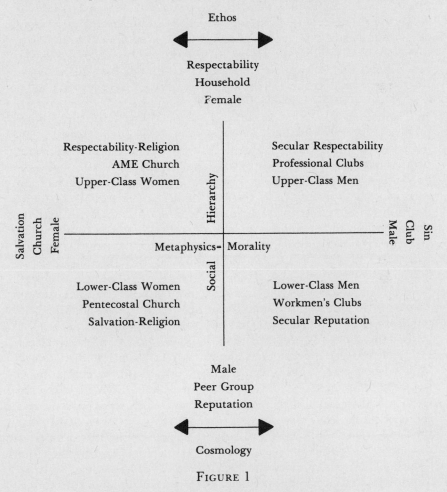

FIGURE 1

*Relationship of the Two Schemes of Classification
of Black Bermudian Thought and Behaviour*

ty. Likewise, the dialectic between reputation and respectability can be played out within either church or club.

Finally, the sin-salvation and reputation-respectability oppositions relate to the division of the sexes. The church constituency is made up mainly of women; the club milieu is primarily the domain of men, both in actual composition and in the emphasis on sport, ritualistic drinking, the machismo complex, and similar male-expressive tropes. Likewise, Wilson (1969) contends that respectability is centred in the household, a setting dominated by women, whereas reputation is symbolized and sustained in the fraternal peer group. Although there are statistical exceptions and other qualifications to this version of the male-female dichotomy, the value opposition between the sexes remains one of the most fundamental socio-cultural features of Bermuda, as well as of other Afro-American and Afro-Caribbean societies (Keil 1966: 18).

To appropriate this symbolic-social structure as a framework of analysis, let us return to the performative context of PLP campaign rhetoric. Like religious revival services, PLP rallies attract what has been termed a "committed audience"[3]—an audience that knows and supports the premises on which the performance is based. Not everyone at a rally is likely to have a previous PLP voting record, just as not everyone at a revival service is likely to be already "saved." But in both cases those present are potential converts, as they are essentially sympathetic with the underlying ideology.

Moreover, PLP rallies are like revival services in that they attract primarily the lower class. Middle- and upper-class blacks, known in Bermuda as "boojees" (bourgeoisie), consider the rallies too crowded, too noisy and emotional, too vulgar—the antithesis of respectability. Aside from candidates, upper-class political activists characteristically remain behind the scenes.

To the rally audience, revivalist rhetoric resonates with the symbols of salvation through religious metaphors and with the symbols of reputation through racial-cultural style. The former set of meanings appeals particularly to women, the latter to men. Data that seem to corroborate this proposition come from post-election survey research showing that increased voting support for the PLP corresponded with increased agreement with party principles among black women, but that among black men there was increased voting support without such a shift of agreement (Manning 1978: 52–59). The female political response is compatible with the salvation experience, which has moral and doctrinal aspects. Alternately, the male response reflects a feature of reputation: the notion that politics is similar to sport and that one should therefore "compete" for one's "team"—a commitment based more on racial identity than on moral or intellectual agreement (Manning 1973: 115-45).

Besides their immediate audience, the rallies reached the general public—a secondary and mostly uncommitted audience—through press and broadcast media coverage. But as religious metaphors and performative styles are not deemed newsworthy, reporting dealt instead with issues. Here PLP politicians served their cause by what they avoided saying as much as by what they said. What they avoided were the major economic and constitutional issues—foreign ownership, national independence, voting rights, labour relations—that have traditionally been the focus of partisan controversy and that, as my surveys show clearly, polarize UBP blacks from their PLP counterparts (Manning 1978: 93-146). What they stressed instead were moral issues related to nuclear family well-being, issues which not only evoke strong agreement among blacks across party lines (*ibid.*: 147-71), but which also symbolize the values of conservative religion and of respectability. As Wilson observes: "The mores advocated by the church, including especially monogamous marriage, are the ultimate reference for respectability. From this follows the emphasis on the nuclear family household as the ideal, not so much from the angle of composition as from the point of view that such a family is the indivisible unit of society" (1973: 100).

Consistent with this analytic orientation, post-election sampling indicates that most of the PLP's electoral gains came from blacks who previously supported the UBP or who previously failed, although eligible, to exercise their franchise (Manning 1978: 38-40). Furthermore, a dramatic shift of ideological agreement was seen among black women, notably in the upper class (*ibid.*: 80-92). In short, what was communicated to the immediate audience in terms of salvation and reputation was paralleled by what was communicated to the secondary audience in terms of a generalized sense of respectability.

Aside from comparisons and generalizations about the relationship of religion and politics (a relationship that has become increasingly manifest in the contemporary world scene), this essay demonstrates a multi-disciplinary analysis of political speech: the exposition of rhetorical content, form and performative style draws from literary and folkloric techniques; the examination of symbolic classification and conceptual domains illustrates the method of Durkheimian social anthropology; and the inquiry into voting patterns and public attitudes utilizes skills developed in sociology and political science. The integration of these perspectives and approaches is essential if we are to come to terms with not only what rhetoric *means*, but also with what it *does* in the arena of mass political action.

Notes

1. Research reported in this paper was done from February to August 1976, although earlier (1968–70) fieldwork shaped my general thinking about Bermuda and furnished important background material. I am grateful to Robert Paine, who helped to relate my interests in symbolism to the field of rhetoric. The Institute of Social and Economic Research of Memorial University gave financial support for the 1976 research.

2. The reference to Flip Wilson, a well-known black American TV comedian, is appropriate in that he has developed a popular routine around the caricature of black revivalist services.

3. This phrase has been used by Keil (1966) in his analysis of black audiences at urban blues performances, and more recently by Newton (1979) in her discussion of homosexual audiences at performances of female impersonators.

Conclusion

10

The Political Uses of Metaphor and Metonym: An Exploratory Statement

ROBERT PAINE

> Men must be contented to be guided by a kind of taste or fancy, arising from analogy, and a comparison of similar things.
>
> Hume, *A Treatise of Human Nature* (Bk. III, Pt. II)

I

The place of analogic construction in Western thought is manifest in religion, literature and science: the fall of man (Genesis), the redemption of man (Bunyan), the concept of gravity (Newton), and so on; it has also inspired some of the most significant work in anthropology in recent years.[1] Our concern with the matter is limited to this question: what place does analogic construction have in political strategy?

The speeches reported in this book are laden with analogic constructions of various kinds, and it is surely noticeable how well they fit both the basic strategy of political rhetoric, which is to induce the appropriate context from which will flow the behaviour that the politician seeks from his audience, and the basic rhetorical technique of this strategy: the enthymemic form of argument (see Chapter 2). But saying that much leaves us with a general thesis only; we now need to consider the role of analogy in political speech as a variable responsive to context.

For example, one too easily slips into supposing that analogic thought is thought about change; there is another common slip too: that analogic thought is (only) metaphoric. These things happen to be true of the historic instances cited above, but looking at the way status relations between men are expressed, for example, it is not difficult to find analogies both supportive of the *status quo* and metonymic in structure. Consider "the employer is to his workers as a father is to his children" (Tambiah 1973: 211–12): notions of loving care and respect are evoked and combined, and transferred analogically—analogy in the service of extending meaning—from the domain of family life to that of work and employment. Or consider "what was good enough for me, is good enough for my son" (father:past :: son:future) as a common piece of rhetoric in England of earlier decades.

Perhaps the two principal tropes of analogic expression, metaphor and metonym, have characteristic 'missions'[2] with respect to change and stability?

The case of the metaphor is quite clear and has been given considerable attention recently (in particular by Brown 1976; Fernandez 1974; Lasky 1976; and Sapir and Crocker 1977). It is the trope of the development and extension of thought; metaphor breaks old boundaries. At the same time, metaphor is widely recognized as evoking *similarity*. Helpful in the necessary reconciliation of similarity with openness is Burke's presentation of metaphor not as similarity as much as "perspective" calling simultaneously upon two domains of experience (1959: 308; 1969b: 503). We can expect, then, metaphoric similarity to be staged by devices of purposive contrast, and often it is an unexpected similarity that is evoked. This leads directly to the elusive as well as allusive (like enthymeme) quality of metaphor's similarity; it resembles similarity, it is partial similarity, it is inaccurate similarity—but not similarity itself.

Such incompleteness, again, is a source of some of the rhetorical power of metaphor; it assists speakers in presenting evocative, arresting and personalized accounts; it encourages audiences to impute a respectability and authority to metaphoric statements (because of cultural/historical allusions they carry) which are scarcely earned (cf. Enoch Powell's speech, Chapter 6).

The role of metonym in symbolic life, on the other hand, has been left relatively unremarked. A likely reason is that metonym is based on the already-known and accepted; its structure is 'closed' and always near tautology. If metaphor affords perspective, metonymy is a process of reduction (Burke 1969b: 503). Whereas metaphor is an instrument in the development of a language of ideas, metonym transposes the intangible back into the tangible so that, for example, "emotions" become "heart" and "shame" becomes "a movement of the eye" (*ibid.*: 506–7). Whereas metaphor may compare something that is known with something that is unknown (positing likeness), metonym brings together 'knowns' so that they 'touch' each other, and (because of the other) each *is*.[3]

But these qualities mean that metonym has a logic of expectancy (one might call it) and invites *gestalt* thinking—attributes of the utmost significance in politics. For example, where metonym prevails over metaphor it can be expected that symbols (needing explanation) will relinquish their place to *signs* that do not need explanation. I suggest therefore that the first 'mission' of metonymy is, contrary to that of metaphor, to withhold the slip into change.

II

Tentatively, I want to draw together the observations made so far into a general proposition of *politics*.

The politician who wants to get into power does well to introduce new options or, if not new, alternative options or, failing that, to destroy, rhetorically, the policy (option) of the government of the day. In short, he tries to open what is closed by the power of others. And that is also the implication of metaphor as a leap of the imagination. "It not only demands that we say 'No' to the organization of experience as it is given to us in pre-ordained categories; it also requires us to rearrange cognition into new forms and associations" (Brown 1976: 176). But having gained power, a politician may be expected to be concerned with the closure of all other options to his public and, given the property of metonym, this purpose would be served by drawing all within his political jurisdiction (persons and symbols, in particular) into metonymic relations.

There could be an absurd conclusion to this general proposition as formulated thus far: namely, that politicians who are in power restrict themselves to metonymy in their public utterances and those out of power to metaphor. We save ourselves from this by recognizing two things about power. First, although all political speech may be about power in the final analysis, a great deal of it is in response to contexts other than that of the gross distribution of power. Oppositions, for example, are not usually *directly* addressing the question of getting into power. The issue here is the necessary sensitivity of rhetoric to context (Chapter 2); and it suggests that politicians are likely to vary their rhetorical stance even within the course of a speech.

Secondly, being in office and having power are, of course, not necessarily the same thing. Along with the office must go influence commensurate to that office (and vice versa) before we can speak confidently of power. I am not attempting in this a Weberian-type law of general political theory but I do suggest that the proposition I have put forward is usually taken into account by politicians when choosing their rhetorical strategy. It sets the limits within which the rhetorical stance can be varied, even directing where the principal emphasis will be placed.

Now, it is in situations where office and influence are commensurate that metonym will prevail over metaphor, perhaps even to the point of its exclusion. Thus Figure 1 below shows metonymy as a line that exactly intersects these two 'arms' of power. The broken lines indicate different scales of power (for example, between municipal and national politics) and we see how the condition governing metonym pertains independently of scale differences.

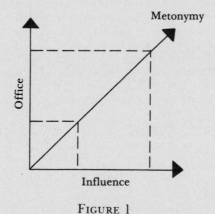

FIGURE 1

Metonymy and Power

Whereas the domain of metonym is bounded in this fashion, metaphor reaches out on either side of the line of metonymy. Metaphor is used to 'attack' this line: its task is to reveal a flaw in the metonymic order—for example, that it is not a natural one but arbitrarily imposed by the power-holder(s). Or, the power-holder himself will make skirmishes, using metaphor, out from 'his' line of metonymy; and the task of this metaphor is to identify and discredit the enemies of the State (or to identify the enemies of the regime as enemies of the State). But often there is no power-holder in the stringent sense that we are using "power"; and it is likely to be metaphor rather than metonym that and were that all, a metonymic style could have been expected. However, the government found itself *in opposition* on this issue. They faced the "all-pervading legitimacy" (Bailey) of Gandhism. Yet, as the government, they determined that their will would prevail. Accordingly, the spokesman devoted himself to exposing the flaw in the Gandhian political philosophy; his rhetoric is iconoclastic in its grandiloquence: his metaphors are deriding. The speaker on the other side, for his part, had less need of metaphor when he could assume the mantle of Gandhian legitimacy: *his* grandiloquence was iconophilic and (therefore) metonymic.

Both of these examples demonstrate, lest the matter be in doubt, how there is a rhetorical arena in political life which places its own constraints on the political process. As the arena of the expressive culture in politics, it is especially here that, on the one hand, there can be a certain power which is independent of office and, on the other hand, that power on the basis of office alone is liable to be devalued. As a consequence of this, speakers can be expected to switch from one rhetorical device to another while making their case. We can suppose that the speeches of the SNP delegate and the Welsh Secretary included metonymic passages in which their 'committed' audiences were treated to a rhetoric of solidarity (solidarity-with-the-cause) containing the *vision* of power. We know that as the debate in the Indian Constituent Assembly continued, the government side, in particular, modified its rhetoric (abandoning the derisive metaphor) in the interest of national unity.

Turning now to our various case studies in this volume, Park's findings concerning U.S. and Norwegian populists (Chapter 5) is a reminder of how a population may demonstrate a cultural bias towards one or the other of the two tropes.[5] In this respect it serves to qualify our present argument; however, his comparison of verbal cultures in politics, based on the alternative premises of "conversion" and "instruction," is epistemologically close to the present argument. As conversion calls upon metaphor most of all, instruction rests upon metonymic knowledge.

The case of the rhetoric of Enoch Powell is illustrative of the conjunction of our two approaches. At the time of the 1968 speech we find him with an "authority over a vast audience despite his apparently weak base in the political structure"; he is "the demon or the prophet of the contemporary British political scene" (Lloyd-Jones, Chapter 6). Clearly, the Powell appeal at that time is, in Park's terms, based on conversion: that is to say, it springs from the expectation that his audiences "seek grandiloquence, persuasion by faith and the courage to call the opposition 'enemy' "; and as Wallman remarks, "he is concerned

competitors for power incumbency will use: both to build up their
options and to tear down those of their opponents.

III

Consider the following examples:

Appearing on the same page of *The Observer*, 29 May 1977
these two items: a report of a meeting of the Scottish Nationalist
(SNP), which stated that ". . . Mr. Henderson was warmly receiv
the conference when he likened supporters of the Union to 'pit p
coming up from the depths, unable to face the sunshine that is Sc
independence' "; and alongside this report was a statement by the V
Secretary in a "Labour counter-attack" on the Welsh nationalist
"Describing *Plaid Cymru's* three MPs as '*cwn bach* Mrs. Thatch
Mrs. Thatcher's little dogs—he told the Welsh Labour Party's an
conference in Llandudno that they would soon be fleeing with their
between their legs." The SNP speech was made from an out-of-
position whereas that of the Welsh Secretary was from an in-office
however, the political context of the issue of devolution withir
United Kingdom is such as to render the power position betweer
nationalists and the Labour Government by no means so dispar
least of all on public platforms—as the factor of office alone w
suggest. The context is one of political competition and the sensitivi
political rhetoric to *this* factor made for a similarity in the circumsta
of the two speeches: the rhetoric was addressed to tearing dow
opponent's position.

Shortly after India's Independence, the Indian Constit
Assembly debated whether the new constitution should be mod
upon village *panchayats*.[4] Two styles within the one rhetorical n
identified by Bailey as "grandiloquent" (Chapter 3) emerge sharp
the debate: one from each side of the issue. The distribution of the s
is along the lines suggested by our hypothesis. Although it was i
tified as a Gandhian idea, Nehru's government refused to accept
panchayat model as practicable. The principal speaker from the gov
ment side scorned the idea in these terms: "What is the village but a
of localism, a den of ignorance, narrowmindedness and c
munalism?" The level of grandiloquence was maintained also
defense of the idea—but with this difference: "Let us strive to reach
goals envisaged by Mahatma Gandhi and all our prophets, sages
seers, the goal—I would not call it, of *sadahnam rajyam* or the Kingd
of God on Earth; I would simply call it *panchayat raj*."

The government representative spoke from an in-office positi

not with planning or the execution of plans, but with ideology"
(Chapter 7). But equally salient, Powell is known by his speeches and
these are remembered for their metaphors: thus the 1968 speech on
immigration is popularly known as "the 'rivers of blood' speech, [and]
the phrase became the media's automatic means of identifying Powell."

The case study of the Cajun politician (Gold, Chapter 8) is an
interesting contrast to that of Enoch Powell, and a number of points
emerge about our two tropes that are worthy of note. In general, Gold
sees Lafleur, the Prairie Cajun, as using metaphors to reduce the
specificity of events and thereby reducing the chance of disagreement
with what he says during the campaign; in particular, "Lafleur's seven
speeches follow a more or less orderly progression of metaphors featur-
ing Police Jury [his opponent] in terms of threats to the community."
Metonyms, on the other hand, are introduced to provide credentials, and
in the fifth week of the campaign, Lafleur, "at his peak of confidence,"
actually bestows a metonym (the nickname of "Black-top") on himself.
But in asking where Lafleur went wrong (for he lost the election), Gold
directs attention to the way in which Lafleur, towards the end, threw
caution—that is to say, rhetorical circumlocution—to the wind and
levelled unveiled accusations against his opponent. For this he used
metonymic (i.e., direct) rather than metaphoric (i.e., indirect) devices,
and in doing so he offended the sense of Cajun Prairie *communitas*.

Most remarkable of all, perhaps, about the Durham miners as
described by Rodger (Chapter 4) is their reserve of political strength,
kept alive through the rituals of their annual Gala. A highly rhetorical
event, it is an occasion when 100,000 people use the "We" in a very
special way, and it behooves any Labour party politician to keep in step
with these Durham marchers. Indeed, when Labour is in power, the
prime minister, "barring some extraordinary crisis," is in attendance.
There, as "one of us," he will also address the Gala; and in 1977 Mr.
Callaghan made a particularly interesting manipulation with the basic
tropes. Very precisely catching the rhetorical mood, he held up a
metaphor only to reject it and to bring together the government and the
miners through metonymy. He said: "The lions can command the lions'
share under a system of free collective bargaining but the Labour
movement and the Socialist movement is about more than the lions. It is
about the weak and the sick and about those whose bargaining power is
not strong." This metonymy proved rhetorically inviolable.

IV

Thus far we have been discussing switches between metaphor and
metonym, but there are also structural transformations between them

(cf. Lévi-Strauss 1966). That is to say, an important part of the human experience is the way in which we are drawn back and forth between our universe and its parts so that relations of similarity 'convert' into relations of contiguity and vice versa.[6] Like the switches, the transformations can occur in either direction; however, there also appears to be a developmental sequence in some of these transformations which, expressed as the 'career' of a trope, is from metonym to metaphor and back again (but with changes, as we shall see) to metonym.

The first stage in this sequence, from metonym to metaphor, is accountable to the fact that a metaphor is a collapsed analogy: the parts of either side of an analogy (A1:A2 and B1:B2) are in metonymic relation to one another; the metaphor (A is 'like' B) developed out of the analogy therefore has metonymic roots. Rhetorically, however, what is likely to be noticed is not the development of a metaphor out of metonym but, on the contrary, the revolutionary aspect of its statement—the "verbal atom cracking" of metaphor, Burke has called it (1959: 308).[7]

But as a metaphor gains in currency, it is likely to lose its suggestiveness: the 'revolution' is over. To borrow from Weber on charisma (1947: 363f.): the revolutionary phase, once accomplished, is likely to be followed by routinization. However, the metonymic relationship emerging at the end of such a sequence (the post-metaphor relation) is, of course, likely to have significantly different import from the one at the beginning. In the final metonym, the symbolic 'revolution' of the intervening metaphor is accepted (routinization:charisma :: metonym:metaphor).

An example of how this transformational sequence can be put to rhetorical use is found in the handling of race in Powellist rhetoric in England. There are legal hazards (and perhaps others) attached to speaking directly about race; accordingly, metaphoric-metonymic circumlocutions are used which all draw upon the basic analogy black: white :: immigrant:native-born, and the following manipulations are undertaken with it. "Black" (separated now from its metonymic partner "white") and "immigrant" (separated from its metonymic partner "native-born") are placed in a metaphoric relationship; that is, blacks are like immigrants (and the metaphor generates a new meaning of the word immigrant). Then, the metaphor established, either of its parts can be used *alone* as a metonym of the unmentionable, "race." By means of this transformation, racist rhetoric can content itself with the word "immigrant" which is legally safe (or safer) while no less pointed and persuasive.

Alternatively, in order to attack racist policies, a politician may liken 'race' to an evil. But with legislative victory there may emerge a new political rhetoric of race based, once again, on metonymy but this time with race as an attribute of an individual along with, for example, language and religion; none of the attributes is considered separately, nor are they presented in any of their particular forms (e.g. "black," "Roman Catholic"). Thus this change in the rhetoric reorganizes our experience in a way least likely to encourage social differentiation on the basis of race. A person now is no more like his race, which he shares with one set of people, than he is like his language or his religion, which he shares with people of different 'races.' It is the individual who, as it were, possesses his race, to do with it what he wants, instead of society possessing (that is, controlling) him through his race.

The politician who would annul this victory must stir men's minds once again with metaphor, this time to disturb the newly won metonymy: he suggests (for instance) that relations between the races are 'like' . . . a cancer. Should he persuade his audience of this, we can expect him, too, to change to a rhetoric of metonomy—but this time racial membership (referred to with appropriate circumlocution) is separated from other memberships so that a person *is* his race; and characteristics of particular 'races' and of inter-racial situations are presented. Thus Wallman (Chapter 7) shows that "once the association of 'race' with immigration is made, the symbolic steps to imputing scarcity, crowding, unemployment, and urban violence to blacks are a matter of simple logic" (cf. the Powell speech in Chapter 6).

Now it is in the transformations rather than the switches that we find the diachronic aspect of political rhetoric. Whereas the switches between tropes simply serve as rhetorical alternatives in the handling of a theme (as in the use of metonym to speak directly of "us," or of metaphor to speak indirectly of "us" through "them"), the *transformation* of a trope signals a *move* along the gradient of power. Thus when discussing Figure 1 and its line of metonymy, I suggested that a politician who was still without power would use metaphor to 'attack' this line; what I am suggesting now is that a successful attack may allow him to rearrange relations, as he wants them, on a basis of metonymy. When this happens one can expect changes in the meaning of key symbols; in the case of switching there are simply changes, to and fro, between symbols.

Consider two possible meanings of "the Bastille" as an example of changes in key symbols: in certain circumstances (say, Bourbon) the Bastille is a metonym of the political constitution in the way that "the crown" is in a monarchy, but in other circumstances (say, Jacobin) it is a metaphor of arbitrary and illegitimate rule. In other words, the Bastille is metaphor or metonym dependent on whether one is defending or storming it—and the lesson is the one made earlier: how political meaning is dependent on context, and the sensitivity of rhetoric to context.

V

When a speaker takes care to relate what he wants his audience to hear and what they want to hear (cf. Chapter 2), the choice of trope may appear to be left to the audience. This is most likely to happen when an appeal has to be addressed to people among whom there are serious differences. In these circumstances, some may 'hear' a metaphor where others hear a metonym: but the merger is achieved between what the politician wants all his listeners to hear and what each of them wishes to hear. The key to this achievement is to have the listeners themselves supply the 'missing' premiss which the speaker has deliberately left assumptive: argument by enthymeme (Chapter 2).

Manning's (Chapter 9) analysis of the electoral campaign of the Bermudian Progressive Labour party (PLP) provides a clear demonstration of this process. The PLP has to take into account how "the value opposition between the sexes remains one of the most fundamental socio-cultural features of [black] Bermuda." To simplify, among lower-class black women religion counts more than race as an issue, and race more than religion among the men. In earlier elections, PLP rhetoric was revolutionary socialism and Black Power—all of greater appeal to the men than to the women; but in the 1976 election "the vocabulary of secular radicalism was replaced by one of religion." The PLP's success in 1976, relative to its showings in previous elections, is accountable to the fact that it increased its support from women while holding its male support; and a key factor here is that "race was relatively muted in 1976, but unequivocally if implicitly communicated through the distinctively black performance tropes of revivalism."

The missing premiss of the PLP platform supplied by the women, then, was that of salvation, and the campaign became a crusade. In the case of the male PLP supporters, their continued identification with the political rhetoric reflects a different perception of the revivalist idiom of the campaign. As performance, the idiom was seen as in keeping with that of the black clubs; and as ideology, the revivalism was seen as in keeping with the prevailing 'conservative' racial ideology among PLP lower-class males that rejects black-white partnership. In short, the missing premiss supplied to the 1976 campaign by these males concerned racial identity and competition, not salvation; for all its

religious metaphor, the campaign was perceived by them as a political
metonym of their blackness.

VI

The various strands of this chapter must now be brought together; but I
will first sketch the perspective of political rhetoric offered by the book
as a whole and on which this chapter elaborates.

Rhetoric has been approached as an instrument by which a
politician can increase his control over his political environment. He is
in competition not only with rival politicians but also with the public
that elects him (or for whom he purports to speak). Few politicians, we
assume, are content to let the balance of power between them and their
public rest where Demosthenes put it when he said: "it is not you [the
public] that aim at what they [the politicians] wish for, but they who aim
at whatever they think you desire" (see Chapter 2). On the other hand, we
suppose that most politicians recognize that what Demosthenes said is
what the public should be led to believe. Here we have the principal task
of rhetoric in politics, and its realization—the dream of any politician—
implies that the meaning of a situation would be found in what a
politician says about it.

This view of the place of rhetoric in politics also sets the principal
task of analysis. Dealing with different empirical situations, the separate
chapters can be seen as combining to demonstrate how politicians strive
to match two dimensions of political rhetoric, the political and the
semantic. The one pertains to the need to handle issues that the public
recognizes (cf. speaking politics: Chapter 2), and the other to the manner
in which an issue is presented and, inevitably, redefined rhetorically (cf.
politics of speaking: Chapter 2). Here I have tried to conceptualize the
relations between these two dimensions of rhetoric *developmentally*.
The notion of *career* is a useful mnemonic.

Presumably, one allows that developments in the political
dimension of rhetoric are found in the 'career' of a political idea, the
'career' of a political party and (at the heart of the matter for us) in the
speaking career of a politician; my question is, are there not
concomitant developments in the semantic dimension of rhetoric? In
other words, we should consider notionally the 'career' of a trope and
look for the conjunctions between it and the speaking career of a
politician. This will also help to uncover the constraints and
opportunities regarding the options and limits of the rhetorical
redefinition of issues.

The link (which I assume is always there) between the political and semantic dimensions of rhetoric may be 'found' through enquiring: which strategy is employed at which juncture in a politician's career? This does not imply identification of 'the' political situation with 'the' trope—such a procedure would be an academic travesty of political process—but the components of a political situation and the serial choices, between metaphor and metonym, that a speaker will probably make. His choices evolve out of *his* formulation of the political context, and aside from his perception of the balance of power between himself and his rivals, is the balance he strives for in the composition of his own political power (see the discussion of office and influence in this chapter). And I would repeat what is perhaps the most important suggestion in our argument; namely, that the transformation of a political metaphor into a metonym may mirror the essential political process of acquiring and maintaining power, or, where the transformation is mishandled, of losing power.

Perhaps the essence of the metaphor-metonym distinction, in its political aspect, is that whereas metonym always endorses power (it speaks 'with' the power gradient), metaphor is used to speak against it as often as it is used to endorse it. Thus we can expect to find politicians using metonym to impress upon their audiences how they enjoy the privileges of living in a political environment of accepted norms; and care is likely to be taken to impart to a people, through the rhetoric of metonym, a 'consolidated' sense of their own worth. Metonym, then, is the trope of social control in which the naked edge of power may be rhetorically concealed and one which is able to give a culturally normative explanation of prejudice—of xenophobia in particular. Metonym is concerned neither with 'other' people nor 'other' standards, not even with an enemy. Although an observer may notice an ambiguity in metonymic address (an example would be the ways in which the use of "we" is stretched), for those so addressed the message is likely to be heard in one consistent way: it is tautology rather than ambiguity that is a social characteristic of metonym.

The sharp contrast with metaphor, on each of these scores, does not need spelling out; but perhaps it is worth stressing that whereas the loose allusive imagery of metaphor may permit people to suppose that they have more freedom—more options—than the political context actually allows, the specificity of metonym ordinarily leads to a perception of less freedom than that which is possible. Also, one is tempted to expand upon the notion of the expressive polarity between metaphor and metonym: as the meta-communication of metaphor is likely to run in the direction of imbalance, indeterminacy and flux, so that of metonymy may suggest balance, determinacy and stability.

These same qualities of metaphor and metonym are also likely to lead to differences—shared by speaker and audience alike—in the importance attached to rhetorical creativity. The politician who has managed to establish among his public an order of metonymy (itself a rhetorical creation) is likely to hold to it; however, the situation of the politician dependent upon metaphor to catch and retain his audience's attention is quite different. His appeal lies in the way his rhetoric opens what people have supposed to be closed, and so it is important for him that his creativity is seen never to abate. But metaphors do not follow each other lineally and they exhibit little interdependence and cannot therefore be expected to generate *gestalt* perception in an audience. Whereas all these things are true of metonym, metaphors follow each other as separate leaps of the imagination. The occurrence of metaphor in politics is, as said, associated with incompleteness of power; put another way now, it is the striving for power, not its possession, that promotes the insistently more creative forms of rhetorical persuasion.

It has been said on behalf of metaphor that its "first mission" is to provide identity for "inchoate" subjects (Fernandez 1974: 120). But to appreciate this particular role of metaphor, it should be distinguished from that of metonym. Whereas metaphor is involved in the articulation of an emerging identity (and this is, I think, where Fernandez's emphasis falls), metonym is likely to reaffirm identity. Yet the role of metonym in this matter is not limited to being a simple alternative to that of metaphor; it also has a role that can be stated as a 'second step' to the Fernandez proposition. As metaphor helps provide identity to inchoate groups, so metonym (but not metaphor) helps to retain political control over these groups as they emerge with an identity.

In sum, there are correlated differences between metaphor and metonym with respect to the control exercised over an audience,

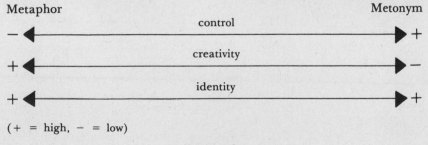

$(+ = \text{high}, - = \text{low})$

FIGURE 2

Metaphor and Metonym: Three General Correlations

expectancy regarding creativity of rhetorical imagery, and contributions to an audience's sense of identity. The correlations are presented schematically in Figure 2. Their significance for us is in the light they shed on the process whereby rhetoric is used to stake a political claim (through metaphor) and even to lay claim to the political environment (through metonym).

Notes

1. On analogic thought in science and the humanities, see Brown (1976), Cameron (1976) and Krohn (1977); on Western and non-Western analogic thought see Horton and Finnegan (1973); Leach (1976) and Turner (1975) are two of the more comprehensive statements of anthropological work on analogic thought.

2. Cf. Jakobson (1956: 76): ". . . in normal verbal behaviour, both [metaphor and metonym] are continually operative, but careful observation will reveal that under the influence of a cultural pattern, personality and verbal style, preference will be given to one . . . over the other." Yet there is still a tendency among commentators on this subject to remark upon the effectiveness of metaphor and metonym, equally and without paying much attention to the context of the speech or the passage within a speech (for a selection of commentaries, see Sandell 1977).

3. As Tambiah (1968: 190) has pointed out, metaphoric and metonymic constructions are (approximately) in the same relation to each other as the Frazerian categories of imitative (or sympathetic) and contagious (or contiguous) magic.

4. The following account, and all citations, are from Bailey (1976).

5. See Douglas (1978) on "group" and "grid" concepts for handling of the problem outside the field of rhetoric.

6. For example, a father's relations to his son (contiguity) can suggest a similarity with employer/employee relations, or, a sense of similarity between fathers and employers can lead to an exploration of father/son relations. I owe this amplification of the general point to James W. Fernandez (personal communication).

7. Consider Sukarno's rhetoric (Anderson 1966; Geertz 1964; Lind 1976), for example. It has been recognized as highly metaphoric, as revolutionary (Geertz)—and indeed it was; however, its imagery drew heavily upon the traditional *wayang* (shadow puppet) plays which "all Javanese, having watched *wayang* performances from their early infancy, know more or less by heart" (Lind, p. 4) and in which the different roles stood in metonymic (part-whole) relationships to each other. Thus considered, the key metaphor that likens Sukarno to *Ratu Adil* (the just ruler) has metonymic roots, a cultural fact of likely considerable impact on Sukarno's audiences.

References

Abrahams, Roger
  1970   "Pattern of Performance in the British West Indies." In Norman
          Whitten, Jr., and John Szwed (eds.), *Afro-American Anthropology:
          Contemporary Perspectives*. New York: Free Press.
Abrahams, Roger, and Richard Bauman
  1971   "Sense and Nonsense in St. Vincent: Speech Behaviour and Decorum
          in a Caribbean Community." *American Anthropologist*, 73: 612-72.
Aldrich, Howard
  n.d.   "Asian Shopkeepers as a Middleman Minority: A Study of Small
          Business in Wandsworth." In David Eversley and Alan Evans (eds.),
          Inner City Employment Problems. London: Heinemann. Forth-
          coming
Allen, David
  1973   "Bermuda: Mid-Atlantic Magnet." In Eugene Fodor (ed.), *Guide to
          Caribbean, Bahamas and Bermuda*. London: Hodder and Stough-
          ton.
Allen, Jim
  1976   "Days of Hope." A series of four plays performed on BBC-TV,
          London.
Anderson, Benedict R. O'G.
  1966   "The Languages of Indonesian Politics." *Indonesia*, 1(1): 89-116.
Angers, Trent
  1977   "The Three Faces of Dudley J. Leblanc." *Acadiana Profile*, 6(1):
          42-58.
Apter, David E.
  1964   "Ideology and Discontent." In David Apter (ed.), *Ideology and Dis-
          content*. Glencoe, Ill.: Free Press.
Austin, J. L.
  1962   *How To Do Things with Words*. Oxford: Clarendon Press.
Bailey, F. G.
  1969   "Political Statements." *Contributions to Indian Sociology* (N.S.), 3:
          1-16.
  1976   "Power and Rhetoric: The Indian Constituent Assembly." Paper
          presented to the ISER colloquium on political rhetoric, Memorial
          University, Harlow, England, 6-8 September (mimeo).
Banton, Michael
  1977   *The Idea of Race*. London: Tavistock.

202   *References*

Bauman, Richard
   1975   "Verbal Art as Performance." *American Anthropologist*, 77(2):
           290–311.
Bauman, Richard, and Joel Sherzer (eds.)
   1974   *Explorations in the Ethnography of Speaking.* New York: Cam-
           bridge University Press.
Beck, Brenda E. F.
   1978   "The Metaphor as a Mediator between Semantic and Analogic
           Modes of Thought." *Current Anthropology*, 19(1): 83–97.
Benn, Tony
   1976   *The Levellers and the English Democratic Tradition.* Spokesman
           Pamphlet No. 54. Oxford: Oxford Industrial Branch, Worker's Edu-
           cational Association.
Berman, Hold J.
   1968   "Legal Reasoning." In David L. Sills (ed.), *International Encyclo-
           paedia of the Social Sciences.* New York: Macmillan.
Bermuda
   1966   *Happy Valley Survey.* Hamilton, Bermuda: Government Statistical
           Office (mimeo).
   1974   *Bermuda Digest of Statistics.* Hamilton, Bermuda: Government
           Statistical Office.
Black Caucus, United Bermuda Party
   n.d.   *Report to the Premier.* Hamilton, Bermuda (mimeo).
Bloch, Maurice
   1974   "Symbols, Song, Dance and Features of Articulation. Is Religion an
           Extreme Form of Traditional Authority?" *European Journal of
           Sociology*, 15(1): 55–81.
Bloch, Maurice (ed.)
   1975   *Political Language and Oratory in Traditional Society.* London:
           Academic Press.
Braithwaite, E. R.
   1973   *Reluctant Neighbours.* London: New English Library, NEL Paper-
           backs.
Brown, Richard A.
   1976   "Social Theory as Metaphor: On the Logic of Discovery for the
           Sciences of Conduct." *Theory and Society*, 3(2): 169–98.
Brox, Ottar
   1972   *Politikk.* Oslo: Pax.
Bunzel, John H.
   1975   "The Eclipse of Confidentiality." *Change*, 7(8): 30–33.
Burke, Kenneth
   1955   *A Rhetoric of Motives.* New York: Braziller.
   1957   *The Philosophy of Literary Form.* New York: Vantage.
   1959   *Attitudes Toward History.* Los Altos, Cal.: Hermes Publications.
   1966   *Language as Symbolic Action: Essays on Life, Literature and
           Method.* Berkeley: University of California Press.

1969a *A Rhetoric of Motives*. Berkeley: University of California Press.

1969b *A Grammar of Motives*. Berkeley: University of California Press.

Burling, Robbins

1977 Review of *Political Language and Oratory in Traditional Society* by Maurice Bloch. *American Anthropologist*, 79(3): 698–700.

Cameron, Iain

1976 "Metaphor in Science and Society." In W. F. Williams (ed.), *SISCON*. Edinburgh: Science Studies Unit, University of Edinburgh.

Cohen, Abner

1969 "Political Anthropology: The Analysis of the Symbolism of Power Relations." *Man* (N.S.), 4(2): 215–35.

Crewe, Ivor, Bo Sarlvick, and James Alt

1977 "Partisan Re-alignment in Britain, 1964–1974." *British Journal of Political Science*, 7: 129–90.

Creyghton, Marie-Lou

n.d. "The Open Body: Notes on Khroumirian Symbolism." In E. Schwimmer (ed.), *The Yearbook of Symbolic Anthropology*, Vol. 2. London: C. Hurst & Co. Forthcoming.

Critcher, Charles

1975 "Race in the West Midlands Press 1963–1970." A UNESCO study (unpublished).

Cross, Whitney

1950 *The Burned Over District*. Ithaca, N.Y.: Cornell University Press.

Dawes, Neville

1974 Excerpt from "The Last Enchantment." In George Lamming (ed.), *Cannon Shot and Glass Beads*. London: Pan Books.

Devons, Ely

1961 *Essays in Economics*. London: Allen and Unwin.

Douglas, Mary

1978 *Cultural Bias*. Royal Anthropological Institute, Occasional Paper No. 35. London.

Douglass, Dave

1973 *Pit Talk in County Durham*. History Workshop Pamphlets No. 10. Oxford: Ruskin College.

Duncan, Hugh D.

1962 *Communication and Social Order*. London: Oxford University Press.

Edgar, David

1974 *Destiny*. A play first performed at The Other Place, Stratford-upon-Avon, 22 September 1976; and at the Royal Shakespeare Company, the Aldwych Theatre, London, from 10 May 1977.

Ellul, Jacques

1965 *Propaganda*. New York: Vintage Books.

Evans, Peter

1976 *Publish and Be Damned*. London: Runnymede Trust.

Fernandez, James W.
    1974   "The Mission of Metaphor in Expressive Culture." *Current Anthropology*, 15(2): 119–46.
Finnegan, Ruth
    1969   "How to Do Things with Words: Performative Utterances among the Limba of Sierra Leone." *Man*, 4(4): 59–69.
Firth, Sir Raymond
    1973   *Symbols: Public and Private*. London: Allen and Unwin.
Flett, Hazel
    1979   "Bureaucracy and Ethnicity: Notions of Eligibility to Public Housing." In Sandra Wallman (ed.), *Ethnicity at Work*. London: Macmillan.
Foot, Paul
    1969   *The Rise of Enoch Powell*. Penguin Special. Harmondsworth, Eng.: Penguin.
Fowler, H. W.
    1937   *A Dictionary of Modern English Usage*. Oxford: Clarendon Press.
Frazier, E. Franklin
    1964   *The Negro Church in America*. New York: Schocken.
Fynes, R.
    1873   *The Miners of Northumberland and Durham*. Sunderland, Eng.
Garside, W. R.
    1971   *The Durham Miners, 1919–1960*. London: Allen and Unwin.
Geertz, Clifford
    1964   "Ideology as a Cultural System." In David Apter (ed.), *Ideology and Discontent*. Glencoe, Ill.: Free Press.
Gellner, Ernest
    1973   "Concepts and Society." In J. Agassi and I. E. Jarvie (eds.), *Cause and Meaning in the Social Sciences*. London: Routledge and Kegan Paul.
Goodwyn, Lawrence
    1976   *Democratic Promise: The Populist Movement in America*. New York: Oxford University Press.
Gustavsen, Finn
    1969   *Rett På Sak*. Oslo: Pax.
Hall, Peter M.
    1972   "A Symbolic Interactionist Analysis of Politics." *Sociological Inquiry*, 42(3–4): 35–75.
Hannerz, Ulf
    1970   "The Significance of Soul." In Lee Rainwater (ed.), *Black Experience: Soul*. Chicago: Aldine.
Hexter, J. H.
    1968   "Historiography: A Rhetoric of History." In David L. Sills (ed.), *International Encyclopaedia of the Social Sciences*. New York: Macmillan.
Hicks, John D.
    1931   *The Populist Revolt*. Minneapolis: University of Minnesota Press.

Hill, Stephen
 1976   *The Dockers: Class and Tradition in London*. London: Heinemann
         Educational Books.
Hobsbawm, E. J., and George Rudé
 1969   *Captain Swing*. London: Lawrence and Wishart.
Homans, George
 1968   *The Human Group*. London: Routledge and Kegan Paul.
Horton, Robin, and Ruth Finnegan
 1973   *Modes of Thought: Essays on Thinking in Western and Non-Western Societies*. London: Faber and Faber.
Howard, Perry H.
 1971   *Political Tendencies in Louisiana*. Baton Rouge: Louisiana State
         University Press.
Husband, Charles (ed.)
 1975   *White Media and Black Britain*. London: Arrow Books.
Hymes, Dell
 1974   *Foundations in Sociolinguistics: An Ethnographic Approach*. Philadelphia: University of Pennsylvania Press.
Jakobsen, Roman
 1956   *Fundamentals of Language*, Part III. The Hague: Mouton.
Johnson, R. W., and Douglas Schoen
 1976   "The 'Powell Effect': or How One Man Can Win." *The New Society*,
         37(720): 168-72.
Keil, Charles
 1966   *Urban Blues*. Chicago: University of Chicago Press.
Kerr, Clark
 1972   *The Uses of the University*. Cambridge, Mass.: Harvard University
         Press.
Kochman, Thomas
 1970   "Toward an Ethnography of Black American Speech Behavior." In
         Norman Whitten, Jr., and John Szwed (eds.), *Afro-American Anthropology: Contemporary Perspectives*. New York: Free Press.
Kosmin, B., and N. Grizzard
 1974   "The British National Front in the Two General Elections of 1974."
         Patterns of Prejudice, 8(6): 18-22.
Krohn, Roger
 1977   "Scientific Ideology and Scientific Process: The Natural History of a
         Conceptual Shift." *Sociology of the Sciences Yearbook*, Vol. 1. Dordrecht, Holland: D. Reidel.
Kuhn, Thomas S.
 1970   *The Structure of Scientific Revolutions*. Chicago: University of Chicago Press.
Kuper, Leo
 1974   *Race, Class and Power: Ideology and Revolutionary Change in Plural Societies*. London: Duckworth.

Lasky, Melvin J.
  1976   *Utopia and Revolution*. Chicago: University of Chicago Press.
Leach, Edmund
  1976   *Culture and Communication*. Cambridge, Eng.: Cambridge University Press.
Lévi-Strauss, Claude
  1966   *The Savage Mind*. Letchworth, Eng.: Garden City Press.
Lind, Elisabet
  1976   "The Rhetoric of Sukarno." Paper presented to the ISER colloquium on political rhetoric, Memorial University, Harlow, England, 6–8 September (mimeo).
Lloyd-Jones, Ioan David
  1976   "Some Methodological Points Concerning Rhetoric as a Discipline Appropriate to the Study of Politics." Paper presented to the ISER colloquium on political rhetoric, Memorial University, Harlow, England, 6–8 September (mimeo).
McKenna, George
  1974   *American Populism*. New York: Putnam.
McLuhan, Marshall
  1965   *Understanding Media: The Extensions of Man*. New York: McGraw-Hill.
Manning, Frank
  1973   *Black Clubs in Bermuda: Ethnography of a Play World*. Ithaca, N.Y.: Cornell University Press.
  1977   "The Salvation of a Drunk." *American Ethnologist*, 4(3): 397–412.
  1978   *Bermudian Politics in Transition: Race, Voting and Public Opinion*. Hamilton, Bermuda: Island Press.
Marris, Peter
  1974   *Loss and Change*. London: Routledge and Kegan Paul.
Merton, Robert K.
  1949   *Social Theory and Social Structure*. Glencoe, Ill.: Free Press.
Miles, Robert, and Ann Phisaklea (eds.)
  1978   *Racism and Political Action*. London: Routledge and Kegan Paul.
Mills, C. Wright
  1956   *The Power Elite*. New York: Oxford University Press.
Moorehead, Caroline
  1975   "Enoch Powell: A Would-Be Leader Deserted by Destiny." *The Times*, London, 12 May, p. 7.
Myrdal, Gunnar
  1962   *The American Dilemma*. New York: Harper and Row.
Newfield, Jack, and Jeff Greenfield
  1972   *A Populist Manifesto: The Making of a New Majority*. New York: Praeger.
Newton, Esther
  1979   *Mother Camp—Female Impersonators in America*. Chicago: University of Chicago Press.

Nisbet, Robert A.
1976   *Sociology as an Art Form.* New York: Oxford University Press.
Overington, Michael A.
1977   "Kenneth Burke and the Method of Dramatism." *Theory and Society*, 4(1): 129-56.
PAG (Populistiske Arbeidsgrupper i Bergen)
1972   *Norsk Populisme.* Oslo: Det Norske Samlaget.
Paine, Robert
1976   "Two Modes of Exchange and Mediation." In B. Kapferer (ed.), *Transaction and Meaning: Directions in the Anthropology of Exchange and Symbolic Behavior.* ASA Essays in Social Anthropology, Vol. 1. Philadelphia: Institute for the Study of Human Issues.
Parkin, David
1975   "The Rhetoric of Responsibility: Bureaucratic Communications in a Kenya Farming Area." In Maurice Bloch (ed.), *Political Language and Oratory in Traditional Society.* London: Academic Press.
Patterson, Sheila
1963   *Dark Strangers.* London: Tavistock.
Perelman, Chaim
1963   *The Idea of Justice and the Problem of Argument,* trans. by John Petrie. London: Routledge and Kegan Paul.
1969   (With L. Olbrechts-Tyteca.) *The New Rhetoric: A Treatise in Argumentation.* Notre Dame, Ind.: University of Notre Dame Press.
1974   "Rhetoric in Philosophy: The New Rhetoric." In *Encyclopaedia Britannica*, XVth edition, Vol. 15, s.v. "Rhetoric."
Phillips, Melanie
1976   "Brixton and Crime." *The New Society*, 37(718): 65-68.
PLP (Progressive Labour Party)
1976   *Campaign Platform.* Hamilton, Bermuda (mimeo).
Popper, K. R.
1961   *The Poverty of Historicism.* London: Routledge and Kegan Paul.
Powell, J. Enoch
1969   *Freedom and Reality.* London: Batsford.
Rabelais, François
1946   *The Uninhibited Adventures of Gargantua and Pantagruel.* In *The Portable Rabelais*, ed. by Samuel Putnam. New York: Viking Press.
Rex, John, and Robert Moore
1967   *Race, Community and Conflict: A Study of Sparkbrook.* London: Oxford University Press.
Ricoeur, Paul
1971   "The Model of the Text: Meaningful Action Considered as a Text." *Social Research*, 38(3): 529-62.
Rosaldo, Michelle Zimbalist
1973   "I Have Nothing to Hide: The Language of Illongot Oratory." *Language in Society*, 2(2): 193-223.

Sandell, Rolf
    1977   *Linguistic Style and Persuasion*. London/New York: Academic Press.
Sapir, David J., and J. Christopher Crocker (eds.)
    1977   *The Social Use of Metaphor: Essays on the Anthropology of Rhetoric*. Philadelphia: University of Pennsylvania Press.
Seabrook, Jeremy
    1976   "A Change in Atmosphere: Race in One Town." *The New Society*, 37(726): 486–91.
Sloan, Thomas O.
    1974   "Rhetoric in Literature." In *Encyclopaedia Britannica*, XVth edition, Vol. 15, s.v. "Rhetoric."
Smith, Bruce L.
    1968   "Propaganda." In David L. Sills (ed.), *International Encyclopaedia of the Social Sciences*. New York: Macmillan.
Smith, William B.
    1969   *The Rhetoric of American Politics: A Study of Documents*. Westport, Conn.: Greenwood.
Smithies, Bill, and Peter Fiddick
    1969   *Enoch Powell on Immigration*. London: Sphere Books.
Snow, C. P.
    1962   *Science and Government*. New York: Mentor Books.
Soyinka, Wole
    1974   "Telephone Conversation." In George Lamming (ed.), *Cannon Shot and Glass Beads*. London: Pan Books.
Tambiah, S. J.
    1968   "The Magical Power of Words." *Man* (N.S.), 3(2): 175–208.
    1973   "Form and Meaning in Magical Arts: A Point of View." In Robin Horton and Ruth Finnegan (eds.), *Modes of Thought: Essays on Thinking in Western and Non-Western Societies*. London: Faber and Faber.
Turner, Victor
    1967   *The Forest of Symbols: Aspects of Ndembu Ritual*. Ithaca, N.Y.: Cornell University Press.
    1969   *The Ritual Process: Structure and Anti-Structure*. Chicago: Aldine.
    1975   "Symbolic Studies." In B. Siegel (ed.), *Annual Review of Anthropology*, Vol. 4. Palo Alto: Annual Review.
Unneberg, Björn
    1971   *Grönn Sosialisme* [*Green Socialism*]. Oslo: Cultura.
Walker, Martin
    1977   *The National Front*. London: Fontana.
Wallman, Sandra
    1968   "Lesotho's *Pitso*: Traditional Meetings in a Modern Setting." *Canadian Journal of African Studies*, 2(2): 167–73.

1974   "Kinship, A-Kinship, Anti-Kinship: Variation in the Logic of Kinship Situations." In E. Leyton (ed.), *The Compact: Selected Dimensions of Friendship*. Social and Economic Papers No. 3. St. John's: Institute of Social and Economic Research, Memorial University of Newfoundland.

1975   "A Street in Waterloo." *New Community*, 4(4): 517-23.

1977   "Introduction." In S. Wallman (ed.), *Perceptions of Development*. Cambridge, Eng.: Cambridge University Press.

1978   "The Boundaries of 'Race': Processes of Ethnicity in England." *Man*, 13(2): 200-17.

1979   "The Scope for Ethnicity." In Sandra Wallman (ed.), *Ethnicity at Work*. London: Macmillan.

Watson, George

1973   *The English Ideology: Studies in the Language of Victorian Politics*. London: Allen Lane.

Weber, Max

1947   *Social and Economic Organization*. New York: Free Press.

Weiss, Robert, and David Riesman

1966   "Work and Automation: Problems and Prospects." In Robert K. Merton and R. A. Nisbet (eds.), *Contemporary Social Problems*, 2nd ed. New York: Harcourt, Brace and World.

Werbner, Richard P.

1977   "The Argument in and about Oratory." In *African Studies*, 36(2): 141-44. Johannesburg: Witwatersrand University Press.

Williams, T. Harry

1970   *Huey Long*. New York: Bantam.

Willis, Paul

1976   "Lads, Lobes and Labour." *The New Society*, 36(711): 407-10.

Wilson, Peter

1969   "Reputation and Respectability: A Suggestion for Caribbean Ethnology." *Man* (N.S.), 4(1): 70-84.

1973   *Crab Antics*. New Haven: Yale University Press.

Wooding, Hugh, *et al.*

1969   *Bermuda Civil Disorders, 1968*. Government Publication. Hamilton, Bermuda.

Woodward, C. Vann

1960   *The Strange Career of Jim Crow*. 2nd rev. ed. New York: Oxford University Press.

Notes on Contributors

F. G. BAILEY   Sometime Reader in Anthropology at the University of London (SOAS) and formerly Professor of Anthropology, University of Sussex, Bailey is at present Professor of Anthropology at the University of California, San Diego. He has done field research in India and Italy, and his publications include *Caste and the Economic Frontier* (1957), *Tribe, Caste and Nation* (1961), *Politics and Social Change* (1963), *Stratagems and Spoils* (1969), *Gifts and Poison* (ed., 1971), *Debate and Compromise* (ed., 1973) and *Morality and Expediency* (1977).

GERALD L. GOLD   Currently Associate Professor of Social Anthropology at York University, Toronto, he has also taught at Laval University. Gold has done field research in Quebec, Mexico and Louisiana, and his publications include *St. Pascal: Changing Leadership and Social Organization in a Quebec Town* (1975) and, with M. A. Tremblay, *Communities and Culture in French Canada* (ed., 1973). At present he is an associate editor of *American Ethnologist*.

IOAN DAVID LLOYD-JONES   Presently Senior Lecturer in the Department of Politics, Glasgow University, and part-time tutor-counsellor for the Open University. In 1966–67, Lloyd-Jones was Gillespie Visiting Professor at the College of Wooster, Ohio. He has written numerous articles in various journals and is completing a book on political rhetoric for Penguin Books.

FRANK E. MANNING   Currently Professor of Anthropology at The University of Western Ontario, Manning has done field research in the Caribbean and circum-Caribbean, and is the author of *Black Clubs in Bermuda* (1973) and *Bermudian Politics in Transition* (1978), as well as of a number of articles.

ROBERT PAINE   Presently Henrietta Harvey Professor of Anthropology at Memorial University of Newfoundland, he has also taught at a number of Scandinavian and other Canadian universities. Paine has done field research among the Coast Lapps and Reindeer Lapps; his publications include *Coast Lapp Society* (2 vols., 1957 and 1965), *Patrons and Brokers in the East Arctic* (ed., 1971), *The White Arctic* (ed., 1977) and numerous articles.

GEORGE PARK   Presently Professor of Anthropology at Memorial University of Newfoundland, Park has also taught at Ohio University and the Claremont Colleges. He did field research in North Norway in the 1950s and again in 1972–73 as Fellow of ISER (Memorial University), and in Africa in the 1960s. He is the author of *The Idea of Social Structure* (1974) and of articles on diverse subjects, including Norwegian local and regional cultures.

IAN RODGER   A graduate of Durham University and sometime reporter with the *Newcastle Journal*, Rodger is the author of three novels, twenty-five radio plays (most of which have dealt with historical subjects), the sixth play in BBC-TV's "Elisabeth R" series and the Amundsen film in BBC's "Explorers" series. He has also translated radio plays from Norwegian and Swedish. In 1977, he convened (at Durham) the first academic conference in Britain devoted to the study of British radio drama.

SANDRA WALLMAN   Presently Director of the Ethnicity Research Programme for the British Social Science Research Council Research Unit in Ethnic Relations, Wallman taught Social Anthropology at the University of Toronto for a number of years and in 1974 at the University of Amsterdam. Her publications include *Take Out Hunger* (1969), *Perceptions of Development* (ed., 1977), *Ethnicity at Work* (ed., 1979) and *Social Anthropology of Work* (ed., 1980).

Index

Index